Mafia Mother-In-Law

Sunny Rubin

Library of Congress Cataloging-in-Publication Data

© 2007 Sunny Rubin
All rights reserved
Printed in the United States of America

This is an original publication of Skunkie Enterprises.

This book is based upon my life and any similar characters, places, and incidents are purely coincidental. Some names have been changed to protect their personal privacy. In regard to Mafia history some of the characters are fictitious to enable the flow of story telling.

This book is dedicated to Minna, my mother. Without her guidance and love growing up I would have never become the woman I am today. Her devotion to our family and her strength during difficult times kept the family together. Always inspiring me to question and never take life for granted. I am my mother's daughter. A special dedication to my hero son, Devin, who restored my hopes, dreams and for little Jackie boy.

ACKNOWLEDGMENTS

Many people have helped me along this long journey. Without their help, inspiration, and enthusiasm I would never have been able to finish this book. Much thanks to special people like Susan Ross, Marty Humphreys, Suzanne Wilson, Gregg Fremer and my publicist Deanne Manning for their support and help.

Prologue
The Clock Was Ticking

The clock was ticking that crisp Tuesday morning at 10 A. M.—10:07 A.M, to be precise, and I can be precise because, as I said, the clock was ticking.

It was round and white with black numbers, one of those generic clocks in hospital waiting rooms. Huge, and with that annoying tick, tick, tick that allowed me to count every second I was spending in the office of Paul Garrison, Esq.

Like the clock, Paul Garrison was huge; plus he had an annoying tic and a squint in his left eye that I thought, at first, was a wink of amusement. I was not amused. I found nothing funny about the sad circumstances that that I might never be able to see my grandchildren ever again.

"Mrs. Rubin," he said with the normal inflection of deference that lawyers use with clients.

"Call me Sunny," I said, because no one called me Mrs. Rubin. Mrs. Rubin was someone from another life I had lived, a long time ago.

"Sunny, this is a complicated case. Far more complicated than I realized when we spoke on the telephone."

He paused and I said nothing. The clock was ticking literally and figuratively; every second was another dollar I couldn't afford to pay to hear bad news.

"Laws vary from state to state. Ultimately, however, the law applying to your visitation rights is the law in the state where the grandchildren live.

"They live in New York."

"Too bad—you'd have a better chance if they lived here in New Jersey."

I knew that already. Countless hours of research on Internet had told me as much. I wasn't in the lawyer's office to hear what I already knew. I was here to put myself in the ring for a fighting chance to be part of the lives of my son's children, my beloved grandchildren.

"Yes," I stated as I glanced to my notes. I'm nothing if not prepared. "Under New Jersey Statute 9:2-7, a grandparent can apply for visitation even if the parents' marriage is intact."

Paul Garrison, Esq. looked startled. Was he surprised I had done my homework? Was he shocked I knew the details and statute number of a particular law? Perhaps he had seen only my blonde hair, not the determination coursing through me. I couldn't even muster any righteous indignation at his surprise. There were more important matters at hand.

"That's correct. You'd have a better chance if there were a death or divorce in the family, and one of the parents was denying you access to your grandchildren, Mrs. Rubin"

"Sunny." I reminded him, or was he hard of hearing?

"Right. Sunny. I believe, in these situations, court should be the last resort. If you can open a line of communication with the parents," he told as his voice and thoughts appeared to move from me to something else on his agenda.

"My son doesn't speak to me."

"Mere animosity between the grandparent and parent may be an insufficient basis to deny a grandparent visitation. Perhaps a neutral third-party mediator could initiate some sort of dialogue."

"I don't think you understand. Joel and his wife have made it clear that they want nothing to do with me."

Saying it out loud reopened my wounds.

How did this even happen? My mind started to roam in the familiar territory of disbelief over the turn of events that I still had trouble digesting. But wait, what was he saying? Was there a way I could again be part of my grandchildren's lives?

"... no hard and fast rules to determine when circumstances exist that would require the law to grant a grandparent visitation with their grandchildren. Every case is determined upon its own facts and circumstances."

So even with an intact family, some grandparents do go to court. I could smell the scent of hope. "Do they win?"

"Some have. Anything is possible."

The chains on my heart broke. Hope and joy flooded my entire being.

Anything is possible. I suddenly recalled the dream I had last night: I was holding my son's newborn daughter at her christening. I could feel her cradled in my arms. Her cheeks, flushed with sleep, were the color of that once-in-a-lifetime pink sunset; her eyelids almost translucent in their delicacy; her mouth a perfect miniature rose. Was that her heart beating, or mine? I inhaled deeply, and smelled her head.

"I'll do whatever it takes," I told the lawyer as I returned from my reverie. "I'll refinance my house. I can give you a check today for--how much is your retainer?"

"I'm sorry, Sunny. I can't take this case," the lawyer Garrison stated in a matter-of-fact way. My joy dissolved. Fear, anger and longing returned.

"But you said anything's possible," I reminded him. Was he contradicting his earlier pronouncements?

"Yes, anything is possible, but, for obvious reasons, I'm going to have to decline to represent you. You understand."

My suspicions were confirmed, but I could not lift myself from the chair, at least not just yet. I sat and stared out the window above his head. Outside, burnished leaves shone gold and terra cotta. Inside the law office, was a world of beige—beige walls, beige carpet, and beige computer befitting Paul Garrison, Esq., a beige man who led a beige life and would never understand something as desperate and powerful as the need I had to see my grandchildren.

Joel was withholding from me the most precious thing he could—my grandchildren. Why? Because I had declined to bow and scrape before his in-laws like the irrelevant peasant they seemed to believe me to be? As clichéd as it sounds, I had given Joel everything, sacrificed my life for Joel and his brother Devin, and this was how Joel chose to repay me? I had learned how to deal with tragedy the hard way, losing a father, mother and husband within a three-year period, but nothing, absolutely had prepared me for this ultimate act of ingratitude and betrayal.

My grandchildren would know me, despite Joel's bizarre behavior. His children deserved to know more than only their maternal grandparents. They were deserved and were entitled to know the Rubin side of the family, Joel's side of the family.

Like an explosion I suddenly knew what I could do—I would write them a long, long letter. I would let them know story of their father's side of the family.

My letter would be a story about love of family, especially after the loss of a husband and father. It would be about dedication to one another, self-sacrifice, respect and standing by one another. It would be about life's most precious treasure—love.

Starting this night, I vowed, I would wrestle my life into a cage of paper and words that could not be hidden from my grandchildren. And someday, when they were old enough, they would read this letter and know of the strength, dignity, loyalty and courage that ran through their veins—from Sunny's side of the street.

Chapter 2
I Am My Mother's Daughter

The flawless October night embraced me. The air was redolent with the smell of early fall--cool and crisp as a gold Jonathan apple. Something about that smell, recognizable yet exotic, stirred me. Or perhaps it was the way the moon hung low and heavy in the sky. Maybe it was the glass of wine I had with dinner. Maybe it wasn't.

Whatever was in the air, I knew it was a powerful force, and it was drawing me to my wedding album, a relic I had seldom opened. That night, though, it beckoned to me, and I answered. The gold embossed white leather cover had gathered a film of dust; it had been that long since I had last looked at it. I flipped through each page slowly, savoring each one like a strong and smooth cordial served after dinner. I realized that the rare times I looked through my wedding album, I had usually focused on my husband Mike, on how tall and handsome he was that day, or how I looked at my 19-year-old self, trying to remember how it felt to be that young. That night, though, something kept pulling me to the pictures of my mother.

My Mother—beautiful, strong, hardworking, stylish, sharp-tongued, bitchy, kind, compassionate, sarcastic, selfless, devoted—a complicated woman.

"I am my mother's daughter."

My mother suffered through a tough childhood and an early marriage to an abusive alcoholic. She endured the pain of temporarily sending her children to be cared for by someone else. She was a single mother and had no means to support them. Later, she became the breadwinner at a time when women simply did not work at a job outside the home. Much later, she would be denied any one-on-one time with her first grandchildren by my imbecile brother-in-law, who contended that she was incapable of babysitting. Later still, she became a helpless bystander when my father suffered a stroke and was confined to a nursing home. In those days it was the only way a patient could have kidney dialysis. Yes, my mother had been dealt more than her fair share of adversity, but she survived.

"I am my mother's daughter."

Despite her circumstances, Minna always dressed impeccably. She accessorized to the hilt with hats and gloves and purses to match her shoes. Her hair style was always *au courant*, and she complemented her lovely skin with just the right amount of makeup. My three sisters have always teased me. They would say I was just like my mother with my penchant for clothes and jewelry and hats, especially hats, and like my mother, I did it all on a shoestring budget.

"I am my mother's daughter."

Minna was raised on New York's Orchard Street. Hundreds of thousands of Jews had migrated from Eastern Europe to New York, where they settled in the Jewish ghettos of the Lower East Side. It was a colorful place with a rich and diverse Yiddish culture, but a world where crime, poverty and disease were common. My grandmother Anna spoke only Yiddish to her daughter. When my mother was in kindergarten, the teachers, in their infinite lack of wisdom, mistook her difficulty with English for stupidity, and she was held back. It was the first of many struggles to come.

My mother married young. She was eager to leave home as were so many young women in the 1940's. She quickly gave birth to two children—my half-brother Billy and my half-sister Becca. Minna's husband was an abusive drunk, a bully who beat her and constantly threatened to beat the children. At that time, a battered wife stayed married. What was the alternative?

Not surprisingly, my mother explored the alternative and defied the odds. She divorced her despicable first husband. A penniless woman, she sent her children to live with her mother in Florida, although it broke her heart to do so. She worked and saved every dime, and she waited for the day when she could send for her two children. She did what she had to do.

"I am my mother's daughter."

Meanwhile, my mother's brother spent a lot of time at a local boxing gym and became quite friendly with Maxie Matozinsky, one of the boxers. Even before my mother divorced her abusive husband, Maxie was silently infatuated with her. In Maxie's eyes she was young; she was beautiful; and she had two small children and an ogre for a husband. To Maxie, my mother's life was right out of a best-selling novel. Maxie was sympathetic and kind, and he was there waiting for my mother when she finally summoned the courage to divorce her husband. My mother and Maxie fell in love and were married. When Maxie was drafted and stationed in North Carolina, my mother went with him.

After he left the army, mother and Maxie returned to New York and settled in Brooklyn. My mother sent for Becca and Billy, who were so young they never realized Maxie was not their biological father. He was kind, and loving, and eventually adopted both of them. He also changed the family name from Matozinsky to Matus.

Soon after, I was born. Two years later, my parents

had another daughter, my sister Cara. Nine years later, when my parents were least expecting it, my mother became pregnant with her fifth child, my youngest sister Nancy.

Maxie was a locksmith and struggled to put food on the table, so my 40-year old mother was dismayed with being pregnant with a fifth child and felt the social stigma of the times. In the 1950's, women approaching 40 did not bear children, especially when they already had four.

Although Minna was upset to be pregnant, I was ecstatic. When she told me she was going to have another baby, I remember jumping up and down with happiness. When my mother brought Nancy home from the hospital, I felt such a rush of tenderness towards this tiny helpless being that I climbed into the crib and laid next to her. I wanted to cherish and protect her. That feeling for my baby sister endures to this day.

Times were not good for the Matozinsky family. Maxie lost his job, and after trying and trying to get another one, he simply gave up. It was as if he had lost momentum and could not recapture it. Still, the bills were there, and seven people needed to be fed. Once again, my mother defied the prevailing social rules. She worked full time at Macy's and assumed the responsibility of supporting our family. It was not easy for her. She was in her late 40's, and her long work days were grueling. Everyone outside our family of seven had something, usually hurtful, to say about my family's situation. Our family was considered to be strange—the wife worked all day, and the husband stayed home cooking and cleaning. Of course, today this husband and wife working arrangement is not unusual, but in the 1960's it was considered weird and downright abnormal.

My mother always forged ahead with her life, doing what was necessary and paying no attention to what people thought. Minna was strong because she had to be. She was fierce in her devotion to her children, and nothing could stand in her way of her taking care of us.

"Truly, I am my mother's daughter."

Chapter 3
Maxie and Bugsy

My father, Maxie Matozinsky, and his family fled religious persecution in their homeland of Russia to come to America with hopes of freedom and prosperity. In 1926, when my father was only 12-years old, his family landed on Ellis Island seeking a new life. However the streets of the Lower East Side of New York City were rife with poverty. My father attended school for only a few years before he had to go to work to support his family. He and his brother Willie worked long hours at any odd job they could find. Today such a situation is unthinkable, but leaving school to support the family was not only common, but expected in those years.

For the half century between 1870 and 1920 nearly two million Jews either passed through or settled in the Lower East Side. They were unwanted and unwelcome. Crowded into unwholesome tenement quarters, often unable to speak the English language, Jews were considered dirty and undesirable. My father's family had left oppression and anti-Semitism in Russia only to find it again in America.

With such intense poverty and ethnic tensions running high, the Lower East Side was a natural breeding ground for crime. A young Jewish man named Benjamin Siegelbaum joined a street gang on the Lower East Side primarily to commit petty thefts. Like my father, "Bugsy" Siegel's father was also a Russian immigrant. Unlike my father, Bugsy was unwilling to work his fingers to the bone to make only pennies a day. Maxie was a kind, gentle, brave protector. Bugsy was a vicious, corrupt, violent sociopath.

During adolescence, Bugsy befriended Meyer Lansky, also the son of Jewish immigrants. Meyer convinced Bugsy that the Jews needed to organize in the same manner as the Italians and the Irish. In 1930, they joined forces with the Italian gangster Charles "Lucky" Luciano and ruled the Lower East Side.

To keep physically strong, to survive in the Lower East Side, Maxie worked out at a local boxing gym. At that time, boxing was one way out of poverty. Many men were aspiring to become professional boxers.

My father regaled me with stories of the gangster so crazy he was nicknamed "Bugsy," although no one used the nickname in his presence. Bugsy often visited the gym looking to recruit men into his company, "Murder Inc." Bugsy's partner, Meyer Lansky, had developed a brilliant plan. Murder Inc. would be a company of hit men for hire. To guarantee loyalty, Murder Inc. paid the men a regular salary, in addition to bonuses for performing a "hit." These hit men actually received health insurance and retirement packages. Their families also received monetary benefits. If they were arrested, Murder Inc. would hire the best lawyers available and pay salaries to the hit men's families while the men were incarcerated.

Murder, Inc. was the enforcement arm of The Syndicate, a tight interstate criminal organization. As a young, strong man, Maxie was struggling to make ends meet like so many others during that time. To Bugsy and Meyer, Maxie looked like a perfect recruit. My father turned down the offer. He was no killer. He had a heart of gold, and at that time, dreams of marrying the woman who would someday become my mother, and raising a family that would be proud of him.

As different as my father was from Bugsy and Meyer, they had one thing in common – they were Jewish. Bugsy and Meyer's involvement in organized crime did not exempt them from the same anti-Semitism that plagued Maxie. Many of the old-school Italian mobsters hated Jews. Around 1930, a Sicilian don named Joe Masseria decided he wanted control of the Lower East Side. Masseria despised Jews in general, and Meyer Lansky and Bugsy Siegel in particular. He constantly demanded that Lucky Luciano stop associating with Jews. So, Luciano arranged for Joe "The Boss" Masseria to be executed at a restaurant on Coney Island.

While Bugsy and Meyer pursued a life of crime, my father pursued that beautiful young woman he had met through the boxing gym. His sister Betty was dating a man from the gym, who happened to be Minna's brother. Through this courtship, Maxie had met Minna, and both couples eventually married.

Though impoverished and desperate, my father would tell us he never considered joining Murder Inc. Such ruthlessness simply did not run through his veins. He was one of the most compassionate and loving men I have ever known.

The only time I ever saw my father use violence was during a visit to his mother in Brooklyn. I was just six-years old. My mother had sewn the three of us matching dresses. We looked quite fetching that day, in our matching dropped-waist, Scotch-plaid chemise dresses. My mother also had made us little matching pocketbooks. The three of us, along with my brother Billy, were playing in the hallway outside my grandmother's apartment.

Suddenly, this enormous man stepped into the

hallway and yelled at us to shut up. My father was a small man—maybe 5'4." The angry man was at least a foot taller, but Maxie didn't care. Defending us, my father yelled, "They're children, they're playing!" The big bully attacked my father. He lifted a chair and charged. Of course, Maxie was a boxer with considerable skills, so he blocked the chair but broke his hand doing it. My father, the hero, still exists in my memories.

During the ride home, I was so distraught and frightened by the events that happened that I threw up— right into my little matching purse and all over my beautiful new dress. Following my example, my two sisters threw up, too. All three of us, drama queens in the making, vomited from the stress. We never wore those dresses again, but we never forgot our hero, my father.

Chapter 4
The Chin

A few blocks north of the Lower East Side, in Manhattan's Greenwich Village, a young Italian man was trying to make it as a professional boxer. Vincent Gigante, the son of Italian immigrants, started boxing first as a middleweight, then as a light heavyweight. He won 21 of 25 professional matches between the ages of 16 and 19. He had a bright future, until a mauler named Jimmy Slade pounded him into submission for seven brutal rounds. Vincent never fought again – at least, not in the ring. In 1946, the lure of organized crime was too strong for this boxer to resist, and Gigante began running errands for the Genovese crime Family.

Gigante's greatest notoriety came from an assassination that he botched—or so the story goes. Historians of organized crime recount that, in 1957, a brutal racketeer named Vito Genovese decided to engineer a coup d'état within the New York Mafia Family that was originally formed by Charles "Lucky" Luciano. Gigante was designated to be the hit-man. At the time, the Luciano family was the strongest of all five New York crime families and, therefore, the U.S.

Luciano had been deported in 1946. From that time on, Frank Costello, a refined, well-spoken man known as "The Prime Minister of the Underworld," pulled strings to allow Luciano to return to the U.S. Author Mario Puzo would eventually pattern many traits of his fictional Godfather, Don Vito Corleone, on the very real Costello. When Marlon Brando was cast in the film to be Don

Corleone, he employed the same raspy voice with which Costello spoke.

Costello was everything that Genovese was not—smooth, politically savvy, a master at bribery and well-respected in the circles in which he lived. He wore three-hundred-and-fifty-dollar suits in an era when a hamburger could be purchased for fifteen cents.

Genovese was a crude, brutal, back-stabbing thug. He pursued the pleasures of a certain Anna Petillo. When he learned the woman was already married, Genovese invited her husband to the top floor of a New York high-rise for a "meeting," threw him off the roof, and did the same to a bystander who happened to witness the murder. Two weeks later, Vito and Anna were married.

Pure ruthlessness had served Genovese well in La Cosa Nostra, an organization that understood the power of fear. Costello still ruled the Luciano Family, but Genovese coveted the crown. He commanded one his captains, Tommy Eboli, to arrange a hit, and Eboli selected an up-and-coming thug named Vincent "The Chin" Gigante.

Gigante spent days in a secure Greenwich Village basement practicing his marksmanship. When the appointed day finally arrived, Gigante brought his shotgun into the lobby of New York's Biltmore Hotel, where Costello was staying. When the Prime Minister of the Underworld appeared, Gigante aimed at his head, squeezed the trigger and saw Costello go down. The job complete, the hit-man fled, thrilled with the new status this important assassination would give him within the Mob.

Gigante's bullets merely grazed Costello's scalp; he did not even require hospitalization. Costello told police he could not identify his assailant, a typical Mafia tactic.

Those in the Cosa Nostra take care of justice in their own way. When Gigante heard the news, he feared for his life, and rightfully so.

Costello's response proved yet again why he was different from a typical crime boss. Instead of launching a bloody war against Genovese, Eboli and Gigante, Costello decided to retire, an act than enabled him to live to the ripe old age of 82, when he died in his sleep.

Genovese stepped into Costello's shoes as the "Boss of all Bosses" in name only, and two years later, he was convicted of narcotics conspiracy. Genovese died in prison, and Eboli was murdered in 1972, shot five times in the head and neck while visiting his girlfriend in Brooklyn.

By 1981, the reins of the most powerful Mafia Family in the nation passed into the hands of the gunman who had botched the Costello assassination—a man who was rejected for military service because of "anti-social behavior" and checked himself into St. Vincent's Psychiatric Hospital in Harrison, N.Y., twenty-two times. That man was none other than Vincent "The Chin" Gigante.

Like shooting stars, my memories are lighting the darkness. My thoughts are going so fast that I fear I may be overwhelmed before I fill in some important details. I don't want to get ahead of myself.

Chapter 5
The Memory Flood

Regrouping after my encounter with the lawyer, I let my mind wander. Sitting at the faded and scratched Formica table that Michael's parents had given us as a wedding gift, I stared longingly at the empty chair directly across from me. I sipped the last drop of Cabernet Sauvignon from my wine glass, and with it came a flood of kitchen-table memories.

Michael using peas and corn to diagram Pop Warner football plays for Joel and Devin. The boys kicking each other under the table and hurling accusations at each other, when it was really Michael who was kicking both of them. Michael helping the boys with their homework, while sorting cards from his football pool. The candlelight dinners I made for Michael before the boys were born. The Halloween night we made love on this very same table.

I was living the American dream: The house in the suburbs, loving husband, athletic boys—a paradise on earth.

"I've opened the floodgates, Koho," I told my Siberian husky, but Koho was asleep. His snoring was interrupted for a phlegm-filled, guttural cough, but continued as if nothing had happened.

As the memories flowed, I wondered how many people knew, really understood, that at any moment their dream could come crashing down. I was exhausted from a long day at work, but I promised myself to start the letter to my grandchildren—tomorrow, first thing in the morning, right after I bought the tulips and, of course, planted them.

In that brief moment, I realized that was exactly how life slips away from us—one moment at a time. While I kept myself busy with dishes, dogs, tulips, purses, hats and goat cheese, life was quietly leaving me behind.

By the time the full weight of the realization hit me, I found myself upstairs in the office, sitting in front of the computer. I looked at the clock. The hands were past midnight. I thought about going to bed.

Instead, I steeled myself to remember the moment my life flew off the rails. It was also in the wee hours of the morning. With determination, I began typing into the computer.

Everything is a jumble. Everything has changed.

It's two A.M. I hear a bell, and wake up screaming "Johnny!" Like a three-year-old, I grab for my doll, but it's not there. Of course not, I'm a grown woman.

The memories erupt from me. I don't know where the journey will take me, but I know enough to trust the images and memories that seemed to be downloading from my mind directly onto the computer screen.

I need no title for this story. I have no time to waste on conjuring a clever title for my thoughts and feelings. I fell compelled to replay my life.

Mom giving me the rag doll when I am one. I refuse pacifiers and want nothing to do with blankets. Ever resourceful, she gives me that rag doll. I take hold of it and never let go.

"We'll give the doll a bath, Sunny."

"No, Mom, Johnny can't swim."

"It's filthy, honey. And it smells like I don't know what."

"I like his smell."

"Well, you can't take him to the store."

"Yes I can."

She relents and lets me take Johnny to the store, and everywhere else, although I later discover she slips Johnny out of my arms in the middle of the night for washings. In fact, he soaks in that washer so many times that his cloth skin begins to wear through. Bit by bit, his stringy hair begins to unravel.

Now, my sister Becca is teasing me, trying to take away Johnny. She pulls the left arm and leg; I hold the right arm and leg. In one horrific slow motion instant, Johnny is tearing apart, shredding into a falling cloud of string, stuffing and buttons.

I was right, Johnny couldn't swim. But that's not what had wakened me.

Was it a bell? In an instant, adrenalin transforms grogginess to panic. "Where are the boys—hockey camp? Billy? Billy is in the hospital with pneumonia. Yes, it is a bell. Did the phone ring? Is the call coming from the hospital? Is Billy OK?" I reach for Michael. He is not there. He is working that night—Casino Night at the Temple. I am comforted knowing he will be home soon.

Memories are my reality.

The doorbell rings. "That's it. Who's here at two o'clock in the morning? Is it Michael? Did he forget his key again? The son of a bitch."

I throw on a bathrobe and tramp down the stairs barefoot. I feel the cold hardwood floors. "Michael's not getting into bed until he promises me wall-to-wall carpet."

At the bottom of the stairs I see the flashlight pointing through my entry window. "What's Michael doing with a flashlight?" I stop cold. "Burglars. Black masks, crow bars.

No. Why would burglars ring the doorbell—twice?" I pull my bathrobe tighter and call out "Who is it?"

"Police, ma'am."

Acid rips through my stomach. I feel my bathrobe fall open as I jerk the door open. "What's wrong? Tell me now. Who is it?"

"May we come in, ma'am?"

"Who is it, God damn it, what's wrong?"

One of the officers hands me a phone number. "Ma'am, there's been an accident."

I go light, airy, drifting out of my body. I can hear myself talk, sense myself moving, but it's not me. It's someone else.

"Ma'am, you need to call the hospital."

"Billy's dead. I know it. Billy—The big brother who came to my rescue when Fat Marty tried to beat me up, because I called him Fat Marty; The big brother who was at my side for weeks last year when Maxie died even though Maxie was not Billy's birth father. Billy would always be my big brother, my first ally, my best friend. Did I say that or just think it?"

I feel the phone pressed hard against my ear, but the voice at the hospital seems so distant.

"Are you Mrs. Rubin, ma'am?"

"Yes," I can hear myself answer, "I'm Mrs. Rubin."

"Mrs. Rubin, I'm sorry to tell you …"

Wait a minute. The police said there was an accident. Billy's in the hospital with pneumonia.

"… your husband is dead."

That must be what the voice said, but all I hear is screaming and crying. I feel tears burning down my cheeks. After the spinning starts to slow, I see a white flash. Michael?

I was in my wedding dress, at 19-years old, like Andrea, my daughter-in-law, my son Joel's wife.

Cherished memories fill me. Michael, so handsome, has the band play "Sunny" for me. He buys me a house on Sunnybrook Lane. He coaches the boys. Leaves work early, so he never misses a game.

"Ma'am, he was shot in a robbery at the Temple."

Yes, all that money at the Temple on Casino Night.

"By the time your husband reached the hospital, he was already gone. There was nothing we could do."

A blur of police, screaming, knees buckling, calling the hockey camp, family emergency, send the boys home.

Everything is a jumble. Everything has changed.

It is 6:00 A.M. Aaron calls to talk to me about Michael. I don't care if he is my sister Becca's ex-husband; I wish it was Aaron who was dead, not Michael. Aaron was in charge of Casino Night, in charge of the money. Michael was such a sweet, good man, and here I am listening to Aaron, a womanizer who openly cheats on my sister, neglects his kids and refused to give my father a job, even after my father helped him get started as a locksmith.

"It should have been you, asshole," I scream.

He hangs up.

Everything is a jumble. Everything has changed.

How did Dr. Rudy get here? He drops a few Valium tablets onto my tongue and pushes a glass of water to my mouth. I feel water dripping down my chin, then two lumps in my throat. More water. I am falling back onto the couch. Dizzy. Faint. Eyes like lead. I close them.

Everything is a jumble. Everything has changed.

Nancy, my six-year-old sister, comes running into my bathroom. "He's here, Sunny! He's here!"

I'm seventeen and dressed for a prom, but it's not prom night; it is my first date with Michael. "Go answer the door, Nance! Tell him I'll be right down."

Dr. Rudy asks me how I'm feeling. My head is pounding. I mumble something, and drift back to seventeen. Nancy runs downstairs and opens the door for Michael.

"You can't be here for Sunny," Nancy says. "You're not handsome enough."

Michael smiles and asks, "What's your name, kid?"

"Nancy."

"Well, Nancy, why don't you take this dollar bill and go tell your sister I'm here."

Nancy runs into the bathroom waving the bill. "He gave me a dollar! He gave me a dollar to get you!"

I walk down the stairs and see Michael waiting. He's not classically handsome, but there's something about him. He's tall with dark hair and a look that says he wants to protect me from everything and anything. I had seen him only once before this date, and that occasion involved Billy.

Yes, now I understand where I am. Billy's poker game in the basement is finished, and he asks me to drive him to the bowling alley for a match with some guy. Fat Marty was supposed to drive him, but he got too drunk. Billy is drunk too, but at least he knew it in advance. He was twenty-one but refused to learn to drive. Drinking, gambling, driving—he didn't like the odds, always knew he'd be safer not knowing how, and everything was about the odds.

I drive Billy to the bowling alley. The match is with Michael, who has already had his share of birthday beers. Billy tells me that Michael's a good bowler and normally would wipe him out, but tonight, Billy holds the advantage, and Michael seems distracted anyway. Billy nudges me with his elbow, and I notice Michael picking up his ball and staring at me. I should walk away from any guy slurring his way through asking for a date. Still, there's something about Michael.

Michael compliments my prom dress, holds open the car door and gets into the driver's seat. "So what do you feel like?"

"Pizza?" For a first date, pizza is the right choice. I try to be calm.

"Pizza it is."

Michael drives through town, passing eight pizza joints along the way. He gets on the Jersey turnpike and heads north.

"Where are we going?"

"You said you wanted pizza."

"Well, what about Angelo's?"

"Sunny, if you want pizza, the only place to go is Ray's."

So we drive to New York City that night for pizza and to Philadelphia the next week for cheese steaks. We go to Brooklyn for seafood; Queens for Italian ices; The Lime House in Little Italy for calamari; and to Chinatown—68 Mott Street—for dim sum.

"Oh Michael, you always want the best for me. You never settle for anything less."

Everything is a jumble. Everything has changed.

Dr. Rudy hands me the phone. I don't know what time it is, but the headache is gone. I don't even feel my body. I'm drifting, drifting where?

"You need to call Michael's mother, Sunny."

Dr. Rudy dials. I'm lost in the haze. "How will I tell

her that her second son is dead?" Michael's brother died at 18. His mother never recovered. Because Michael's brother died on August 15th, Michael's mother lives in fear of that day every year. She makes Michael call her at 12:01 A.M. on the 16th of every August, just to let her know he is safe.

"Millie." I hear my quivering voice say.

"Sunny, my God!" Millie sounds terrified. "Does she already know? She couldn't possibly."

"Millie, it's Michael."

Somehow she knows. She is sobbing, gasping, heavy, uncontrollable sobs that rip an even bigger hole in my soul. I am as broken as she sounds, but Valium blocks my grief, my tears, my cries.

"Millie, there's been an accident."

Silence at the other end of the phone, then, more tears and short breaths. I know Millie. She is trying to compose herself enough to say something. Finally, in a tiny, weak voice, she whispers, "He's dead?"

I can't bring myself to say the words, but she knows the answer anyway. I think she knew the instant she heard my voice on the phone. She is his mother. Intuition, sixth sense, whatever you want to call it, I understand it. As deeply as my pain cuts through my own heart, I also feel anguish for this woman who has suffered the worst fate of all—living long enough to see her child die. Millie has endured that agony twice.

My tears finally conquer the Valium and pour through. "I don't know what to do, Millie."

"Sunny." Millie speaks in a strangely calm whisper. "It's August 15."

Everything is a jumble. Everything has changed.

I walk through Newark Airport. Everyone in the

sprawling terminal is staring at me, pitying me. My older sister Becca holds me on one arm, my younger sister Nancy on the other. I feel like my old rag doll, Johnny, being pulled apart from both arms, my insides spilling under every step I take.

Becca's bright red beehive hairdo reminds me that I once was a redhead. Nancy's brown hair reminds me I was a brunette, too. "Blond is better," I tell myself, though I'm not sure why. "Maybe it's all about change. Can we really re-invent ourselves? Maybe Michael is still alive?"

Dr. Rudy has loaded me with Valium before we leave for the airport. I think that maybe the Valium is helping the pain. What I do not realize that it also is making me a bit too honest. "It should have been Aaron." I tug on Becca.

"Don't say that, Sunny," Nancy says. Becca is either too mad to say it herself or too humiliated by Aaron's philandering to admit it.

"Well, it should have. He slept with half the woman in Queens before you finally got around to divorcing him."

Becca pulls away. "Aaron's broken up about this, Sunny. He loved Michael."

"The man wouldn't even give Daddy a job on Casino Nights, Becca."

"Sunny," Nancy warns.

Daddy was out of work. It didn't have to be much—taking tickets or making change, just some job. Aaron could have let Maxie help in some small way."

"Let's not talk about Daddy," Becca whispers.

"I agree," Nancy says.

"So let's talk about Mommy," I said, but I couldn't let Aaron's affairs rest. "After all these years, I still remember how Aaron wouldn't let her baby sit your kids when they were little. He didn't trust her. Mommy raised five kids, and your son-of-a-bitch husband didn't trust her with her own grandchildren."

"Sunny, it doesn't help anything to talk about this now." Nancy was always the peacemaker, but this time it's not working.

There's no peace for me now. The memories are so real.

"We always knew how much that hurt her. When Joel was born, Michael handed him right to Mommy and said, 'Here's your baby.' He always did the right thing. When Daddy died, he was right there to support me. Now I don't know what I'm going to do." I break down crying, which now seems as easy as breathing. Nancy holds me closer.

I want to disappear. "I can't even take care of myself, how am I going to take care of the boys? Michael was the one who guided them, disciplined them, connected with them. I don't know how to do any of that. I can buy them clothes, cook for them, but then what? I can't raise two boys alone."

"I wish Billy were here," I say, hoping to make them both feel unworthy, but Billy is in the hospital with pneumonia. He had planned to be at Casino Night with Michael. Billy is pit boss at the tables. He's the professional gambler, who knows the numbers backward and forward. He always ran the games at Casino Night. If he had been there last night, he'd be dead, too. "Thank God for pneumonia," I think. "Billy really does have nine lives. Always had luck, always will. Both luck and pneumonia."

Billy's first pneumonia episode came when he was in military service. His unit was about to ship out for

Vietnam. Billy started taking cold showers and going outside in freezing weather. Sure enough, he came down with pneumonia, couldn't ship out and was stationed in Germany for the remainder of his enlistment. No Vietnam. No risk to life or limb. Only a successful bookmaking ring in Germany. He was making so much money and partying so much, that he missed his flight home and had to stay in the military an extra month to wait for the next transport.

After that, he could get pneumonia whenever he needed to. The first day of a real job; Billy's got pneumonia. Temple Casino Night gets robbed; Billy's got pneumonia. Thank God. The lucky son of a bitch.

"I'll need Billy now more than ever," I think.

Adam, Becca's oldest child, walks toward us from the airline gate. I wish Michael were here.

Adam is accompanied by an airline agent who, like a mortuary director, solemnly says, "Mrs. Rubin, I'm terribly sorry about your loss. The boys have arrived and are waiting in our private lounge."

I want to get on one of these planes, fly away and never come back. "I can get through this myself alone," I think. "I don't know how, but somewhere deep down I have to believe I can survive this. But raising the boys? Getting them through this? I don't think I can do that. I truly don't."

As the agent leads us toward the lounge, a sharp, bottomless pain slashes through my body as if Dr. Rudy and Valium never existed. I mumble. "How will I tell them?"

Walking into the private lounge, I have a brief moment's view of Joel and Devin before they see me. At seventeen and fifteen, they are so young. In the next moment, I watch their youthful innocence give way as they turn and see the distraught pain on my face.

Devin slowly walks toward me. "Mom, is it Uncle Billy?"

They saw him in the hospital before they left for camp. In a way, I'm glad they had that to hold onto for the flight home. I start to sob as I rushed to hug Devin. I know I can't tell them I need their support. I have none to give. Crying on Devin's shoulders, I see Joel, still standing in place.

"Where's Dad?" Joel asks.

I feel Devin's arms loosen their grip. He slowly pulls back and eyes me with a look that begs me to tell him, "Dad's parking the car."

With my arm still around Devin, I lead him closer to Joel. "Sit down, boys."

Joel stands in place. "Where's Dad?"

I sit down with Devin, hugging him tightly as if that alone will protect him from ever having to feel the pain.

"Joel, please sit down."

I hear Becca and Nancy crying. Not the kind of help I need. I start crying harder myself.

Joel crosses his arms. "Where's Dad?"

"Honey," I look Joel in the eyes. "There's been an accident." My voice is either hoarse, or I just don't have the nerve to say it out loud. Joel's eyes turn angry. He's already blaming me. I feel Devin start to collapse beside me.

I reach for Joel, who finally sits down beside me. I hug the boys, pulling them as close as I possibly can, feeling like a bad mother for not looking them in the eyes, but I just can't. "Your father's gone."

"What do you mean, gone?" Joel's not going to let

me off easy.

I open my mouth, but nothing comes out. I struggle, hear a soft wail, and finally whisper, "Your father died last night."

I break down sobbing. Devin goes limp. I feel Joel breathing heavily. "It's OK, Joel." I squeeze him. "It's OK to cry this time."

Joel pulls away and storms to the window, looking out at the rows of planes on the tarmac. I look over to Becca and Nancy, who both move toward Joel. "We're gonna be OK," I whisper to Devin. His face is blank. Pale. I'm not even sure he's breathing.

I watch Becca put her arm around Joel. Joel jerks away and screams "No!" He picks up a chair, screams again and throws the chair straight at the window. The glass cracks, but doesn't shatter. Joel picks up another chair and aims for the window, but Adam and the airline agent quickly hold him back.

I want to get up and rush to Joel, but the Valium is like an anchor around my legs. I cry harder instead. Joel struggles with the agent, Becca and Nancy try to calm him down, but they are helpless. His arms are flailing. He storms to the corner of the room, screaming, kicking chairs, punching a hole in the wall. Even as he drops to his knees and buries his head, I can't move to help him. I can't comfort Joel because his anger is in the way. I can't pierce Devin's silence.

"Devin," I whisper. "Are you OK?"

Devin doesn't say a word, doesn't cry a tear. Just silence. I want him to cry instead of hold it in. I want Joel to cry instead of lash out. Michael always told the boys not to cry, so they never have. They didn't want to disappoint their dad. They don't want to disappoint him now. Even though he's dead, he's giving Joel and Devin more support than I can give them being in the same room.

I know it now. I can't raise these boys alone. Now I don't even think I can take care of myself.

Now, it is a slow-motion blur of people and sounds. Joel slamming trash cans. Devin catatonic. Joel screaming. Devin walking through security doors. People pointing and frowning. Baggage claim tickets not matching. Hockey bags too heavy to carry. Becca and Nancy hurting more than helping. Skycaps ignoring everything, and Valium making it all seem like the horror is happening to everyone but me. We stagger out of the terminal, onto the turnpike and head home.

From my bed, I hear the boys screaming. I put the soggy pillow over my head and cry into the sheet. I hear something break. A glass, a picture frame. I take another Valium and hope that when the sun comes up, this will all have been a bad nightmare.

Everything is a jumble. Everything has changed.

Joel is holding one of my arms, Devin is holding the other. I'm Johnny the rag doll again, only this time they're holding me together so I don't fall apart. We walk into the Temple and find a sea of faces—faces crying, faces pitying us, faces smiling—as if that's supposed to comfort us. Even in deep grief, I know I must find a way to put money in my bank account—to pay for hockey lessons, camp, tuition, the mortgage.

So many faces. Michael's fellow electricians. Neighbors, aunts, uncles, cousins. Friends I haven't seen since high school. Boys whom Michael coached. "We could field an entire Pop Warner football league with the kids in this funeral hall," I think. Their parents are here, but I don't even know most of them. Teammates of Michael from the adult basketball league. Friends from the Casino Night group. People are spilling out of the seats, crowding the aisles, pouring out the doors.

We approach the front of the funeral hall. I thank God that Joel seems calm. I hope he stays this way. I hope Devin eventually says something, shows some emotion. I hope at some point, I can rise above my own pain and support and comfort them.

The Rabbi speaks words and words and words. What a great guy Michael was, an asset to the community. More words and words and words.

Our Rabbi has no idea how great Michael truly is. No idea how Michael is my protector. How he has a way of balancing my emotions. No idea how he calms my hysterics—how when I'm throwing plates at him, he just smiles, hugs me and tells me what a big mess I've made.

I know the words should be, "Was. Had. Calmed. Threw. Smiled. Hugged," but I can't even think the words, for now, at least.

The Rabbi talks of how much Michael was loved, but he doesn't know that at first, I didn't want to marry Michael. I was afraid it wouldn't be the fairy tale I held in my mind. The Rabbi has no idea that Michael knew I loved him, even before I knew I did. Michael opened up my world, took me on adventures. With Michael, I traveled for the first time in my life. He became my protector. With Michael I felt secure and safe, stable for the first time in my life.

He supported and encouraged everything I ever did. He built a kiln in our basement for my ceramics. He was my best friend. He gave me the perfect life. Michael would never let anything bad happen to me, but now the horrible has happened.

He's gone. He's gone.

I'm starting to believe he is gone. He is not going to walk through the door tonight. He is not going to change the oil in my car this weekend. He is not going to pay the mortgage next month, and I don't know who will. My party planning business was good for pocket money, for shopping trips to New York and maybe a facial once in a while, but Michael kept us going. Michael took care of it all.

Suddenly I realized that I had never had to take care of myself. I married at nineteen and went straight from the bedroom I grew up in to the home Michael bought for us. Between my parents and Michael, I have never had to fend for myself. I have never been independent. I have never, not once in my life, been alone—until now.

I feel Joel and Devin take me by the arms and lift me to my feet. I'm not alone. Maybe it would be easier if I was alone, but I have the boys.

The service is finished. The Rabbi hands me the urn of Michael's ashes with a look that admonishes me, "We don't cremate bodies in the Jewish faith."

I know that, but cremation is what Michael wanted. It is also what my father wanted, because he and my mother wanted their ashes to be together. My mother's wishes also are for cremation. She wants her ashes and Maxie's to be blended to become one.

Michael liked the idea, so he made me promise to cremate him. Even though he always joked about living a short life, I never thought I would actually have to do this.

Not this soon.

Everything is a jumble. Everything has changed.

I hear my mother's voice. "Sunny," she says, "Sunny, wake up." I feel her hand gently touch my shoulder. "You'll be late for kindergarten."

I pull my rag doll, Johnny, close to my face and roll over, keeping my eyes shut tightly. Every morning mom tries to wake me before she goes to work. Every morning I try to get a few more minutes of sleep.

"Sunny, wake up."

Mom hated going to work. She hated the fact that my father could never make enough to support the family. She hated having to cook, clean, raise us and support us financially. My father won her heart by promising to take care of her and her two children—and not to beat her, as her first husband had. He kept that promise, but he never found quite enough work as a locksmith to make ends meet.

My mother had to support the family. She may have resented it, but life had handed her many disappointments, so she learned to do what she had to do to care for those she loved.

"Sunny, wake up."

Her hand is on my face now—warm and soft, but to my surprise, wrinkled. I open my eyes. I'm at home, and it is after the funeral, sitting Shivah for three days, as is the Jewish custom. Time eludes me. I'm not sure what day this is.

Everything is a jumble. Everything has changed.

I look up to my mother, but can't speak. Every new Valium plunges me deeper into an abyss, further from the pain, further from reality. I faintly hear Joel yelling in the background, but I can't understand what he is saying. He throws something, pushes Devin into a wall.

"Sunny." My mother shakes me a bit. "Joel's taking the car. He's furious. He'll kill himself."

Her words seem to cut right through me. I leap up, trying to shake off the Valium, trying to sweep away the haze, trying to climb from the abyss. Sharp fragments of the world get through to me—Michael's new red sports car. Joel in a rage, perhaps even drinking. Now Joel's yelling right at me. In my face.

My instinct is to slap him for this behavior Michael would not tolerate, but my heart says Joel needs me. He needs my love, my support, my strength.

For the first time in my life, I feel a strength I never knew I had.

I rise to my feet, steady and determined. I reach for Joel, but he pushes me away. I reach for him again, he turns away screaming. I reach for him again, taking him by the shoulders and pulling him into me, hugging him, holding him, letting him know, without words, that I will hold him for the rest of his life and never let him go, never let him down, and that he can count on me to take care of him, to be there for him, to love him endlessly. I let him know that I will be a provider and a friend, a mother and a father, and that we, as a family of three, are going to make it through this, and I am going to lead the way.

Devin steps forward and puts his arm on my shoulder, not so much to support me, but to let me know that he senses my new strength, that he understands things have changed. I sense he feels cared for and safe. I look in his eyes and see them turn from fear to trust, from anxiety to contentment. I can feel Joel making the same shift, his tense muscles relaxing, his anger melting into acceptance.

I bribe him with a promise of the red sports car. He feels my strength. He stops fighting me and surrenders into a hug. He's still not crying, but I can feel him let go, overcome with the relief, He feels he will collapse if he lets himself cry.

All the pieces are coming together. Even though I'm afraid, even though I'm drowning in doubts, something is stirring in me, telling me to trust that I can somehow do this. I don't have a plan, but I know, accept and embrace that everything is up to me.

This is just a more intense level of parenting. Not knowing how to do it, but making sure the boys think I do. I will find a way. I know in my heart I will. I will do, now and forever, whatever it takes to give these boys a normal life, to make sure they are know how much they are loved, to provide for them, to guide them, to inspire them, and to make sure they achieve all their goals.

I don't know how, but in my heart I know I will make this broken family whole again.

Things change.

I pull back from the computer, my cheeks flushed with tears. It was 5:00 A.M.

I pick up a picture of Michael from the desk, softly kissed him on the check and turned out the light.

Things have changed indeed.

Chapter 6
Alone Again, Unnaturally

I woke up alone, again. One month and I still was not used to Michael being gone, being dead. I didn't know how I ever would. The first thing I used to do every morning was kiss Michael. Now the first thing I do was get nauseous. My gut churned when I thought about how I couldn't make the mortgage payment; how I couldn't pay the boys' tuition; how Michael had no life insurance; how Aaron had no workman's compensation insurance.

Churn, churn, churn. I didn't qualify for victims of violent crimes benefits, because I own a home. If I didn't own a home, I would have been eligible. In a cruel legal twist, if I lost my home because I could not pay the mortgage, I still would be ineligible. The reason? I owned a home at the time of the crime.

No one could cut through the legal entanglements. No one could help. Something, anything would help, but there is nothing. The only thing I could do and would do was to stand tall and proud, and make a way for my family by myself.

Stumpy, a friend of Michael's from Casino Night, had tried to take up a collection for me, but Aaron wouldn't permit it. Stumpy told me Aaron not only did not have worker's compensation coverage; he had also let his gaming license expire. Aaron wanted to sweep this whole thing—a murder—under the carpet. A collection for the victim's family might draw attention to Aaron's mistakes, so a collection just would not be taken. Aaron didn't want any reminders that someone was killed at Casino Night.

He just pretended it never happened.

I wondered, "Did Aaron even care that Mike was dead, murdered?" I doubted it. Aaron cheated on my sister when they were married. Now, his sister-in-law is broke and alone. True to form, all he could think about was saving his precious ass and making everything go away. Again, I wished it was Aaron who was shot that night. How I wished it was Aaron.

Using the anger within in me as fuel, I got out of bed and headed for the bathroom. Anger was the only energy I could muster. If that son of a bitch Aaron thought I was going to let him get away with this, he didn't know me as well as he thought. Stumpy had given me the name of a lawyer. I would call that day: No it would have to be tomorrow. That day, I had to get the boys packed and ready for school.

The boys were leaving. I questioned whether they be OK at boarding school. Should I keep them home? Find them a school closer to home? Perhaps a public school?

I turned on the shower and started to cry. I would be alone for the first time in my life. The house would be empty, except for the faint echoes of the boys' joyful pranks and jokes. No laughing, no excitement, no life. I was clueless how I would manage the burdens of mortgage, tuition and bills. Would the boys have to be on their own?

"Alone," was my only answer. I was falling apart, everything was falling apart. Michael was the one who was supposed to keep it all together, not me. I couldn't do it. I just couldn't.

I stepped under the shower and closed my eyes, letting the hot water wash the mortgage and tuition and bills down the drain. By the time my mind finally started to clear, the water was cold.

I walked into the kitchen and saw the boys were already eating cereal.

"I could've fixed you something," I said.

"We got it, Mom," Devin answered.

It felt good having the boys here. I started a pot of coffee, trying not to cry. I was surrounded by pain. This morning's pain was not losing Michael, and it was not the debt that drowned me. I knew the source of that morning's pain—I was going to miss the boys. I would have been crying even if Michael had been here.

"Mom," Devin says, "it's not too late."

"Devin, we've talked about it already. That's enough."

"There are great schools around here, and I could look after you."

I wanted so much to say "Yes, go to school in the neighborhood, stay at home, take care of me," but I bit my tongue.

"The Pierce Academy is a once in a lifetime opportunity, Devin. Ask Joel. This is something we all talked about as a family."

Joel didn't look up from his cereal.

"And you boys will be able to play hockey together again. It's a Godsend."

"It's charity."

"Don't say that, Devin. You deserve to go there. The Pierce Academy is the best school in New England. Why do you think members of the DuPont family attend there? Why do you think the heirs to the Gulden Mustard business send their kids there?"

"I'm not a condiment, Mom."

"Forty thousand dollars tuition for the both of you

to go there, and, thanks to my begging and tears, they're letting you both go for eight thousand. We're not passing it up."

I couldn't tell him the eight thousand might as well have been forty thousand. I couldn't pay the tuition costs for either son, but I was not about to say so.

"It wasn't all begging and tears," Joel finally said. "Our hockey scholarships are half of that."

"I want you boys together. You have to stay together."

Devin looked me straight in the eye and, for the first time since he was six, he looked ready to cry. "If we stayed here, we'd all be together, Mom."

He was the one who always wanted to protect me.

I turned away as the tears start to flow. I fumbled with a dish towel, then poured a cup of coffee and took too big a sip. "Owww." I jerked the cup away from my mouth, spilling hot coffee on my white blouse. "You're both going. Together. That's the plan. That's what your father would've wanted. We made this decision together."

Devin held back tears, but the look on his face was ripping through me. Not even trying to hide my tears, I walked over to the table and put one arm around Devin, the other around Joel. "I'll be there for all your games."

Joel ate cereal as if I were standing in the living room. Devin looked down at his bowl, then slowly turned away.

Another day. I untied my bathrobe so I could bend down and pick up the morning paper from the sidewalk. I didn't look at the paper, I didn't retie by bathrobe. Why bother? As I shuffled up the driveway to my front door, I saw Sharon, my next-door neighbor, sweeping her porch. I waved, and she waved back. As I started across the lawn to talk to her, I smiled, maybe for the first time in a month. The boys had been gone a week now, and I had not left the house once, had not picked up the phone. I'm not even sure if I had gotten dressed. My bathrobe was my new best friend. My only friend. But now there was Sharon. My old girl-talk buddy.

The wet grass felt good on my feet. It was good to feel anything besides pain. It would be good to talk to someone. Just chat, like the old days. Maybe even have a cup of coffee. As I started to step over the flower bed between our homes, I looked up and saw Sharon rushing into her house. Her screen closed. Her door closed. I closed my bathrobe and pulled it tight.

That's why I hadn't spoken to anyone or anyone to me. No one knew what to say. That's why I hadn't picked up the phone and no one had called. I was alone. No Michael. No sons. No friends.

Days pass. I set the newspaper on the kitchen table next to a stack of unread papers and unopened mail. Companies must have known I wasn't opening my mail, because now they were stamping "past due" on the outside of the envelope. I pulled out the envelope from the mortgage company and slipped it under the bottom of the stack.

I needed to find work. There was no way my party-planning business could support me. I had a feeling my partner Georgina wanted to dissolve the business, because I had become a burden. I was missing too much work so I could attend my sons' hockey games. Oh hell, I was tired of playing the bad guy all the time anyway. If a client's napkins were candy pink instead of pale pink, I was supposed to be the one who dealt with them while they freaked out. It all seemed so pointless and trivial. Maybe Georgina was thinking she could do it alone.

I picked up the phone and dialed.

"Georgina, it's Sunny."

"Listen, Sunny, can we talk later? I'm running out the door."

"When, later? I have some ideas …"

"I'll call you. Take care, Sunny. And please, call me if you need anything!"

As the phone clicked, I thought, I do need something. Money. And I just did call you. Was she trying to run the business without me? Or was she just hiding from me, like Sharon? I had thought with Michael gone, at least my friends would step in and give me a hand, a shoulder to cry on, help me get back on my feet. Instead, they were treating me like I did not exist, or worse, like I just didn't matter to them. I had lost my husband, now I was losing my friends as well, and right when I needed them most.

Another week or another day? Time was fluid.

Dishes were piling in the sink as fast as the bills on the table. I didn't know why I was hardly eating at all. I had no appetite. I saw Joel and Devin's cereal bowls from last week at the bottom of the pile. That's how the pile had started. I didn't want to wash away that memory just yet.

I opened the cupboard for a coffee mug, but there wasn't a clean one to be found. Didn't matter. I didn't have the energy to make coffee, anyway. I grabbed a dirty mug from the sink and poured a cup of cold coffee from yesterday's pot. I had gotten used to cold coffee. I didn't know why people didn't drink it more often.

The phone rang. No calls in a week, and now two

calls in one morning. Well, at least somebody cared. I picked up the phone, excited to hear a friendly voice.

It was not to be.

"Mrs. Rubin, this is Dean Eccleson at The Pierce Academy."

"Oh God, is something wrong with the boys?"

"No, ma'am. Well, yes, but ... "

"Which is it?"

"Mrs. Rubin, under the circumstances, we thought it would be wise for Joel and Devin to pursue a course of psychological counseling."

"What? They need a shrink?"

"We have a doctor on staff, and he offered to visit with the boys. They've already met."

At least they weren't in trouble, right? The last thing I needed was for my sons to get kicked out of school. But a shrink? My mind raced and quickly came to a logical stop.

"I think it's a good idea, Mr. Eccleson. The boys could use someone to talk to so they could define and share their feelings. God knows I haven't been much help to them this past month."

"It's a difficult time. I'm sure you're doing your best."

Tears welled in my eyes. I was doing my best, I thought, but it wasn't good enough. Nothing was working. Nothing was making sense. When will this nightmare end so I can wake up and have my happy life back?

"The thing is, Mrs. Rubin, well, Joel became violent during the session. Quite violent."

"Violent?"

"He threw a chair through a window."

"He lost his father, Dean Eccleson."

"The doctor was very upset."

Tears flowed, and my voice sounded odd to my own ears, shaken with uncertain fear. "I'll pay for the window."

"Our concern is with Joel, Mrs. Rubin."

I sobbed. Why hadn't I said that? Why hadn't I thought of Joel first? "Is Joel OK?"

"He wasn't hurt. However, we're concerned his behavior, if left unchecked, might cause problems in the future for himself and possibly others."

"He was never violent. Never a problem."

"It's understandable that he's upset. But he needs help."

What was I supposed to do? Go up there? Should I bring the boys home? "So what's next, Dean Eccleson?" I did not know what else to say.

"For now, I think we encourage Joel to continue counseling, if I can get the doctor to agree to see him again."

I broke down completely. I'd been crying for a month straight, but this felt like I had not cried in years. I could not stop crying long enough to even get a word out my mouth. I just hung on the phone sobbing.

"Mrs. Rubin, are you OK?"

OK? Was I OK? I was so far past OK I didn't think I would ever find my way back. "I'm fine," I sobbed. "It's just so hard."

"If there's anything we can do," he said with his vice trailing to someone or someplace else.

"Just take care of my boys," I managed to blurt out. "Take care of my boys."

I moved from one place to another in a haze of confusion. Time moved in fits and starts. That day, I sat in the stark lobby of the Mathews Paint Factory. It was my fourth job interview this week, if you can call them interviews. The first two refused to even see me because I could not produce a resume. The third potential employer had cut the interview short and given me a brochure about adult education.

"You want an education, interview lady? Try living my life for a few days, "I thought.

At Mathews Paint I went straight to the owner, Charles Mathews. I was learning.

Charles Mathews had attended school with Michael and played in the basketball league with him. At the funeral, Charles had told me, if I needed anything, to come see him. If I couldn't get a job here, I might as well put the house up for sale and look for a women's shelter.

My mind was racing recounting my attempts to get a job. Why did every lobby in New Jersey look the same? The same shiny vinyl chairs, the same worn Formica tables, the same dirty shag carpet came with the same smug, condescending looks from the receptionists who were much better at looking busy than they were at actually getting any real work done.

"I could do your job in a heartbeat, honey. Experience? You want my experience? Try raising two boys. Try running a household full of men. Try having your husband murdered. You want my experience? Trust me, you don't want it." My smile masked my silent thoughts.

Selling paint. I never thought I might be selling paint, but a job is a job and nothing is forever. I just needed someone to give me a chance. Let me show what I could do. I would move up the corporate ladder in no time, if someone would just give me a chance. Charles would give me a chance. He had to.

The receptionist's phone rang. Even though she

wasn't doing a thing, she didn't answer on the first ring. I guessed she couldn't let anyone know she was just sitting around. Second ring.

"Yes?" The receptionist cooed. "I'll send her right in."

The receptionist smiled at me like we'd been friends for ten years. "Mr. Mathews will see you now."

Charles closed his office door and gave me a big hug. It occurred to me that he'd never hugged me before. Then again, I'd never been a widow before, either. I was touched. At least someone was showing some support.

"Can I get you coffee? Soda? Water?"

"Coffee's great," I said, just to buy some time and to have some hot coffee, too. I mentally ran through the notes from *Glamour Magazine's* article on "How to Land Your Dream Job." Be assertive, but not pushy. Confident, but not arrogant. Sexy, but not raunchy. It wasn't my dream job, but the tips should work for this as well.

Charles handed me the coffee. I didn't know where it came from, but I reached out my index finger to lightly touch his wrist. I didn't plan it. I didn't even know I was doing it. It was like instinct. Are women somehow programmed at the DNA level to use their sexuality to get what they want?

My stomach tightened. I felt like I was betraying Michael, but I could not deny that touching another human being felt good. How could I throw myself off balance like this? Luckily, Charles let it go. It didn't mean anything. Something that happens when one person hands something to another.

Charles motioned for me to sit, then took his place behind the safety of his desk.

"So, Sunny, what can I do for you?"

Oh, God, I thought. He was going to make me ask? He was going to make me beg? "Well, as I'm sure your receptionist told you, " I began.

"No, she didn't tell me anything."

"She didn't tell you why I was here?"

"No. But it's good to see you, I've been thinking about you."

My *Glamour Magazine* demeanor crumbled into *Mad Magazine* confusion. I felt like a fool. That receptionist was probably laughing at me right now. Tears welled in my eyes, a sensation so familiar by now it was like feeling my skin. "I need help."

"Of course, Sunny. I know it's rough getting used to not having Michael around. What can I do for you? Help you move some furniture? Start your furnace? Take the boys to a ballgame?"

"Charles, I need a job." I hadn't thought it would be that easy. I hadn't thought pride would crumble so quickly under the weight of desperation, but it did. I felt good. Relieved. The ball was in Charles's court. Unfortunately, it looked like it hit him in the balls.

"Um, Sunny," he paused, "That's a tough one. We don't have any positions open at the moment."

"Really? Because I heard you needed another paint salesperson," I couldn't believe the words coming from my mouth. "Charles, I need the money."

Suddenly I realized that pride isn't a great friend to have. Look how fast it deserted me. Desperation, I found out, was much better at sticking by my side. "You know, Charles, I ran my own business."

"Party planning?"

He was killing me. Couldn't he give me even a little

break? He was going to make me work this hard?

"Event planning. It was very successful and growing. Business is business, Charles." *Glamour Magazine* comes to my rescue. "I built my business, I can build yours. You know I'm a people person. In the end, selling all comes down to relationships. Who do you know that's better at relationships than I am?"

"Sunny," was all he said.

"Charles, you and Michael go way back." Had I just said that? If I had an ace in the hole, desperation must have had a whole stack of aces.

"Sunny, please. I want to help. I really do."

"Then help, Charles. Why is it that everyone wants to help so much, but no one ever does? Is it all just words?"

"Sunny."

I did not want fear to take over. I could not allow fear to undermine my determination. Fear was simply an opportunity to show courage and strength. My tears stopped. I resolved to turn this negative into a positive. I knew I could meet this challenge.

"I'm sorry, Sunny. If there's any other way I can help …"

I smiled, shouldered my purse and, with a pleasant "Thank you, Charles," I headed for the parking lot. The engine was running and I was about the shift into gear when I was startled by a knock on the driver-side window. It was Charles. I rolled down the window, happily anticipating his change of heart.

"Listen, Sunny. I've known you and Michael a long time."

"A lot of good times, huh, Charles?" My composure remained intact. I would accept his job offer with dignity.

"Too many to remember. The thing is, I always felt like we were special friends."

"Michael did too, Charles. He always said so."

"I know, but I mean you and I."

"Of course we were, Charles. That's why I'm here."

Charles leaned into the window, a little closer than a good friend would.

"Sunny, maybe it's too soon, I don't know, but I've always had a crush on you, and I was hoping maybe we could, you know, have dinner sometime?"

I didn't know what a black hole felt like, but I imagined this was it. My life, my memories, what I knew to be true seemed to implode into a burning rage of anger and tears. I threw the car in gear and pulled away, maybe taking Charles's left arm with me. I didn't know what had happened. Everything I saw was red. I heard him yell, "Sunny! Wait!"

I skidded out the parking lot and onto the street. I pressed the gas pedal to the floor, running a stop sign that I didn't see, until I was halfway through the intersection. I heard a horn honk but not a crash, so I kept going. I rubbed my tears like a windshield wiper, but the road appeared blurrier. I heard another long honk, then jerked to the side of the road and screeched to a halt. I turned off the motor, rolled up the window and screamed. Not a fearful scream, but a long, guttural wail of anguish, like my insides were being ripped from my body and strewn across the road for all to mock.

Was this hell? I really did not know where I was. It felt like hell. Where else could I be in this much pain? My scream turned into sobs as my head fell back on the headrest. Had Michael's murder not been enough of an emotional beating? Did I now have to live through all of this mess?

Now I wished I had been murdered. Now I wished that I was the one who was dead.

Chapter 7
A Rose by Any Other Name

Georgina would not return my calls. I made appointments with her, but she never showed up. After eating lunch alone three times, I had had enough. I wanted to talk about our party planning business, but that wasn't all. I also needed a friend. I needed to tell someone that Charles had asked me out. I needed someone to agree with me that he was a worm. I wanted someone to tell me that I should call Charles's wife and tell her what had happened, or I wanted someone to stop me from doing it. I didn't know. I just needed a friend.

I decided if Georgina did not call me, I would go to her house unannounced. I did just that, but she wasn't home. Her husband, Rick, answered the door.

"Sunny, how are you?" Rick smiled.

"How the hell do you think I am, Rick?" I wasn't mad at him, but I had no one else to absorb the anger I felt.

"Hey, if there's anything." His reply had a familiar ring to it.

"Don't even say it, Rick. Is Georgina here? She hasn't returned calls. She's been standing me up."

Rick stepped outside and closed the door behind him. "I'm sorry, Sunny. I know she's behaving badly."

"Badly? My only friend left in the world, and she's ignoring me. I need her, Rick. I want to get the business off the ground."

"I know, Sunny. The thing is, Georgina can't do it."

"Can't do what?"

"She can't be around you anymore. She says you

depress her."

"I depress her? I depress her?" I felt myself starting to cry. "What the hell is that?"

"I'm sorry, Sunny. I really am. I don't agree with her, but she wants to close the business."

"Close?"

I couldn't utter another word. I wanted to say how I have been depending on that income to keep my house; how the rug had been pulled from under my life. I didn't need my best friend and business partner to kick me while I was down, but I could not speak. My mouth wouldn't make the movements to form words. I slowly turned and walked down the path to my car, ignoring Rick as he called something out to me.

Now I understood I was operating alone. I learned that when people said they understood, when people said they wanted to help, the words came much easier than the actions. Since Michael had died, I couldn't think of one time anyone had ever actually meant it.

Reality can be hard to accept. I cried for a few weeks after going to Georgina's house. When those tears subsided, I put my resume in order. After a dozen dead-end interviews following the ugly encounter with Charles, I finally found a job as an office temp.

I was fired the next week.

The reason was simple—I was going to go to the boys' hockey game on Wednesday.

It was a four-hour drive up to the boys' school. For me was six hours, because I was afraid to drive, so I took off the entire day. By itself, that might have been acceptable, but when I told the boss I needed the next Wednesday off, and the next, and the one after that, he fired me.

I didn't care, the job was worthless, and the pay worse, but I could see I had a problem. The boys had games every Wednesday, and there was no way I was going to miss a single one. Michael had always been the cheerleader. He had never missed a game. He had been the parent who started the cheering in the stands. He had been the guy leading the Y-M-C-A dance. He had been the loudmouth who got the dirty looks from the referees.

He also was the man who had beamed, his eyes glistening from pride, whenever Joel or Devin made a good play. It didn't have to be a goal; it could have been a great pass or a well-timed assist. The boys would make the play, then instinctively look to the stands for his approval and, like clockwork, Michael was standing and cheering them. I didn't know a lot of things about how to raise my sons, but I knew I had to be in the stands to cheer. I could do that. I had learned from the best.

At some point, I discovered I didn't care if I did lose the house. I didn't care if I was afraid to drive. I didn't care if the games were four, six or ten hours away. I didn't care if it was raining, snowing or if the roads were a sheet of ice.

I made a vow to myself to be in the stands at every game, leading the parents in cheers, starting the Y-M-C-A dance, and standing and cheering every time my sons made a play. No matter what happens, they'll always have that memory. Even if I couldn't hold a job, my sons would always have my cheers and support at the hockey games.

Of course, I could not convince potential bosses that I would work extra nights, weekends or whatever it took to make get the job done, just so I could attend the Wednesday games. No one understood. The bridal shop fired me. The market research firm fired me. The leather store fired me, and there were others I don't even remember, but I do know I never missed a game.

I was moving forward. I had no work, no income, but things were changing socially. Arthur and Rose, old friends of Michael's, called and asked me to dinner. Arthur knew I didn't like to drive at night, so he offered to pick me up. Finally, I thought, friends acting like friends.

Arthur was a little jumpy in the car.

"Are you all right to drive, Arthur?"

"I'm fine, why?"

"You seem nervous."

"To tell you the truth, I'm a little unsure about what to say to you. With, well, you know. "

Arthur was one of Michael's wise ass friends, the kind of guy who didn't have many friends of his own, let alone popular friends like Michael, but Michael had always felt sorry for Arthur in high school and took him under his wing. Michael was like that, always standing up for people who needed help, and Arthur definitely needed help. He was always starting fights or smoking pot.

Michael didn't care what others thought. He wanted Arthur to be his friend, and if people didn't like it, forget them. Now, I finally saw why Michael felt sorry for Arthur. I felt sorry for him, too. He was so nervous and unsure of himself.

"You know what, Arthur?" I looked at him warmly. "That's about the most honest thing anyone has said to me since Michael died. I can't tell you how many people say all the right things, but do nothing. Here you are actually inviting me over for dinner."

Arthur smiled nervously.

"Michael would've been happy," I told him.

Boy, was I wrong,

At the house, Rose greeted me with a long hug and led me to her living room couch. Arthur disappeared into the kitchen while Rose and I sipped wine.

"I've been thinking about you so much, Sunny," Rose said with the standard sympathy face. She seemed sincere, so I didn't bother telling her how many times I'd heard that line.

"It hasn't been easy, Rose, but I'm starting to get back on my feet."

"You're a strong, dynamic woman, Sunny. I've always admired you for that."

"Well, I'm nothing like you."

Rose was like Michael, good-looking, popular and kind to people who needed it most. People like Arthur.

"I'm nothing compared to you, Sunny."

"What are you talking about? You've always been popular. You've always had it together. Things always go right for you."

Rose blushed, taking a sip of wine to hide it. She ran her fingers through her dark brown hair, the way she always did when she was nervous. With her tan, smooth complexion, she looked the same as she had in high school.

"Well then," Rose smiled, "I guess we're just two women who admire each other." Rose raised her wine glass to toast mine. We smiled as the glasses clinked and took long sips of wine. I hadn't been this happy since before Michael died. Just sitting, chatting normally, enjoying the company.

Rose swished the wine around in her mouth, savoring the flavor, and then slowly let it trickle down her throat. A moment later, she brightened.

"Hey, I'm taking masseuse classes. I'm hoping to pick up some extra cash."

"Well, let me know when you graduate. I'll be your first customer."

"I will." Rose smiled.

"Michael always gave great massages. I miss that."

Rose nodded in sympathy. "Well, hey, I'll give you a massage now. I think we have time before dinner, and we're supposed to find people to practice on anyway."

"Sold," I laughed.

Rose set both our wine glasses on the coffee table so she could kneel on the couch.. "Turn around."

I knelt as well, turning my back to Rose, who gently began massaging my shoulders. I hadn't realized how tense I had become. I felt tightness in my back. As Rose's fingers slowly kneaded my shoulders, the tension drifted away. I felt amazingly calm.

As I closed my eyes, I realized I had become so alone and isolated during the last few months that I had forgotten what it was like to have someone do something nice for me. As I melted into relaxation, Arthur's voice suddenly whispered, "Want a line?"

I opened my eyes and saw Arthur holding a mirror with a few lines of cocaine drawn out. He was rubbing his nose and sniffing.

"No thanks, Arthur. I'm good."

Cocaine definitely was not something I had ever used, but I didn't want to rain on his parade. One thing was sure—I wouldn't let him drive me home. No wonder he was so jumpy when he picked me up.

"What about a joint?" Rose asked. "It might help you

relax."

"Oh, my God, it's been years!" I never would have accepted the offer of a joint with Michael around, but suddenly I said, "Why not? It'll be fun."

Rose lit the joint and took a big puff. As she gave it to me, her hands returned to my back, working their way down my spine, deeper and more intensely. I took a long hit of the joint, and Rose slid her legs alongside mine, so I was almost sitting in her lap. The massage got more intense, and my mind slowly spaced out. I was in another place. My worries dropped away, my body glowed. I felt supported, loved. These were real friends. This was the way real friendship should feel. It had been so long, I had forgotten.

I took a sip of wine, while Arthur turned on the TV. I didn't open my eyes to see what he was watching. Why would he want to watch TV when just being here together felt so nice? To each his own, I guessed. Rose and I finished the joint, and the massage got better with every hit. Her fingers were like heated magic running up and down my spine. I took another sip of wine, and as I set the glass on the table, I peeked at the TV. Arthur was watching a threesome porn video. How strange, I thought.

Rose's hands caressed my shoulder blades, and then slowly worked over to my sides. Before I knew it, her hands had reached around to the side of my breasts. A little close, I thought, but she was a masseuse, so she must know what she was doing. In one fluid motion, her hands cupped my breasts, and her fingers started massaging my nipples.

I opened my eyes just as I felt her breath on my shoulder, then her lips, warm and wet, nibbling my neck. I jerked away. "What are you doing?"

"Just relax," Rose whispered.

"What do you mean, relax?" I yelled.

Rose whispered in my ear, "I've always wanted you, Sunny. You know, there's nothing like the tenderness between two women."

Rose kissed my neck again, and I jumped off the couch. My stomach tightened. I felt dizzy, wobbly. I felt a tingly, cold sweat flush from my skin. Arthur looked at me with his homely eyes, but didn't say a word. Rose took my hand. "Don't be scared, Sunny, It'll be fun. Exciting. Think about it for a minute."

"I don't need to think about it." I didn't know if it was the pot or the situation, but I suddenly felt sick to my stomach. I rushed to the bathroom, slammed the door shut and locked it. I was shivering in a cold sweat. My back cinched up tighter than before the massage. I felt faint and started to see white and red flashes.

I felt panicked. I was stuck in the bathroom of perverts.. I didn't have a car, I wouldn't let Arthur drive me. What was I going to do? How did I get into this? How could people treat me this way?

I dropped to my knees. The cold tile of the bathroom shot through my body. I opened the toilet, leaned over and gagged. My stomach heaved. I was vomiting into the toilet like a drunken, high school girl. Tears streamed down my face, until I finally broke down sobbing, resting my head on the toilet. I didn't care that my face was inches from the vomit, I didn't care that my hair was dangling into the toilet—I just wanted to die.

I sat there for ten, maybe fifteen minutes before I heard a knock on the door. "Sunny?" It was Arthur. I flushed the toilet, wiped my tears and rinsed my face in the sink. The cold water felt good, bringing me back to life.

"Sunny? I can explain."

I looked at myself in the mirror and saw a woman I barely recognized, living a life I never imagined. Where did I go from here? How could I protect myself? Who could I trust?

I heard a screwdriver fiddling with the lock. There was nothing I could do. I was helpless. Arthur was going to force himself on me, and there was not one thing I could do to stop him.

The lock clicked and Arthur slowly opened the door. His face wore the same pitiful look that Michael saw when he befriended him. "I'm sorry, Sunny. I really am."

I started crying again. "What do you want from me?"

"It's Rose. She's never been happy with me. Sexually, I mean. I'd do anything for her, Sunny, you know I would. So when she asked me to set this up, I agreed. I didn't want to hurt you, but at the same time, I would do anything to keep Rose happy." Arthur started tearing up. "She'd leave me, Sunny. I can't please her in bed."

They say a baby's natural defense is innocence. That's what Arthur was. A big, innocent baby. I couldn't help but see the pain in his eyes. He wasn't just telling the truth, he was feeling it.

"Can you drive?" I asked.

"I'm OK. I promise."

Arthur led me to the front door. I didn't see Rose anywhere. Like a repentant gentleman, Arthur opened doors for me, drove like a grandma and safely took me home. Michael's instincts were always right. Arthur was one of the good guys. Still, after this, I didn't think I could ever trust him again, and, believe me, I wanted so much to trust somebody. Anybody.

  After that night, I didn't even trust myself.

Chapter 8
Don't Brake

I woke up early with a headache and the taste of bile in my mouth. The house was freezing. I was too hazy to think about turning on the heat or to try to figure out why it wasn't working. I was too hazy to remember why I was hazy. As I stood up and my head started spinning, it all came back.

Walter and Rose. The wine. The pot. Throwing up in the bathroom. There were so many reasons for the headache I didn't even bother trying to focus on the main one.

I popped two Tylenol and went to take a shower, but there was no hot water. A shower—the one perk of living alone, and even that was taken from me. I threw on my bathrobe and walked down the hall to check the water heater. It was ice cold. What would a plumber cost? What did that matter? I didn't think I could afford a plumber anyway.

I couldn't think with my head throbbing. I went to the kitchen to put on coffee, but the coffeemaker wouldn't work. I flipped the switch back and forth – nothing. Not even the blinking red timer.

I opened the refrigerator and noticed the light was out, then smelled the rank odor of warm, rotting food. The electricity was out? Is that why there was no hot water? No, the water heater was gas. Was the gas out, too? I looked around the kitchen, and then flipped on a burner on the stove. It didn't light. My temples were throbbing dully, but when I saw the gas and electric disconnection notices on the counter, the pain spiked to a sharp piercing. They had shut off my utilities.

I had seen the notices, but never thought they'd do it. What were the dates? I had thought I had more time. I was going to walk the payment into the office after my next paycheck. Hadn't I talked to someone about that? Hot tears swelled in my eyes, making my head throb even harder. I slid down the kitchen counter until I was sitting on the cold linoleum floor. I raised my knees to my chest, rolled to the ground, crouched into a fetal position and cried.

"Don't brake," I said out loud, repeating it to myself over and over, "Don't brake. Don't brake. Don't brake."

The highway was patched with ice, and I remembered Michael always saying it was a "rookie move" to brake on ice. That's why so many people spin out. Michael was the driver. Always. I never drove, especially on the long trips to the boys' hockey games.

I was scared to death of driving, so much so that I had willingly endured Michael's radical, high-speed, lane-changing, car-passing, driver-cussing trips. With Michael behind the wheel, I had felt that every trip could be our last, but he turned a four-hour drive into three-and-a-half hours. I was turning it into six.

I knew enough to leave three hours early so I wouldn't miss the beginning of the game. Besides, with no heat, the house was freezing. At least the car was warm. The drive was nice. It felt good to get out of Cream Ridge, out of New Jersey. My thoughts were clear. Problems seemed more solvable on the open road.

I had a social security check coming in the morning. It would be my second payment from Michael's death benefit. It wasn't much, but it did cover the basics. I had used the first one to make a mortgage payment. That had put me only three months behind. Not good, but enough to keep the bank from foreclosing. This one would go to utilities, gas and food. I never thought I'd be so excited to see eleven hundred dollars.

I'll get another job. That seemed easy. After all, I was good at getting jobs. I just had to learn how to keep them.

Unfinished business kept me occupied during the drive. The lawsuit was at the top of my list. It had been eating away at me for months. I had to call Stumpy's lawyer friend about suing Aaron. The creep had let his workman's comp policy lapse. Upshot of that was I could not be eligible for any payments in connection with Michael's murder.

"Son of a bitch." My foot hit the brake, and I felt the car skip under me. I slid across the lane into oncoming traffic. I screamed as my foot jerked away from the brake. The tires spun, but then gripped the road. I steadied the car back into my lane.

Brother-in-law or not, I was going to sue Aaron the minute I got home. I had never been to a lawyer in my life—didn't even know one. Stumpy's suggested legal mind would be my first. Yes, I needed the money. Yes, I was angry as hell at Aaron, and I vowed I wouldn't let him get away with this one. Problems are so easily solved on the open road.

Of course, while I was running from my problems at home, I was speeding closer to the problems at school. I was grateful that the boys were able to attend a pricey private school on a full sports scholarship. They were getting an education I would never have been able to afford, but it was painful to have them so far away from me during such a challenging time in their lives.

Joel had been combatant with the psychologist again. The doctor had refused to see him. I hadn't heard much about Devin, but I was sure he was all right. He hadn't taken Michael's death as hard: He seemed to have found his way through the grief and emerged on the other side.

Joel was trapped in a downward spiral. As I pulled off the open road and navigated through the town to school, my thoughts went from clear to shadowy and, by the time I pulled into the parking lot, my thoughts were a thick, muddy murk.

From the look on his face, his body language, and the immediacy with which he extended his hand, Dean Eccleson had been waiting for me.

"Mrs. Rubin, so good to see you."

"Were you waiting out in the cold for me, Dean?"

"On my way to the game and saw your car. It's good you come to all the games. Means a lot to the boys."

"I'm excited to see them."

"Before you do, perhaps we should talk."

The "oh-God" pit in my stomach was old hat now. "It's Joel, isn't it?"

"No," Dean Eccleson said. "Actually, Joel's doing quite well. He's starting on the front line today. Our first sophomore to start varsity in ten years."

"Joel's starting?"

"He's the leading scorer. Coach didn't have a choice."

"Then it's Devin?"

"Joel's been making progress in the sessions. He's still quite sullen, but not violent, or even tending toward violent. Dr. Meter takes this as a very significant development."

"But Devin?" I was worried. Joel was predictable. He'd be violent, but wouldn't really hurt anyone. What could Devin have done? Fights? Attempted suicide?

"Devin's having some trouble in class," Dean Eccleson said in a hushed tone, as he led me toward the indoor rink.

"Are you sure? Devin's always had good grades."

"His grades are good, but he walked out of English class and refuses to go back."

"That's not like Devin at all. Did he say why?"

"Not to me. I let it go the first day, but it's been three days now. If he doesn't go back, well. I don't know"

"I'll take care of it."

We walked into the rink, and Dean Eccleson was suddenly surrounded by parents shaking his hand, pulling him away and inquiring about their children. I took my seat in the stands and watched the boys warm up on the ice. As they circled by me, skating one after the other, they raised their sticks to me and, still young enough to want to impress me, picked up their speed on the ice.

I never felt comfortable in the stands at games. The school was for rich WASP families. I was a poor, single, Jewish woman. No one had said it, but I thought Joel and Devin were the only Jewish kids in school. They were definitely the only ones without trust funds. As I watched the game, I felt that everyone in the stands was watching me, judging me to see if I validated their pre-formed opinions of "those people".

The boys were on fire. Joel scored two goals. Devin made an assist. I smiled and waved, but didn't jump up and cheer. It wasn't the same crowd as youth hockey, and I didn't want to stand out any more than I already did. But I cheered inside. Yes, inside I was on my feet, dancing with the crowd, screaming at the refs, whooping with every play

Joel and Devin made. Inside, I was climbing the glass and jumping onto the ice when they won the game, while the rest of the crowd applauded politely, as if it was a tennis match.

"I know everything they're teaching," Devin said, as he squirted ketchup onto his fries.

"That doesn't mean you can walk out on class, sweetie," I said, wondering how much this steakhouse was going to cost me, and why I hadn't taken the boys to Denny's.

"My classes are pretty tough," Joel said. "You can't be getting off that easy."

Devin took a bite of steak and looked out the window. He could hide his feelings from anyone except me. He was hurting, but I didn't know why. I was blank. I had nothing to say. I took a bite of my salad, and as the chewing amplified through my head, I realized I had never really dug in deep with the boys. I had done their laundry, I had cooked their meals, I had driven their carpool, but Michael was the one who had pushed them. He was the one who had known how much pushing they could take, and when not to back down. I had been the easy one. The one they had come to when they wanted to get away with something.

I took another bite of salad and tried to chew softer. What do I do here? I had no idea. Michael could make the boys know he meant business just by the tone of his voice. I can't do this, I thought to myself. I can't raise my boys.

Another bite of salad for me, as Joel elbowed Devin, and they both eyed a cute girl walking by. I wished my life was that easy. I wished for Michael to come back, to be here now.

As Joel and Devin turned around, pretending to look for the waitress, but actually catching a glimpse of the girl's cleavage as she bent down to her seat, I suddenly felt warm. The boys thought I didn't notice what they were doing, but I knew. I always knew, like Michael had always known.

The warmth surrounded me. I felt as if Michael was sitting next to me. I could hear him gulp a beer, I could smell his silent burp. I could feel him scoot closer to me in the booth, put his arm around me, tell me everything was going to be fine. Whispering into my ear that he never knew what he was doing either, he just went on instinct. "The boys didn't know," said Michael's soft voice, though it was more of a thought than a real voice. "They thought I knew what I was talking about. Besides, you don't need to know what you're doing, you just need to love them. Engage with them. The rest will take care of itself."

I swallowed the bite of salad and didn't even hear it go down. "Devin," I said, as confident as a rich parent, "tell me what's going on."

Devin spun his head back around. "My Coke. I need a refill."

"I'm not talking about the girl, Devin, I'm talking about class."

Devin blushed as Joel elbowed him. "It's nothing, Mom, I'm just bored by it."

"Devin," I said, surprising him by not giving up easily, "tell me what's wrong."

Devin twisted his fork into his steak and started cutting fat off the edges. "Hope we're not paying by the pound."

Joel laughed. I didn't take my eyes off Devin. "Grades

were important to your father, Devin. They're important to me."

Both boys looked up and stared. I stared myself. It was the first time any of us had mentioned Michael outside of the context of his death. It was a moment that could have turned us back on the hard road we had just traveled, or a moment that could build a bridge to a new way of being together. I didn't know which way it was going to go.

"Hockey was important to him too," Joel said. I was glad he said it. It was the first step on the bridge.

"It's important to all of us," I said. "But it's not the only thing. You're in a great school, it's a great opportunity, and I don't want you to miss out on it. We're not quitters here. We don't run from our problems. Your dad always taught you to face your fears, face your problems head on."

I was ready to cry, not from sadness, but from joy. I had spoken about Michael out loud. It had seemed taboo, because so often it would set Joel off into a rage of bitterness or anger, but why couldn't we remember the best of him? Why couldn't we still live our lives with his love and guidance, even if he wasn't there to see it? It felt so natural. I didn't know why I had avoided talking of Michael for so long. The boys, I could tell from their eyes, were as relieved as I was. After a long, warm silence, Devin put down his fork.

"He wants us to do a project on family," Devin said softly.

"Who?"

"My teacher. He wants us to write a paper about our parents. How they raise us. Our relationship with them."

No wonder he walked out, I thought. He wasn't ready to talk about Michael. "Did you tell him about your father?"

"He didn't care. He said to incorporate it into the project."

Joel eyed me, letting me know I had to back Devin up. I appreciated the direction. "Devin, sweetie, I'll talk to the dean. I'm sure we can work this out."

Devin looked up, surprised.

"If you don't want to write that paper," I suggested, "maybe the teacher can give you another project."

Devin almost smiled. I felt the warmth again, only now it wasn't coming from my imaginary Michael, it was radiating between the boys and me. In that moment, the boys and I connected in a way we hadn't since they were infants in my arms. As I reached across the table and took their hands in mine, I swore to myself I wasn't ever going to lose that connection again.

"Mom," Joel said. I knew it was either going to be heartfelt, or, like any kid, he was taking advantage of the moment to get something he wanted. "Devin and I are the only ones in school without a stereo in our rooms."

Definitely taking advantage, but t it was ripping my heart at the same time. With his eyes watering up, I couldn't say it was manipulation. God, I thought to myself, it must be tough for these boys being around so many rich kids. Peer pressure in high school was tough enough without money issues, particularly when you were up against some of the biggest trust funds in the country? I wondered if it was worth the education they were getting.

"Joel," I said, tears welling up in my eyes, "I'm sorry. We just can't do that right now."

"We're not talking about anything expensive, Mom," Devin said.

This was killing me. I couldn't tell them I was about to lose the house. I couldn't tell them the utilities had been cut off. They hadn't asked for anything since Michael had died, and the one time they found the courage to speak up, I had to shoot them down.

"I'm sorry," I squeaked, starting to cry. "I just can't."

"It's all right, Mom," Joel said.

"Yeah, we can just go to our friends' rooms," Devin added.

"I wish I could. I really wish I could."

"Don't worry about it, Mom. I don't even know why I asked," Joel said.

"We're playing hockey all the time anyway," Devin said. "It's not like we're in our room that much anyway."

I wiped my tears and nodded, thankful for how much like Michael they truly were. I would have sold my car and bought them the stereos, if I didn't have to come for the games. I didn't want to just give them whatever they asked for; I just wanted them to have a normal life, not feel deprived. I wanted to provide for my boys, the way Michael had, but I couldn't. That's what hurt the most. I didn't care about myself. I just wanted to provide for my boys.

Chapter 9
Money and Balls

It wasn't an easy decision to take Aaron, my sister's ex-husband, to court.

Aaron had been a bastard from day one. It wasn't just the way he treated my parents, or that he had openly cheated on my sister for years. He was the kind of person whose goal was to make everyone around him miserable.

The night before my wedding, I was at my mother's house in Queen's, going over last minute details. Becca was there with Aaron, and Nancy of course, who still lived there. We decided to order Chinese food for everyone. Aaron offered to drive me to pick up the food. While we were waiting for our order, Aaron actually started trying to convince me that I shouldn't marry Michael. He told me that he had feelings for me. This idiot was actually coming on to me the night before my wedding! I suppose he assumed he could take advantage of the pre-wedding jitters a 19-year old girl might have. Unfortunately for him, I didn't and he couldn't. I told him, with a few well-chosen expletives, that he was crazy.

After returning to my mother's apartment, I told her what had happened, and she told me he did the same thing to Billy's girlfriend. As the saying goes, "Pigs is pigs."

All that aside, I was entitled to some type of workman's compensation from Michael's death, but Aaron was my sister's ex. I worried the lawsuit would put even greater stress on a relationship that had been strained for years

I also didn't want to involve myself in a lawsuit that

would create more stress in my life. When Becca heard I was thinking of taking Aaron to court, she started calling me. Pleading turned to bullying, and that turned to abuse. I held off until the day Billy asked me, "If the situation was reversed, do you think Becca would hesitate, for one second, to take Michael to court?"

I called the lawyer the next day.

The night before the case was to be heard in court, Becca phoned me. She was screeching so loudly her voice was distorted.

"How can you do this to me?!!"

"I'm not doing anything to you, Becca."

"You're taking food from my children's mouths! You're sending me to the poorhouse! You're destroying my poor Aaron!"

Her poor Aaron? Her poor Aaron?

"What do you think he did to me, Becca?"

"You blame him for Michael's death, but did you ever stop to give him credit for giving Michael a job?"

If only there had been a way to slap her right over the phone line.

"How can you talk to me like that? Michael was murdered. He's not coming home, ever. Do you understand that, Becca?"

"That's not Aaron's fault."

"It's Aaron's fault that he let his worker's comp policy expire. I have nothing, Becca. Can you see that? Nothing! At least the insurance would've helped out some, and it wouldn't even have come out of Aaron's pocket."

"Well, now it is," Becca said. "Not that he'll have any money left once you're through with him!"

She hung up me, and called me back, and hung up

again. I couldn't believe she was defending the man who had made her look like a fool, over and over again. Her frenzied phone calls rattled me to my very core. I slept very little that night.

Stumpy, who looked like his name sounds, picked me up bright and early. He looked wrong in a suit. I don't think I'd ever seen him in anything but Levis and a T-shirt. He drove me to the courthouse. He was going to testify against Aaron in the workman's comp case.

"With Billy and me testifying," Stumpy said, "Aaron doesn't stand a chance."

"Let's hope Billy makes it," I said.

"Atlantic City isn't far. He'll be there."

"As long as he's losing."

Billy, wearing slacks, an open-collared white shirt and a tan sport coat, met us at the steps. He gave me a big hug and whispered, "Today's your lucky day, huh, Skunkie?"

I smelled Billy's pungent aroma: smoke, whiskey and perfume. Somehow, the familiarity made me feel safe.

"Thanks for coming, Billy."

"Are you kidding? A chance to kick Aaron's ass? This has nothing to do you with you, kid. I'm here to see the cocksucker's face when you stick it to him."

"I'm trying my best to keep my emotions out of it," I said, knowing that was impossible.

"Well, he didn't keep his emotions out of it when he made those death threats. Did you bring the tapes?"

Once Aaron found out I was taking him to court, he called and left messages on my answering machine, threatening to have me killed. I wasn't actually afraid of this sniveling weasel as much as I was outraged by his audacity.

Billy had advised me to tape every last threat. I had. "Yes, I brought the tapes with me," I told Billy.

"Believe me, I wish you would go the whole enchilada and get this guy for harassing you and threatening your life. It's not your fault he was so cheap, that he let his workman's compensation policy expire. I've never seen anybody cheaper with his workers than Aaron. The guy's a crook. Believe me, I'm gonna' make sure he gets his."

The judge – a woman, thank God – moved things along quickly and smoothly. She actually told Aaron to keep his mouth shut unless spoken to. Aaron took the stand and admitted that when the shot was fired, he grabbed all the money from the tables and hid in a garbage dumpster. What a fitting image—a rodent. He said he didn't see Michael get shot. I'll never know if that was true or not. It's not like he would have tried to do anything brave, like help Michael as he lay dying, so I guess it didn't matter.

Stumpy and Billy took the stand and told the judge the Temple made twice the amount of money the night of the murder than what Aaron had told the court. Billy let everyone know that Casino Nights was a full-fledged operation, and that he and Michael, were paid in cash under the table. As I heard Billy say this, it occurred to me how much he must really love me. Here was a guy who lived his whole life on cash under the table. He never filed tax returns. Never put money in the bank. He flew under the radar and stayed out of the spotlight. Yet here he was, in a court of law, admitting under oath that he was being paid cash, putting it on record, and he was doing all that for me. A tear rolled down my cheek. My sweet brother Billy.

We never told the judge that Aaron had threatened

my life, we didn't have to. After I testified, the judge called me to the bench and whispered to me, "This case is a no-brainer, Mrs. Rubin."

She was outraged at what Aaron had done and wasn't going to let him squirm out of it. She awarded me $300 a month until the boys graduated from college. The money came out of the state's uninsured fund. To hear Aaron tell it, it was coming right out of his pocket.

Aaron looked at me like I had stabbed him in the heart. Of course, he was facing a pretty big fine for the insurance lapse and letting his gaming license expire, but those were his mistakes, not mine. On the courthouse steps, Stumpy said, "Aaron will be fine, seeing as how he's transferred most of his property out of his name like a chicken-shit." Aaron's father, who lived in Vegas, had been buying strip malls in Aaron's name, and Aaron, just as Stumpy said, transferred every piece of property back to his father's name, hiding his assets and making sure I received as little as possible. He was as worthless as the trash he covered himself with while Michael was dying.

Stumpy pulled up with the car and opened the door for me, but Billy held me back. "I'll take her, Stumpy. We're going to celebrate."

"Where?" Stumpy asked. "I'll meet you there."

Billy hailed a cab and smiled at Stumpy. "Vegas."

"Las Vegas?" I asked. "I can't go to Las Vegas."

"Sure you can. They'll take anybody there. Especially losers like you."

I playfully slapped Billy, happy to have him back in my life. "I need to pay my bills," I said. "I need to find a job."

Billy ushered me into the waiting cab. "You need to

get away. Take a break from it all."

A break did sound good, I thought. I didn't know if I deserved one or not, but I sure did need one, and spending some time with Billy would do me some good.

"OK," I smiled. "I'm in. I just need to pack a bag, set up someone to take care of the house and let the boys know where I'll be. You can stay at my house tonight, and we'll leave in the morning."

"Good enough," Billy said.

"Where to?" The cabbie asked in the rear view mirror.

"JFK Airport," Billy answered.

"Billy!" I screamed. "I need to pack. I don't have a thing with me."

"You only need two things in Vegas, Skunkie. Money and balls."

"I don't have either."

"Well, I have money," Billy said as he pulled a flask out of his coat pocket with one hand and lit a cigarette with the other, "and we can use the money to buy you some balls."

Chapter 10
What Happens in Vegas…

We landed in Las Vegas five hours after we left the courthouse. I was wearing the same clothes I wore for court, but I stopped worrying about it somewhere over Kansas. First-class air travel has a way of helping you forget these things.

What a life Billy had. A black stretch limo picked us up at the airport and took us to Caesars Palace. As we approached the resort, I admired a picture-perfect view of Caesars Palace across a row of cypress trees and fountains, the tallest of which sprayed 35-foot columns of water in the air. The hotel manager met our limo and gave Billy the keys to a master suite.

Caesar's was indeed palatial; a fusion of what I imagined to be classical Greek and Roman architecture. Heroic arches curved gracefully into elaborate domed ceilings rimmed with ancient mosaic. The main entrance to Caesars featured sculptures of Roman emperors and other ancient luminaries. Among the proud golden charioteers, plumed centurions and Greek Goddesses, I recognized replicas of several famous statues: Venus de Milo, Bacchus and Michelangelo's David, larger than the original in Italy. The gorgeous white marble statues stood atop intricately detailed gold pedestals. Even the floors boasted gleaming gold marble. Toga-clad waitresses and tanned muscled Roman soldiers stood, ready to do our bidding. The overall effect was a mixture of lavish and over-the-top ostentatious; the perfect atmosphere in which to forget all my problems.

"Meet my older sister, Charlie," Billy yelled to the

manager. I was jolted out of my reverie.

"I'm his younger sister," I protested. "By ten years."

Billy held his face up to mine. "Does she look younger than me, Charlie? What do you think? She's at least ten years older, right?"

"She got the looks in the family." Charlie winked at me. "I can see that much."

Billy grabbed the chauffeur, who was unloading bags. "Hold it, Dan, we're going to the MGM."

Charlie quickly took Billy's bag from the chauffeur and handed it to a waiting bellhop. "Mister Matus' room." He handed a gold key to Billy. "Twenty-third floor."

"Our room's on the twenty-third floor?" I asked, excited about the view.

"Our room is the twenty-third floor," Billy said, as he tipped Charlie a hundred-dollar bill. "Use this to buy some glasses," he said, patting Charlie on the back.

"That tip would've paid one week's tuition," I told Billy.

"After this trip, you'll be able to pay the boys' entire college tuition," Billy said, heading straight for the tables.

"They're in high school," I reminded him.

"I know." Inside the casino, Billy pointed down a long hallway lined with shops and window displays. "Great shops down there. Go buy whatever you need. I'll meet you in the room in three hours."

"I don't have any money, Billy." I felt embarrassed to have to say it, but he's the one who dragged me here on the spur of the moment.

"Just tell them you're with me."

I thought he was kidding, but he suddenly made a beeline for the craps tables and left me standing alone.

Why not? I thought. Maybe I can charge it to the room and pay him back later. I wandered into the first shop and was quickly greeted by Sofia, a classy-looking woman who appeared to be around 50-years old, but she had those blonde, bronzed good looks of a Swedish schoolgirl.

"Can we help you, madam?" Sofia shook my hand.

"Well, I kind of came here on a moment's notice. I don't have a thing to wear."

"I understand," Sofia said.

"No, I mean I really don't have a thing to wear."

"Oh." Sofia looked me over. "I see."

I felt like a hooker on the strip, but I was not going to let it stop me. I didn't have a choice.

"Why don't we start with everyday wear," Sofia said. "You're a four, no?"

I nodded. As Sofia disappeared into the back, Charlie noticed me in the shop and came inside. "Ms. Rubin, are you finding everything you need?"

"I'm getting there, Charlie. Beautiful hotel you have here."

"Thank you, madam. I'm certain you'll enjoy every moment of your stay."

Charlie walked into a back room, then returned seconds later. With a nod and a smile, he left as quickly as he came in. After a few moments, Sofia brought out six casual outfits, not one under five hundred dollars. "They're beautiful," I said. "But a little out of my price range."

"Compliments of the hotel, ma'am."

"Excuse me?"

"For our special guests. Compliments of the hotel."

I looked around. "Am I on 'Candid Camera'?"

"You're a guest of Mr. Matus, and Mr. Matus is a

guest of the hotel. Our compliments."

I was amazed. I knew Billy pulled weight, but this was beyond belief. "Wow," I gasped. "Well, I guess I'll take the black outfit."

"No, ma'am," Sofia smiled. "They're all for you."

"All?" I couldn't hide my shock. I tried to be cool, aloof, but I was beside myself. "This is just too much."

"Not at all, ma'am. Let me get your evening wear." Sofia stepped into the back, but not before making a phone call. When I finished trying on the casual outfits, Sofia brought out three beautiful, elegant evening gowns, all exactly my size. A hotel clerk walked into the store and handed me two Caesar's shopping bags filled with panties, underwear, bras and nylons, a toothbrush, hair brush, shampoo, body wash, makeup, bathing suits, shoes and sunglasses. By the time I was in the suite, I had more clothes and toiletries than I would have packed myself.

"I don't think I'm in Kansas anymore," I said, talking to myself. I walked through the marble rotunda entryway of the suite, past the living room with gorgeous floor-to-ceiling windows and a full wet bar. The marble and brass bathroom had a gigantic whirlpool tub, which I could not resist. After a hot bath, I picked out the nicest evening gown and put on makeup. I had to admit, I was looking good. I walked to the living room bar, knowing that was where I would probably find Billy. I searched for excuses since I was a half hour late. The shopping, the bath. Truth was, he probably wouldn't care.

I was right. He wasn't even there.

I waited until eleven o'clock, then midnight. Then one. Then two. I was in Vegas. I thought to myself, "Why aren't you out on the town?" I didn't need Billy. "Why don't

I go by myself?" I started to get up and then realized, "I don't need Billy, but I sure do need his money."

I started to get ready for bed when the door bolted opened, and Billy, along with one of his gambling friends, burst into the room like it was midnight on New Year's Eve.

"Skunkie!" Billy yelled. "Are you ready?"

"I've been ready for four hours."

"Can't leave the table when I'm winning, now, can I?" Billy smiled.

"How much did you win?"

Billy leaned down and whispered in my ear, "Forty thousand."

"What?" I was suddenly wide awake.

"That's just the beginning," Billy laughed. "Skippy, you need a drink?"

"Vodka martini, extra dry," Skippy said, although he was already holding what looked like scotch on the rocks.

"Skunkie." Billy put his arm around me. "Meet Skippy. My best friend in Vegas."

"Charmed," I said sarcastically.

Skippy—a kind-looking man about 20-years older than I was—gulped his whiskey, then kissed my hand. A nice gesture, except for the scotch leaking out of his mouth.

"Skippy," I said, pulling my hand back, "I can't help noticing you already have a drink."

Skippy winked at me. "The martini's for you."

The three of us hit the casino floor and headed straight for the craps tables.

"I thought we were going to eat," I said.

"Skunkie, dear, when will you ever learn? We're on a roll, here. We can't stop to eat."

"Then why'd you stop to get me?"

Billy whispered in my ear again, "Skippy needs a good-luck charm."

I couldn't remember Billy ever whispering in my ear, now he'd done it twice in one night. Something was up here.

"Where'd Skippy go?" I asked.

"I can't keep track of everyone in this town," Billy said as he threw a wad of cash onto the center of a craps table. "Change, Jim."

The croupier smiled. "You got it, Mr. Matus." Jim started handing stacks of chips to Billy. "Ten thousand, fifteen thousand, twenty thousand, twenty-five thousand and thirty thousand. Good luck, Mr. Matus."

Billy left one stack on the pass line, took the dice and grinned. "You're the one who's going to need luck, Jim." Billy rolled and hit seven.

"Seven, a winner!" Jim cried out. The table cheered.

"How much did I win?" I excitedly asked Billy.

"Nothing, Skunkie. You have to place a bet if you want to win."

Billy handed me a stack of chips.

"A thousand dollars," Billy said. "Use it to play. When you win, give me the thousand back and keep the rest."

"What if I lose?"

"You won't." Leaving the original bet and his winnings on the line, Billy rolled again.

"Seven, a winner!" Jim yelled.

"Wait for me this time!" I laughed. "I don't know what I'm doing here!"

"Just do what I do, except with fewer chips," Billy said. He picked up two stacks of chips and left two on the line. I quickly dropped a single chip on the line next to his. He rolled and hit eleven.

"Shit," I yelled. "Just my luck."

"We won, Skunkie," Billy said. "Eleven wins on a come out."

"We won?" I screamed. "How much?"

"Don't ask, and don't count. Just play."

A cocktail waitress with bulging boobs and slender thighs, all wedged into a tiny swatch of velvet, put her arm around Billy. "Something to drink, Mr. Matus?"

"Wild Turkey, rocks," Billy said as he picked up my empty martini glass. "And you see this, Marci? I don't ever want to see this again. You bring my sister a new Grey Goose martini whenever she's half done. I don't want to see ice sitting alone at the bottom of her glass. Got it?"

"Got it." Marci smiled, knowing Billy was joking, sort of.

Billy picked up another two stacks of chips from the line. I left my winnings on the line. Billy rolled an eight.

"Is that good?" I asked.

"So far." Billy winked.

"He has to hit eight before he hits seven," Skippy said, suddenly squeezing in beside me.

"Don't even say that number," Billy said.

"Where'd you go?" I asked Skippy.

"To get you dinner."

Behind him, a waitress held a tray with various hot dishes, all looking and smelling delicious.

"Skippy, thank you so much. I'm starving. That's so thoughtful."

"Cut out the love fest," Billy joked. "I'm trying to play here."

"My own brother wouldn't buy me dinner," I said to everyone at the table, "but this old man, who doesn't even know me, brings me a feast."

The table booed Billy.

Billy feigned outrage with onlookers at the table. "Hey, dinner's always on the house for us. And why would I buy my older sister dinner? Isn't she the one supposed to be taking care of me?"

"I'm not older." I played along, knowing Billy was working the crowd to get the energy up.

Billy grabbed my cheeks and pulled my face over the table. "What do you think, people? She's no spring chicken, is she?"

Everyone laughed, including me.

"Are you here to lie about your age or are you going to roll?" I joked back to Billy. The crowd applauded.

"You want to see me roll?" Billy asked. "Watch this." Billy threw the dice and, like magic, they came up eight.

"Eight's a winner, pay the line," Jim yelled, working the crowd himself.

Billy rolled for what seemed like hours. The chips kept stacking up. After one big roll, I couldn't help counting my chips, careful not to let Billy see me.

"How much?" Billy asked.

"How much what?"

"I can feel you counting your chips, Skunkie."

"How? I wasn't even touching them."

"This is my business, Skunkie. It's my life."

"Fifteen hundred," I said.

"Don't count 'em again."

Billy picked up the dice and rolled a seven.

"We win!" I screamed.

"Seven out, take the line," Jim said.

The croupier picked up all the chips on the table.

"What are they doing?" I asked. "We won."

"Seven after the point. We lost." Billy explained. "I told you not to count your chips."

"Well, let's go to bed then," I suggested. "It has to be five in the morning."

"I'll say three things to you, Skunkie, then I won't say any more."

I was having fun. I really enjoyed being with Billy. He always had a way of sweeping me away from reality. I didn't know anyone else as colorful.

"First, it's only four," Billy said. "Second, I told you we don't leave when we're winning."

"You just lost, though," I pointed out.

"One roll, Skunkie. We don't win every roll, but overall we're winning. We're not going anywhere."

"And what's the third thing?"

"It's your turn to roll."

The croupier across from Jim slid six dice over to me with his stick.

"I can't roll," I told Billy, who playfully zipped his lips to remind me he can't say another word to me.

"Just pick up two dice and roll," Skippy said.

I decided I didn't like Skippy. He was much older than Billy, maybe sixty, I didn't know. He was making a big scene out of getting me drinks and dinner, telling me how to roll, but I wasn't fooled. He wanted to get laid.

"Just throw the dice and make sure you hit the wall on the other side of the table," Skippy said, leaning closer as he motioned a fake throw of the dice.

I saw Billy put three stacks of chips on the line, more

than he had bet on any of his rolls. He smiled at Jim, "Beginners luck. Never fails."

I put a few chips on the line and threw the dice.

"Seven a winner," Jim yelled. The table crowd burst into cheers.

"Not bad for an old lady, huh?" Billy yelled.

"If I'm old, you must be dead," I yelled back. The table crowd laughed and started betting heavily. I had never seen so much money in one place. People were packed against each other two deep. During Billy's roll, a crowd had grown behind the betters. The table was hot, as they say, but I couldn't help wondering what all these people were doing here at four in the morning. Even a few extra pit bosses had gathered to watch the excitement. I picked up the dice and rolled again.

"Seven a winner! Pay the line!" Jim yelled.

This was out of control. The chips kept coming. The drinks kept coming. The crowd kept cheering. Billy kept joking. And Skippy kept leaning closer and closer with every roll.

We got back to the room at sunrise, drunk, exhausted and flush with cash. I tried to give Billy his thousand dollars back, but he refused to accept it.

"What'd you win?" he asked.

"Two thousand!" I smiled. "What about you?"

"Ninety."

"Thousand? My God, Billy."

"Sometimes you're up, sometimes you're down," he said, taking off his jacket. "Skippy, you sleep in the blue room. Skunkie, you take the master. I'll sleep on the couch."

"I won't have you sleep on the couch," I protested. "It's your suite."

"And I'm going to do what I want in it. I want to sleep on the couch."

Skippy disappeared into the blue room. I walked to the bathroom and started taking my makeup off, then decided to just sleep with it on. I went back to the living room to say good-night to Billy. Just as I got there, I saw Billy quietly slip out the front door, then softly close it, careful not to make a noise.

Chapter 11
...Stays in Vegas

I woke up and glanced at the clock, which said 7:30, but I wasn't sure if it was morning or evening. Billy was still gone. A dozen red roses were waiting on my nightstand, but there was no card to tell me who they were from. I showered, then put on one of my new pantsuits. I joined Skippy for a room-service meal in the living room, compliments of the casino. In the daylight, after a long, hard night, I decided he had to be closer to seventy, and not the healthy kind of seventy. But he did have hot coffee waiting for me, along with some Danish.

"Sweet rolls for a sweet woman," Skippy gushed.

"Is your real name Skippy?" I asked.

"Don't I look like a Skippy?"

"You do," I said, "but Billy calls me Skunkie and my name's Sunny, so I was just wondering."

"Skippy's my real name, all right, but you can call me Skip, because my heart skipped a beat when I met you."

I was thinking fast for a putdown that would sound firm yet gentle when Billy walked through the door.

"You two drunks finally wake up?" Billy said. "Can we go have some fun now?"

"You've got to be kidding," I said. "You haven't slept at all."

Billy pointed to Skippy's matted, gray hair, pale skin and sunken chest wheezing for air. "Look what sleep does to people. Not me. I'll sleep when I'm dead."

Skippy looked at me, realizing for the first time he must look like hell. "Nothing a hot shower can't fix," he said.

"Well, make it quick," Billy said. "I've got a lot of money to win back."

"I'm eating a proper breakfast," I insisted, "or dinner or whatever."

"Anything for you, Skunkie. Tables are too cold to play now anyway."

I didn't want to ask Billy how much he had lost, but he knew I was dying to know. With Skippy in the shower, Billy mixed me a martini.

"At eight in the morning?" I asked.

"It's eight P.M.," Billy said, handing me the glass and pausing before answering my unstated question. "A hundred and twenty thousand."

I was shaken. "Maybe you should take a break tonight, Billy."

"And let them hold my money overnight? Forget it." Billy saw the look on my face. "It's a game, Skunkie. I win, they win. Same money goes back and forth. The secret is to quit when the money's in my hands."

"Then why'd you go out again this morning?"

"Well, it's no fun if I don't give them a fighting chance. Now drink this. We have a long night ahead of us."

"I can't. I haven't had a thing to eat."

"Why do you think I put an olive in it?"

Showered and wearing a suit and tie, Skippy was back to pushing sixty. Billy, still in the same clothes from last night, was the one who was starting to look like hell—and smell like it as well. I was casual in my pantsuit, so we were quite a threesome when we walked from the hotel into the waiting limo.

Cocktails in the limo, dinner at an elegant French restaurant where prices weren't listed on the menu and every bottle of wine was older than the last, cigars and cognac. Everything was "Compliments of the house" with a "Come see us again, Mr. Matus." As I took a puff of Billy's cigar and choked on the hot, tar-laden smoke, I couldn't help wondering just how much money Billy had in this town, and how much he'd blown.

"Care to dance, Sunny?" Skippy asked.

A live orchestra was playing swing music. I raised an eyebrow and decided. "Why not?"

Skippy led me out on the dance floor and into a dozen slick dance moves, spinning me out, then twirling me back in. He'd done this before, I thought, probably during the Forties.

During the second song, I saw Billy walking toward us on the dance floor. "May I cut in?" Billy asked.

"Not on your life," Skippy answered.

"Just one dance," I said, touched that Billy had asked.

Billy took my arm and quickly led me to the front door. "Time to play."

"Hold on," Skippy yelled, "I'm coming."

It was another late night and early morning at the craps table. Money flowing in and pouring out, drinks replaced before they're finished, and crowds cheering Billy and me on. Skippy was not betting much and didn't quite get into the banter with the crowd like Billy and I did. I was starting to think that Skippy was the calm and boring counterpart to Billy's wild and boisterous Vegas life. Everyone needs balance, I guessed. For the first time since I hit Vegas, I thought about Michael. I missed him. My balance was gone, and I didn't know how to get it back.

The dice came to me. I picked them up and rolled

craps. The croupier swept everyone's chips away, and I realized that maybe attitude had something to do with luck in this game. So for my next roll, I doubled my bet. "Let's see what your spring-chicken sister can do now," I joked to Billy.

"You better do something, or I'll send you back to New Jersey." Billy doubled his bet. So did Skippy.

"Bring me back to life, hun," Skippy yelled.

I rolled a seven.

"Seven, a winner," yelled that night's croupier, Frank.

Skippy jumped up and down, picking up more chips than I'd seen him win in two days. He grabbed me, pulled me in for a hug and kissed me hard on the lips. I pulled back fast. "Not the kind of luck I'm looking for," I said.

"I call 'em as I see 'em." Skippy laughed.

Billy sensed my discomfort. "Come on, Skunkie, keep it rolling."

I threw the dice and won again. And again. The table heated up. The crowd grew. By six in the morning, Billy had won all his money back and was up another forty thousand. "What I could do with that kind of money," I thought to myself.

"That's a night," Billy said, as he tipped each of the four croupiers a hundred dollars. Five hundred to the pit boss, another hundred to the cocktail waitress. One thing about Billy, he might have been living for free in Vegas, but he knew how to tip. Five hundred to the waiter, a hundred to the limo drivers. He tipped a guy in the elevator fifty bucks, and the guy was just another guest at the hotel.

"Are you crazy?" I yelled. "He doesn't even work here."

"He pushed the elevator button for us, didn't he?"

I loved Billy, but it was hard seeing that kind of money disappear.

Six in the morning. We were getting to bed earlier than last night, but like last night, Billy sneaked back to the tables, and like last night, when I woke up, there was a gift waiting for me. This time it was a Fendi handbag. I had seen it in the shop downstairs for six hundred dollars. No note, no wrapping, just a brand new handbag.

"I could get used to this," I said out loud.

It's noon. I had only slept for five hours, but after coffee, I felt great. "I'm turning into you," I said to Billy when he walked back into the suite, "but I'm not too sure I'm proud of it."

"That's the nicest thing anyone's ever said to me," Billy replied with a cough. "But you don't have time for small talk. I made you an appointment at the spa. Massage, manicure, facial, hair style, mud wrap, the works."

"I can't afford that."

"You don't learn very fast, do you, Skunkie? You don't have to pay for a thing. Just make sure you tip big. Fifty dollars at least."

"Do I have time for breakfast?"

"Always time for breakfast," Skippy said, walking out of his room looking showered and fresh. "I'll take you myself."

I glanced at Billy, who smiled. "Lucky lady. I think I'll stay home and try one of those things they call beds."

"Try one of those things they call showers while you're at it," Skippy said.

"We hit the tables hard tonight," Billy yawned. "No more pussy-footing around for you two."

I checked into the spa for four blissful hours. I was starving, because I missed breakfast, but the spa was worth missing breakfast. Fifty dollars nothing, I tipped a hundred dollars, and I didn't bat an eye, until I walked out and realized what I had just done. The relaxation from the massage, the refreshing invigoration from the mud bath, the elegant pride from the manicure all slipped away, forming a lead ball in the pit of my stomach. One hundred dollars? Even though Billy gave me the tip money, I wondered if I'd gone insane. "Is this what Vegas did to people? Take away all sense of time and money? I don't have a job. I don't have a dime in the bank. Now, just because I have three thousand dollars in winnings in my new Fendi purse, I am tipping like a millionaire."

Of course, I argued to myself that I wouldn't have had any money had it not been for Billy. He was the one who staked me. So, it wasn't really like I was wasting my money, and I was having fun, enjoying myself for more than a hour or two for the first time since Michael died. Didn't I deserve that? I started to feel better.

My self-satisfaction didn't last long. I wondered, "Don't the boys deserve a stereo in their room?" The lead pit turned to cement. "I can't stay here," I thought to myself. "This place is dangerous." I didn't know how Billy was staying for three more weeks. I didn't know if I could make it through the night.

Walking through the casino to meet Billy at the pool for lunch, I decided to tell him I was going home. I'd had enough. I had three thousand dollars. I'd give Billy back his one thousand at lunch, so that left two thousand in winnings. That would buy me some time.

As I was about to step through the door toward the

pool, I heard screaming and cheering. I turned around and saw a crowd gathered at a craps table, someone obviously was winning. I looked outside and spotted Billy waiting at a table by the pool. Then I had a revelation. If I could take my three thousand and double it, I could give Billy his thousand back, and still have five thousand to pay some bills, buy the boys' stereos, and maybe have a couple hundred left for pocket change. "Pocket change," I thought, that was Vegas talking again. I couldn't keep my utilities on at home, but in Vegas, two hundred dollars had become pocket change.

Home. Mortgage. Utilities. No heat. Reason returned. There was no way I was taking a chance with my two thousand dollars. This Vegas life was Billy's, not mine. He thrived on the adrenaline rush, and he could absorb the losses. Vegas was in his blood, but not mine.

I'd found out that Skippy owed Billy a hundred and fifty grand and that he was on the casino payroll. His job is to wine and dine big-time players like Billy. He had a girlfriend, yet he told me he loved me. Skippy was a scam artist, and he was playing me for a fool, but the old guy had zeroed in on the wrong woman. I was no mark. I was no fool.

Stronger and wiser than when I arrived, I walked outside to the table by the pool where Billy sat.

"I'm going back to New Jersey." My voice filled with conviction.

I packed my bags, dressed for the flight home and waited in the living room of the suite. It was eight P.M., and I had a red-eye flight that landed in Newark at five in the morning. Talk about a rude re-awakening to reality. Billy was supposed to take me to dinner at six P.M., but he didn't show up. I wasn't mad, just disappointed that I wouldn't see him again. He was the rock in my life: The one person who had been there since I was a kid, and the one person I knew would always be there.

The bellhop didn't show up either. Arriving in Vegas was a lot more fun than leaving. I picked up the Gucci suitcase that was mysteriously waiting for me after lunch—again no note, no message—and lugged my new clothes downstairs. Walking through the casino, I passed a craps table that was exploding in cheers. I didn't even stop to look. As I headed for the front door, an arm grabbed me and jerked me back. I grabbed for my purse, thinking I was being robbed. "I don't have a dime!" I yelled.

"Then take this thousand dollars," yelled Billy, holding a wad of cash, Billy put an arm around me and led me to the cheering craps table. "You don't think I'm going to let you go home without one last round, do you?"

"I've had enough, Billy."

"It's winning time."

Billy motioned to a bellhop who rushed over and took my suitcase from me.

"I have a flight."

"They're a dime a dozen in Vegas," Billy laughed. "Same deal on the thousand."

The first thing I noticed when we got to the table was Billy's chips. More than I had ever seen, and in colors I hadn't seen before. Billy noticed me eyeing them and whispered, "Two-hundred."

I know he means thousand, but I couldn't believe it. Reluctantly, I got change and dropped a five-dollar chip on the line. Billy rolled a seven.

"Winner," the croupier cried.

"Let it ride," Billy yelled back.

Instead, I picked up my winnings and yelled for the bellhop, who was heading for the registration desk.

"Sir, may I have my bag, please?" I turned to Billy, who wore a look of confusion. "It's time to go home."

I slept the entire flight and awoke in chilly, windy New Jersey, ready to get started on my life one more time.

I had won the lawsuit and put those lawyers behind me. Amazingly, I was rested from the trip and felt centered. I felt I knew myself a bit more, than I ever had before. I felt strong, protected and confident. I felt that perhaps I was finally starting to put Michael's murder behind me. Move on. In fact, I knew the worst of it was behind me, though I knew it would be hard, I also knew in my heart that my life was about to take a turn for the better.

I had two messages on my answering machine. One was from the D.A. They had arrested Michael's murderers. They wanted me to clear my schedule for a two-month trial. I'd have to re-live Michael's murder all over again.

The other message was from my sister, Nancy. Mom was dying.

Chapter 12
Death Comes in Three's

Home at last, I flipped through my bills, unpacked the Vegas suitcase and packed a new one.

The next morning, I headed again to Newark Airport, feeling as if I had never left it. I had to fly to Florida, where my three sisters and mother lived. The morning commuter traffic had me at a standstill on the New Jersey Turnpike. One hour to make my flight. If the traffic broke I would make it, I hoped.

I played back the phone call from my sisters over and over in my head. Mom had called Cara complaining of asthma, difficulty breathing and gasping for air. Her asthma hadn't sparked up in years. Worried, Cara called Nancy, who lived down the street from Mom. Nancy rushed over and found Mom on the floor, barely breathing. The ambulance driver had been the first to call it a stroke, and the doctors in the ER confirmed it.

Damn. Construction in the fast lane was forcing four lanes into three, and I was in the lane that had to merge. Why couldn't they do road work at night? Did they really have to do this during morning rush hour? Still, if I got past the bottleneck, maybe the road would open up.

I had to get there in time to see my mother. They didn't think she was going to die, but "they," that faceless meld of hospital personnel who make such pronouncements, were usually wrong. I had been able to spend a great deal of time with my father before he died, and I believe that the time I spent made it easier. After my father became ill, he had to stay in a nursing home, because my mother couldn't care for him any longer. She didn't have the strength to lift him in and out of bed. He needed total care. He also needed kidney dialysis, which, at that time, could be provided for him only at a live-in facility. With a heavy heart, my mother had checked her husband, best friend and lifelong companion into a local nursing home. Even there, he needed constant attention and care giving from family. My sisters lived locally, but they had full-time jobs, so I went to Florida to help my mother.

It's a horrible experience, going to see the hero of your childhood only to find him wasting away in a hospital bed. When I first went to see my father, the nurses told me he wasn't eating, that he just refused his food. Slowly, he was dying of starvation, and I couldn't figure out why. Then I realized that my father disliked the nurses intensely. He was tense, cold, and even rude when they were in the room. Now, I knew my father. He was a kind, gentle man with a loving disposition. It just wasn't like him to dislike someone, let alone a whole group of "someones." Sadly enough, it turned out the nurses were being cruel to him, rude, uncaring, antagonistic, and my father, enfeebled by sickness, protested his behavior the only way he could—by starving himself. I immediately started feeding him myself, and he ate right away. My sisters and I set up a schedule. Becca would feed him breakfast. I did lunch. Cara and Nancy took turns with dinner. Cara was the best at it. She was firm and stubborn. Cara surprised me. I never thought she had it in her, but she was like a drill sergeant with him. I, on the other hand, was a marshmallow. I pleaded with him to eat, and he did, but he made it hard for me. Still, he was getting better. He'd never be completely well, but he was getting his strength back, his sense of humor, his playfulness.

He had even started telling me stories again, about his youth, and his courtship of my mother.

He would start with a far-away look, as if he had gone somewhere else for a moment, and then the clarity would return to his eyes and he would say, "Sunny, did I ever tell you about the time?"

I loved those stories. The ones about the old-time crime bosses and thugs that my dad had known growing up, and most especially, the stories about how he had fallen in love with and married my mother.

One such day, his memories had taken him back to the days when he had first met my mother.

"She took my breath away, Sunny, right from the very start."

He smiled when he said that, and then suddenly something dark seemed to pass across his face, like a thundercloud passing overhead, just briefly.

"She came into the gym one day with my sister. I knew she was married, so in the past I had always tried to keep things casual. I didn't know much about her personal life at that point, except that my sister had mentioned she was married to a loser, and she had two babies.

That day though, something was different. For one thing, she was wearing too much makeup. I had noticed right away, because in the past I remembered thinking what an amazing natural beauty she was. She also didn't seem to be looking directly at anyone. I had said hello, like I always did, and instead of her usual radiant smile, she looked down at the floor and returned with a whispered hello. I knew something was wrong. I put my fingers on her chin, and tilted her face up to the light. Under all of that makeup, I could see the bruises. Her face looked like mine sometimes did after a few rounds in the ring. I don't even have words to describe all the emotions that went through me then, Sunny. I was angry and sad and frustrated all at the same time."

My father stopped there for a minute. Then he looked up at me, and taking my hand, he said, "I knew I had to put a stop to whatever was going on in that nightmare she was living. My business, or not, I didn't care anymore after that."

That day, she wasn't truthful with Maxie about her situation. She tried to say she had fallen, but he wasn't buying it. He tried to get her to say she would leave right then, but she wouldn't do it. He told her that she knew where to find him, if she ever needed his help, and he would be there when she decided she'd had enough.

Maxie continued with the story. "A few days later, she came back to the gym. She told me she was ready to leave, and she asked if I could pick up her and the kids later that night and take them to Betty's house. I agreed. That was the first time I kissed her. It was just a peck, really, on her cheek, but I'll never forget the sweet way she smelled, or the feel of her warm skin on my lips."

He smiled again, and then went dark.

"That night, I showed up at the time we agreed on. I was worried right away, because the house was all dark. When I got close to the front door, I could hear the babies crying inside. I didn't care if the son of a bitch shot me, I walked right in. Little Billy was sitting in the front room. He had something all over him, at first I thought it was chocolate. His little face was red and swollen from crying. When I picked him up, I realized it was blood. He was covered in it. I panicked, thinking he was hurt and bleeding somewhere. I tore off his clothes, scaring the poor little guy even worse, and I realized there was no blood on his skin. The blood wasn't his. I asked him where his mama was, and he pointed towards the back of the house. As we were headed down the hall, I could hear Becca's cries get louder. I found her in the first bedroom, scared, but safe in her crib. I sat Billy next to her, and told him to take care of his sister, and I would go find their mama. God, Sunny, I had seen a lot in my life up to that point, but nothing that ever shocked me like that."

Maxie shuddered a little at whatever frightening image was being called up from his memory. His eyes filled with tears as he continued.

"I found your mama in her bedroom. She was crumpled in a corner like a rag doll. There was so much blood. I was afraid to touch her, because I thought for sure she was dead. I called out to her, but she didn't answer, so I got close enough that I could see a little rise and fall of her chest. I was so thankful she was breathing. I picked her up, and laid her on the bed. Her clothes were torn, and all saturated with blood. Her hair was matted with it, and when I pushed it back from her face I realized there was a big gash in her head. That was where most of the blood was coming from. I'm not sure where the rest came from, Sunny, what was I gonna do? It wasn't what I had done before, but cleaned her up, kept talking to her, trying to get her to wake up. I stopped the bleeding and bandaged her head. Her poor little body was covered with bruises. I put some cool towels all over her, I didn't know what else to do. When she seemed more comfortable, I went and checked on the babies. They were hungry and scared, and Becca needed changing awful bad. I fed them and cleaned them up, and rocked them both in my lap until they fell asleep.

Afterwards, I found your mama, still in her bed, but awake. She was confused at first. It took a lot of reassuring to make her believe that she and the kids were going to be okay. I would see to it. From that point on, they were my family, and no one would ever hurt them again. I made sure that son-of-a-bitch would never come back, Sunny. I don't think you need to hear anymore about that. Let's just say, it's the closest I ever came to being a member of Murder Inc. I never had it in me, to do what old Bugsy and Meyer and their boys were doing on the streets, but I made sure your mama's worthless husband thought I did. He never came back, and you know the rest of the story, I married your mama, and made those babies mine, and she and I made the rest of this family together."

He smiled again, this time, his memories recalling all the good times.

After a few weeks of feeding, the nurses suddenly announced that we could no longer feed our father. We weren't licensed, and it was against policy.

"Against policy?" I shouted.

"Only our nurses are licensed to feed patients," the head nurse said.

"Your nurses are bitches," I yelled. "My father refuses to eat for them, because they treat him so poorly, and if he doesn't eat, he'll die."

"It's company policy," she said. "Only licensed nurses are allowed to feed patients."

"He's not a patient!" I went ballistic. "He's my father!"

I had to take my case all the way to the director

of the nursing home. After threatened to go to the news media, they finally relented and let us feed our father. The time spent, caring for the man who had cared so much for me, was some of the best I ever had with him. Just being together, sitting and talking, had allowed us get to know each other in an entirely new way. I was always his favorite, I knew, because I was his first-born. Billy and Becca were from my mom's first marriage, although they never talked about it, and he loved them like his own, but that didn't change the fact that I was his first-born.

As a child, I craved this man's attention constantly. If Cara sat on his lap, I would snuggle up onto his lap, pushing her off in the process. Now he was dying. Maxie, my hero, was dying. I spent every moment with him that I could, and somehow, it made it all easier.

Having Michael made it easier, too. He was strong, he was attentive, and he was there with whatever I needed. I couldn't have gone through my father's death without Michael. He was my support system. But what happens when your support system dies? How do you get through that? Every time I thought I was getting back on my feet again, something else would happen. My father. Then Michael. Now my mother.

That goddamned traffic.

I pulled into Newark International twenty minutes before my flight. If there was no line at the check-in counter and I carried on my luggage, I could make it. Barely. I made a quick left into the long-term parking lot. It was full. I was routed to a satellite parking lot, bused back to the airport and missed my flight by six minutes. Six minutes. I broke down crying at the gate. Partly for missing my flight, partly for the fear of losing my mom, partly for having lost Michael, and partly for still not having gotten my life together a year after Michael's death.

Nancy picked me up at the airport, twelve hours after my original flight was scheduled to land. We went straight to the hospital. It was so unsettling to see my strong, proud mother lying helplessly in that bed, hooked up to oxygen, heart monitors, blood pressure machines, IVs.

She was sleeping so peacefully, like a baby.

It struck me at that moment. Somewhere, somehow, everything in life changed.

I had been taken care of so long by my parents, but somewhere along the line I was called upon to take care of them. Feeding my father until his death. Protecting and caring for my mother, who could no longer care for herself. I knew taking care of one's aging parents was part of the cycle of life, but I was still grieving for my dead husband, and of course, I was caring for Joel and Devin. So many to care for, yet no one to care for me.

Life had pulled a fast one on me. I would meet my responsibilities, I knew. I wouldn't let down the people who counted on me, but at the same time, I decided that I would turn this all around, perhaps not now but someday. I promised myself to get in a position where caring was not my central and only function in life. I promised myself that someday I would enjoy life again, and maybe I could even have someone who would care for me.

I stayed at the hospital for three days. My sisters came and went. They worked during the day and came to the hospital at night. I couldn't tell them I didn't have a job, except the one caring for Mom. She was getting slightly better; at least enough to be awake and recognize us. She was "stabilized," as the doctors call it. I needed rest, not to mention a shower. Nancy offered to take me to her house, so we left Becca with my mom.

Becca was still angry at Mom for so many things. I never understood it. Why was she so angry with my mother? For stepping in and working like a dog to support our family? For making sure we always had beautiful clothes, even though she had to sew them herself? Becca was the kind of person who used anger to deflect what she was most angry about—the shitty choices she had made in her life. My mother had never liked Aaron. Why should she? He wouldn't trust Mom with her grandkids, so she was never allowed to spend unsupervised time with her grandchildren. Aaron sure wasn't Michael. He loved my mother, and he made sure she spent as much time as possible with Joel and Devin. The loving relationship between my mother and my husband infuriated Becca even more.

We always hoped that crisis would bring out the best in family. Nancy and I decided time alone with Mom would be good for Becca. It would be a chance to reconcile, heal, or even to just have the chance to tell Mom she loved her.

As we left the hospital, we ran into the doctor, who told us he was so happy with Mom's progress. He predicted she would be home in a week or less. I was so relieved. I left the hospital without any pangs of guilt for taking the brief respite I so desperately needed. My brief time out of the hospital would be restful.

In the shower, I planned my trip home, knowing that I would have to come back at least once a month to help my sisters with Mom. It would be a struggle, but a happy one. I was grateful I could do something for Mom. I felt better than I had in days. Yes, better than I had in days, until I got out of the shower.

Nancy was on the bed crying. She'd gotten a phone call. Mom was dead. Both of us thought the same thing, but neither one said it: How did a woman go from stable, making progress and almost ready for release to dead in thirty minutes? What the hell did Becca do? What did she say? My God, I thought. Becca's anger killed our mother.

Chapter 13
Life, Death ... and an Airport Caper

The feeling in my mother's house was devastating. Cara was sobbing and wailing uncontrollably. Nancy was grief-stricken. She couldn't speak, she couldn't cry. Even as a grown woman, she was the baby of the family, and I felt terrible for her. I imagined that was how I must have looked after Michael's death.

Becca wasn't having too hard a time dealing with Mom's death. She was an ice princess, acting sympathetic while silently divvying up Mom's belongings in her mind.

I was lost and heartbroken. I cried at the sight of Mom's picture, the ring of her phone or the smell of her perfume. We were four sisters who were so busy grieving and, in Becca's case, conniving, that we could not begin to lend each other support.

Joel and Devin flew to Florida from school, and both had packed everything they needed. The right suits, the right shoes, the right expressions. We were all getting too good at funerals.

Nancy and I picked them up at the airport. It was a nice break from the house. Fresh air. New scenery. Seeing the boys, I realized how much I truly missed them. I'd been so preoccupied with surviving that I forgot who I was surviving for—Joel and Devin.

The boys both gave me a big hug, then hugged Nancy as well.

"Is Uncle Billy here?" Joel asked.

"Not yet," I whispered, "But I hope he gets here soon. We need him to brighten things up a bit."

"And to put Becca in her place," Nancy added.

"So when's his flight?" Devin asked.

"It's Uncle Billy, sweetie," I answered. "No one knows when he's getting here."

"Or if," Nancy added.

The night before the funeral, Billy still hadn't shown up. Nancy, Cara and I had met with the Rabbi, and let him know Mom was to be cremated without question. The Rabbi took issue with this, since it is contrary to Jewish tradition for a Jew to be cremated. The Rabbi reminded us that the body must be interred, intact, in the earth, and that this ruling was almost 2000-years old. Of course, he then told us he would make an exception. Mom was cremated that same day. We had purchased a beautiful urn for the service and reserved space in a nearby mausoleum. After the service, we had planned to blend Mom and Dad's ashes, then place them in the mausoleum for their eternal rest.

Joel sat with Nancy, trying to console her. Devin was doing the same with Cara. I was so proud how strong these boys were, and how mature. They had been very close to their grandmother. Michael and I had always made sure of that. Those boys had been the sparkle in my mother's eyes, and yet, they were putting their own pain aside to help their aunts. I was proud at how responsible they had become, yet regretful for what they had to go through to get that way.

I was making final arrangements for the funeral, crying my way through phone calls at the thought of now living life without my mother. Though she had lived in Florida, Mom had been a big support to me for my entire life, and especially after Michael's death. She had stayed with me a month after the funeral, cooking, cleaning, consoling. She had called me daily to check on me, giving advice, direction or just listening. When all of my friends had disappeared, Mom had showed up stronger than ever.

I had three people in my life who were always there for me – Michael, my mother and Billy. Now two of them were gone. How would I get through this? I had Michael to help me through my father's death, I had my mother to help me through Michael's death. Now there was only Billy, and he wasn't even here yet. God must have wanted me to be an independent woman, because he had taken two of the three people in life I had always relied on, trusted and needed. Well, I still had Billy. My first friend. My first ally.

Car tires screeched outside. A car door slammed. Becca stormed into the house and flew upstairs. I was too tired to even think about it. A few minutes later, Billy showed up with his two daughters, Brittany and Kristen. Both were about Joel and Devin's age. Both girls, slender and red-headed with sparkling eyes, were beautiful in their own way. Billy may not have seen the girls as often as he should have, but there was no denying how important they were to him. There was no way he could say good-bye to his mother without his daughters there.

Billy took one look at all of us in various stages of crying, sobbing and exhaustion. "You see, this is why I never come home."

We all smiled. Billy could always make us smile.

"How are you, Billy?" I asked, hugging him.

"Better now, Skunkie." He hugged me tight and whispered, "You missed the streak. It started the night you left and hasn't stopped yet."

"And you left?"

Billy pulled back, looked me in the eye and started to well up. I hadn't seen him cry since—well, never. Cara and Nancy now joined us in the hug, all consoling each other. I felt Billy shaking in my arms, his chest heaving. I was comforted to smell that familiar Billy smell of whiskey and cigarettes, but it worried me to see him so hurting.

"Where's the bar?" Billy suddenly pulled back, acting strong again. "Never mind, I can sniff it out from here."

Billy poured himself a straight Wild Turkey. I hugged Brittany and Kristen. "So good to see you both. And you're both so beautiful!"

"What'd you expect?" Billy said, swigging his drink. "They take after their father."

"I hope not too much," Cara laughed.

We all laughed, including Billy, although when he took another drink, I heard him mouth into his glass, "Me too." Maybe I was just projecting. All I knew was that, although Billy was still the life of the party, his eyes looked sad and beaten. I hoped it was just Mom's death, but I couldn't help feeling that being with his daughters again had stirred something in him—maybe a sense that even with all his gambling winnings, he might have been losing the bigger game of life.

"Shit!" Billy yelled. He ran toward the door and sorted through the suitcases, tossing aside his own, then Brittany's and Kristen's. He was searching for something, and whatever it was, it must be important.

"Let's go!" Billy grabbed my arm, then Nancy's, and dragged us outside. He threw me into the driver's seat of Nancy's car and jumped in the passenger seat. "To the airport. C'mon, Skunkie. Floor it."

"You're not leaving already, Billy." I didn't understand

what was happening.

"Drive!" He was panicked, I could tell, so I didn't argue. Nancy got in with us. I drove as fast as I could, while Billy nervously tapped his feet and drummed his fingers on his lap.

"What is it, Billy? What's wrong?"

"My bag," Billy said. "I left it in on the plane."

"Well, relax, they'll have it in the lost and found."

"It's fifty thousand cash, Skunkie."

"Fifty thousand dollars?" Nancy sounded as astonished as I felt.

My heart started beating faster. I pressed down on the accelerator and started changing lanes a bit quicker. Every second I drove faster was a better chance the money would still be there. I drove in silence for a few minutes, but the thoughts wouldn't stop spinning in my head. I knew Billy didn't have a bank account. I knew he didn't have a credit card. Never paid taxes. He lived his whole life in cash, under the radar. Still, I couldn't help it blurting it out. "Why do you carry so much goddamned cash, Billy?"

"No paper trail, Skunkie. I've tried to teach you that."

"But why so much?"

"I don't know how long I'll be here. How do I know how much I need?"

"But fifty thousand?"

"What if I want to bet?"

Nancy was having trouble understanding all this. "Bet on what?"

Billy always amazed me. As much as I knew how he lived on the edge, his life still fascinated me, not so much because of the thrill of it anymore, but because he really believed it. He wasn't trying to be cool, he wasn't trying to impress anyone. He sincerely believed he had found the best adaptation to life possible. But as that night proved, no way of living was without its drawbacks.

We parked at the curb, and Nancy decided the excitement was a little too much for her. She offered to stay with her car.

"No, I might need you, Nance. Let's go!" All three of us ran to the gate.

Billy, sweating, stopped to brush back his hair, straighten his jacket and wipe his brow. "Better look official." He winked.

"Maybe I should be the one to ask," I said.

"You can't lie fast enough," Billy says. He walked up to the agent at the gate and calmly smiled. "I seem to have left my bag in the overhead compartment. Would the plane still be here?"

"The plane is still here," the agent said, eyeing all three of us, "but it's been cleaned out." She was a middle-aged, overweight brunette whose cynical frown made her look like she'd never had a day of fun in her life. Maybe it was just me, but I sensed that she knew Billy was a wild one, and she was all too happy to have the upper hand with him. It was validation that her choice of a safe, no-risk, boring life was far superior to his life of non-stop excitement.

"Then maybe you found my bag? It's a brown gym bag with a—"

"Oh, we found it all right," the agent interrupted.

"Did you look inside?" Billy wasn't one to ignore the obvious.

"Yes, we did." She was making it as hard as she possibly could, but Billy knew better than to react.

"So you know it's very valuable to me. Can you tell me where I can find it?"

"We turned it over to the FBI." It's the first time she smiled during the entire encounter.

"Why would you do that?" I jumped in. "Don't you have a lost and found?"

The agent glared at me. "Airline policy. Anything over ten thousand."

"Can you tell me where the FBI took the bag?" Billy was the smart one. He didn't care about putting this bitch in her place. "Follow the money," his look said to me. "It's all that matters."

"There's an office on Level Two, C Concourse."

We got off the elevator, and Billy headed straight into the men's restroom, then came back out way too fast to have relieved himself.

"What was that about?" Nancy asked.

"Betting stubs. If the FBI sees those, I'm in trouble. I'll pick them up after we get the money."

We saw the FBI logo on the door and stopped outside. Billy gave me a one-armed hug, then led me and Nancy inside. I was moved by the hug of support, then I realized he was not letting go of me. He was just trying to make it look like we were husband and wife. Any piece of evidence to show the FBI he was a responsible, everyday guy, the better. He was good at what he did. He knew how to take advantage of every shred of opportunity, and his poker face was so good, you'd have sworn it was only his morning newspaper he had left on the plane.

The FBI men gave Billy the third degree. "What's the cash for?"

"Down payment for a condo in Florida."

"Why no driver's license?"

"I don't drive."

"No passport?"

"I don't leave the country."

"What's the cash for?"

"Down payment for a condo in Florida."

"Drug dealers carry this kind of cash."

"Lucky fellows."

"Drug dealers don't carry ID."

"Sounds like you know a lot of drug dealers."

The questioning went on for half an hour, then Nancy and I were asked to wait outside while Billy was escorted into another room. We waited another half an hour, pacing, sitting, tapping, pacing. I was ready to call a lawyer when Billy walked out with the bag in his hand.

"Let's go."

"How'd you get out of that?"

Billy didn't stop to answer. He just kept walking briskly toward the exit. He looked back once, not to see if Nancy and I were following, but to see if the FBI was following. We caught up with him just as he stepped outside, then looked around for Nancy's car.

It was gone.

"The car's been towed, Billy," Nancy said. "I should have known better than to leave it at the curb."

Billy didn't skip a beat. Didn't say a word. He walked straight to a taxi and got in. We jumped in after him. "What about the gambling stubs?" I asked.

Billy looks at me and smiled, "You're learning kid, you're learning." He took a hundred-dollar bill out of his pocket, ripped it in two and handed half to the cab driver, an old man who flashed a toothless grin. "Wait for me."

I held the bag of cash. Billy headed back into the airport. A few minutes later he walked back out carrying three see-through, industrial sized bags of airline trash.

"I forgot which trashcan I put them in," Billy said, throwing the bags in the trunk and then jumping in the cab. "Let's go." He was as calm as if he had just gotten back from a business trip and was headed to the office.

Nancy and I shook our heads in amazement. The taxi drove off with us and a truck filled with the trash of a thousand different lives.

Chapter 14
Life Is Like a Box of Chocolates

The weight of Mom's death hit me again, when we got back to the house with Billy's bag of cash. I hadn't realized it, but the airport fiasco with Billy took me out of my reality. For a few short hours, I didn't feel any pain, I didn't think about my problems, I didn't worry about what obstacles life had in store for me next. For a few short hours, nothing really mattered. No wonder Billy loved that life. No wonder he was so good at it.

Billy walked in the front door and picked up where he left off as if he had never been gone. He poured a drink for everyone in the room, then fake-boxed with Joel and Devin, anxious to give them a strong male presence. The boys loved him. Even before Michael's death, he was special to them. After Michael's death, Billy had become a god. As he sat them down to teach them poker strategies, Brittany and Kristen took their bags upstairs.

"You lose," Billy cheered. "Gotta pay attention. Watch the faces, not the cards."

"It's only the first hand," Devin laughed.

"We're just warming up," Joel added.

"Pussies warm up!" Billy yelled. "By the time you're finished warming up, the sharks will have already eaten you alive and shitted you out."

I worried that he was being too harsh on them, but they seemed to enjoy his tough-guy attitude, plus they did need a male perspective on life.

"Just deal," Devin said in a playful challenge.

Soon Billy was taunting them again, "You lose!

Losers! Both of you!"

Joel and Devin were still smiling, so I let it go. What was I worried about? A lot. Life was tough, but I hadn't taught them that. I'd only protected them. It was good for them to hear it from someone.

Brittany came downstairs with a strange look on her face. "Why is Aunt Becca going through grandma's jewelry?"

"What?" Cara yelled.

"She's putting it in her purse," Brittany said.

I just collapsed on the couch. I didn't care anymore. I hadn't felt like Becca was my sister for some time. She was just someone I used to know, used to love, and if she ever wanted to be my sister again, that would be fine with me. Until then, I didn't have the time or energy to give her.

"Losers!" Billy yelled, ignoring Brittany's announcement. "I'll eat you two pussies alive," he shouted at Joel and Devin. "And if your Uncle Billy will do this to you, imagine what someone who doesn't even know you will do!"

I saw Joel and Devin's smiles slip away. Their faces grew more intense. Billy didn't let up.

Cara and Nancy argued with Becca upstairs. Kristen and Brittany watched their father, who hadn't seen them in quite a while, but was ignoring them to spend all of his time with his nephews. Joel and Devin were learning the ropes of gambling and life from a brutal teacher who loved them as much as he loved gambling. I poured myself a glass of wine and soon fell asleep on the couch.

Hours later, I woke up to a crashing sound. Everyone had gone to bed. The house was dark, except for a dim light in the kitchen. I walked in to see the refrigerator open. Its light offered a pale view of Billy sitting on the floor shaking, along with a bottle of Wild Turkey shattered by the trash can. I couldn't go to him. I didn't know how to console him, because I didn't know what he was crying for. He had loved our mother, he was hurting about her death, but that wasn't all. I knew it wasn't. There were the daughters he didn't know. The life lived alone in a false sense of thrill and excitement. The emptiness of running, struggling to stay one step ahead of feeling any loss, monetary or emotional. I cried for him, but I couldn't help him. Not with this one. I wasn't strong enough. I didn't have the answers, not for myself, not for Billy.

I walked softly back to the couch, laid down and shut my eyes. Boom. I heard another crash, then a long, guttural moan. The anguish and despair of Billy's breakdown shuddered through me like the destruction of death I had become far too familiar with.

The next day, Billy's façade was as strong as it normally was. He was laughing, joking and pouring drinks for everyone who came by Mom's house for Shivah. It was day one of three, and we were already exhausted. Cara, Nancy and I sat on the couch, paralyzed. Becca wouldn't sit down. She was polishing furniture, counting china settings, mentally appraising the house. Devin, Joel, Brittany and Kristen were outside catching up, comparing schools and favorite bands.

Why were we sitting Shivah? It was boring, depleting, yet I wouldn't want to be anywhere else. It was a way to honor Mom and to hear things we never knew about her from friends we never knew she had.

What I don't understand is why they all brought fruit. It's against Jewish custom to send flowers when a loved one dies, so most people send a fruit basket. Every person who came to pay their respects brought a fruit basket, or a bag of fruit, or a fruit plate.

"For sitting Shivah," they said.

"Thank you," we said. "Mom would have been so grateful, but you really shouldn't have."

What we didn't say was that we were serious. They really shouldn't have. How much fruit can a person eat? We moaned every time another visitor left us with a basket of oranges and grapes. We figured Billy had had enough, because all of a sudden he was gone. Mrs. Simpson was visiting, and she wanted an old fashioned, and no one knew how to make the drink, not even her. No one knew where Billy had gone. He didn't say a word to anyone. He was just gone. Knowing Billy, he was probably on his way back to Vegas. I didn't blame him. Three more days of being cooped up in a small house with his four dysfunctional sisters and nothing to eat but fruit was too much for a guy who lived in hotel suites and ate at five-star restaurants every night without spending a dime. Honestly, I hoped he did leave. It would be better for him. The combination of being out of his element, Mom's death and seeing his daughters again was too much for Billy. It was not the world he lived in— family, life, death and everything that goes with it.

"We'll never hear from him again," Nancy said.

"Of course we will," Cara answered. "He comes and goes when he wants."

"Mom was the common thread," Nancy said. "Without her, there's no reason for him to come back."

"I'll ask him when he's coming back next time he calls," I said.

"He calls you?" Becca sounded indignant.

"Often," I said. "Doesn't he call you?"

"Not in ten years," Becca said. "And I'm the only real sister he has."

"We're all his real sisters," Nancy said.

"You know what I mean," Becca said.

"Great." Nancy fell back on the couch.

"Don't be such a drama queen," Becca said.

"Leave her alone, Becca," I said.

"She's a big girl, Sunny. I think she can speak for herself. Even if she doesn't have a clue."

"Well, now I know why Aaron left," Nancy said.

Becca jumped over to Nancy and cocked back her arm, ready to slap her. Just as she started to swing, Billy grabbed her arm and stopped her. He was back. He was back with several giant, shiny pink shopping bags with fuchsia vinyl bows. I recognized the bags. They were from the most exclusive chocolate shop in the area.

"Ladies," Billy smiled. "I think you need a little relief."

Billy reached into one of the pink shopping bags and started handing out boxes of expensive chocolate to everyone. "Truffles for Nancy, milk chocolates to Cara, dark chocolate with nuts for Skunkie the nut, and caramels for Becca. No more fruit for this Shivah. It's time to get my sisters fat!"

Billy unloaded a dozen more boxes of chocolates and stacked them on the coffee table, then poured drinks for everyone. "You're going to be my big, fat sisters," Billy sang, as he danced across the room. "You're going to be the big, fat Matus sisters."

I picked the receipt out of the bag. Billy had spent close to a thousand dollars on chocolate. He knew how to make people happy—even a grieving, cat-fighting group of sisters like us.

Chapter 15
Trials and Tribulations

The job search. The hirings and firings. The past-due notices. The lawsuit. The whirlwind trip to Las Vegas. My mother's death. The tension with my sisters. Now, it was the plane ride back to New Jersey.

We rose to 30,000 feet, and I looked out the window over Florida. I couldn't help feeling like I was a pinball being tossed around the game board. Plunked here, bounced off there, kicked back ,and then spun around again. My life didn't feel like it was mine. I didn't feel like I had a say. Everything that happened to me was a reaction to something outside of me.

I had to take control of my life again. I was a capable woman. I had faced some of the worst that life could throw at me, yet I was still standing. Through the scammers, the schemers and the deaths, I had kept my head up, always found a way to keep going. I had done things that made me proud. Focus on that, I told myself. Not all the negative stuff.

I woke as the plane started descending into New Jersey. I didn't even know I had fallen asleep, but I felt rested. After all I had been through, I'd developed a sense of calm. Some of it was the nap, but there had to be more. The realization that I was getting stronger and could take control gave me a new perspective, which was freeing for me. New steps, one by one. I looked over at the magazine that the man in the next seat was reading. The lead article was about the booming insurance industry. Unlimited growth, stability, expanding marketplace.

I can do that, I thought to myself. Teach me the rules, and I could sell insurance. I was confident. I had years of experience dealing with people through my party planning business, and who could possibly be better at explaining the importance of insurance than someone who had lost a spouse? Insurance is protection. Insurance is what people need when they go through what I'd been through. It was knowing that somewhere, someone is watching out for you, ready to catch you if you fall. If I couldn't sell that, I might as well go back to Las Vegas.

"Can I borrow that when you're done?" I said to the man, feeling bold and sure of myself, knowing I had to say something to get what I wanted. I was ready to reach out and grab what I needed to get my life together. I was brave. Dynamic. In control. And was excited about my future for the first time in a long time.

"Take it." The man handed me the magazine. "I'm just trying to kill time."

"Thanks. I saw the article on the insurance industry and thought it might be something for me."

"Are you in insurance?"

"No. Looking for a new career, though."

"What was your last career?" He smiled, and I hope he wasn't flirting. I was in a business mood and didn't want to have to deal with that at every turn.

"I had a party planning business. Very successful."

"So you do catering?"

Oh, God, I thought. He was flirting. "No, it wasn't catering. I hired caterers. I handled all aspects of big events, weddings, corporate parties." Please, mister, don't flirt. Just let this be a normal conversation.

"My wife's always wanted to start a catering business."

Thank God.

"She's always got something on the stove," he said, leaning back in a very non-flirting way.

"Well," I said, relieved, "I believe people should follow their dreams."

"And your dream is insurance?"

I looked out the window and saw New Jersey rising up to meet me. "I'm trying to re-invent myself."

"Well, if you need any help," he muttered

I smiled at the man, then looked back out the window. My mind started racing. Did he just offer to help me? Did I just ignore him? I had gotten so accustomed to people trying to take advantage of me, I didn't know what a true offer of help sounded like. Was it too late to answer? Did I miss the opportunity?

"Are you in the business?" I asked, emboldened.

"No. But, I've got a friend at Certified. He's always looking for eager new agents."

"I don't have any experience." Let him know exactly where I stood. If he could help, fine. If not, I would move on to the next opportunity.

"They'll train you, as long as you have the right attitude." He looked at me and nodded. "And you do."

I was usually warm and friendly, and men often took it the wrong way. I was glad this man hadn't.

"Well, I'd appreciate the chance to prove myself," I said sincerely.

"I'll give him a call tonight."

Tonight, I thought? Can it happen that fast?

"Here, take my card," the man said, reaching into his suit coat pocket. "Call me in the morning, and I'll put you two in touch."

I took the card, fighting the skepticism in my head. This could be the break I needed.

The wheels touched down in New Jersey. For a broke widow, I sure felt like I was living the jet-set life. Reality set in as soon as I got home.

Ten messages on the answering machine—all from the District Attorney. He had been trying to reach me all week, but I never once checked my messages. With Joel and Devin at the funeral in Florida with me, I figured that there was no one I needed to talk to. My entire life had been right beside me.

I unpacked while listening to the messages. Each was about a trial date for Michael's murderers, but I didn't hear the date. Every new message became more urgent, until finally, the tenth message was from this morning. The trial was starting tomorrow. The D.A. would send a car for me at 8 A.M.

Thoughts raced through me head. "Tomorrow morning? Was he kidding? What do I do? What do I say? Where do I go? What do I wear? Do I really want to do this? And what about the insurance business? How long will the trial last? What if it is months? Just when I got a break for a job, a career, I get sidetracked."

I set my makeup bag on my dressing table and saw the picture of Michael at the lake. So young, so strong, so kind. My chest started heating up. I knew that more important than any bills, any job, any career, was Michael, and I wasn't going to let those thugs slip away, even if I lost everything. If my presence in the court would help the case, then I would be there every day, looking sorrowful for the judge, weeping for the jury, vindictive toward the two punks on trial. One thing was for certain, they would believe it all, because it was all true. I wouldn't have to act. I would drag myself through misery again, so Michael would be vindicated. I would go toe-to-toe with those scumbags. I wished I could put them away for life, the same as they did to Michael, and to me.

The car pulled into the driveway at 8 A.M. sharp. Why did all unmarked law enforcement cars look the same? Square models, dull, non-descript colors, vinyl seats and a crew-cut, stocky guy at the wheel.

The stocky man in a gray suit came to the door. "Morning, ma'am. Ready to roll?"

Ready to roll? He has to know he was taking me to my husband's murder trial. Still, I know he wasn't being cold, it was just the language they used. I handed him a hot Styrofoam cup of coffee. "Cream or sugar?"

"Black, ma'am. Thank you very much. This'll hit the spot, but we should get going."

"Call me Sunny."

"I'm Jim, ma'am."

I took my coffee, my purse and the weight on my shoulders and stepped into Jim's car. He didn't say much on the trip, but I could tell he was enjoying the coffee, and that made me feel good.

At the courthouse, Jim escorted me inside. I felt important as he opened the doors and led me around the lines of waiting people, through back hallways and to the third floor, and even more important with Bill Johnston, the D.A., waiting for me outside the courtroom.

"Mrs. Rubin? Thank goodness you're here. I left so many messages."

"I'm sorry, I was out of town. Just got back late last night."

"Pleasure, I hope."

"My mother's funeral." When the words came out of my mouth, I started to cry. I realized he was the first person I'd told. Everyone else I knew was at the funeral. This was the first time I actually said it out loud. This was the first time I realized she was truly gone for good.

"I'm sorry, Mrs. Rubin."

I shook my head and wiped my tears. He led me into a courtroom with more clerks and lawyers swarming around the bench than people in the gallery. Mr. Johnston sat me down in the third row, behind where he would be sitting.

"Shouldn't I be closer?"

"This'll be fine," he said.

I turned around and realized Jim was gone. I didn't say goodbye.

I started to feel the same haze from Michael's funeral overtaking me. Something was lifting me out of my body, so maybe it wasn't the Valium after all. Maybe this was just the way we cope with unspeakable pain. I began drifting dizzily. In a fog, I saw the jury enter. The two defendants couldn't have been be older than twenty, but they looked like pure evil. Smirks, scowls, apathy. They acted more like they had jaywalked than murdered my husband.

The days went by. Jim picked me up. I gave him coffee. We talked about dog racing. I was comfortable with the subject, because Billy used to take me to dog tracks in Florida. It was the only thing Jim seemed to like talking about, and I enjoyed listening to him. It was better than being left alone with my thoughts. Bill Johnston met me every morning at the courtroom door, and every day, those two kids walked in chewing gum, slouching, shaking off the deputies who escorted them to their seats.

I thought of my own two sons, and how they couldn't be more different than these two punks. Thank God. I had decided not to let Joel and Devin attend the trial. I just didn't want to expose them to the horrific details of Michael's murder. I would have liked their company, though, or anybody's, for that matter. I felt so alone. I wondered, "How did I get to this place of such utter loneliness?"

I listened with the jury as we heard about the thugs' criminal records—blowing up a police department, robbing a jewelry store, raping a man's wife while they held him at gunpoint, and now, murder. They murdered Michael, just because he was there. They were junkies. Life had no meaning to them.

I cried on the stand, so much that it was difficult to talk. "My children will never see their father again," I sobbed. "I have no money. No source of income. My husband's union benefits died with him. The love of my life is gone."

I went on for ten minutes. I was in such a pain-induced altered state that I couldn't even remember everything I said. When I was done with my testimony, most of the jury members wiped their tears as I did mine.

I thought being on the stand would be the worst part of the trial.

I was wrong.

One of Michael's murderers took the stand and recounted what had happened. I sat, listening to the two telling how they had worn ski masks when they entered the

Temple on Casino Night. Michael was walking towards the door, and when he saw them, he turned away. Not quickly enough. They were intimidated by his height, and shot him in the back. Michael dragged himself down the hall, but it was too late. The bullet had ripped through his body to his heart. Hearing these details, I sobbed more violently than I had while on the stand. I pictured my love, my Michael, my gentle knight in shining armor, fighting to save his own life. The raw agony ripped through my heart, as well.

The one who pulled the trigger got 14 years, the closest thing to a life sentence that was allowed in New York for the crime he was charged with. I felt relief that these animals wouldn't be allowed to ruin other lives, at least not for a long time. I found myself hoping he would be murdered in prison, or worse.

His friend was sentenced to two years. The life was drained out of me.

My thoughts were a jumble. I still hadn't called the man from the airplane. I wouldn't know what to say to him. I wouldn't have been available until after the trial, which went on two months, and I didn't want to start the job by dropping a mountain of garbage on day one.

Who was going to hire a widow going through a murder trial, her mother's death and with no current job? Bold, brave and unemployable.

Even if I had called him, even if I was going to spill my life into the heart of a new job interview, I just didn't have the strength. The trial took every ounce of energy I had. All the boldness, all the bravery, all the dynamism, all the determination to reach out and grab life—I left all of that on the worn linoleum floor of a cold, plain, wood-paneled courtroom.

Chapter 16
Chance of a Lifetime

The trial was behind me. I was coming to terms with my mother's death. The boys were doing well in school.

Joel and Devin were doing very well indeed. They had been invited to Hockey Night in New England, where all the NHL scouts and college coaches would be. It was a showcase of all the top high-school talent, a chance for players to make big impressions. Just being invited was a good indication that they had what it took to make it. I couldn't have been happier for them.

And then there was the job. Or, better put, the lack of a job. I was fed up. It was time to take action. I didn't call the man from the airplane, but I called every other insurance company in the state and landed a dozen interviews. I got a shot with a company that would hire me and pay for my classes and license. There was an unwritten agreement that I would stay with the company once I got my license, and that was fine with me. If they were going to give me a hand up, I was sure not going to bite it.

So I started working, and I was thrilled. Exhilarated. Working with other people in a real career was a whole new world for me. I felt like doors were opening to a brighter future. I was learning, I was working toward my insurance license, and I was getting paid. I was moving on with my life. Picking up the pieces and starting new. What more could I ask for?

Midway through my insurance classes, I got a call from Bill Johnston, the D.A. He had found more evidence and wanted to retry the second man with additional charges. He was sure he could get a longer sentence.

Another trial. Another jury. Another chunk of my life taken from me.

I had been a model employee, one without any apparent baggage. Now I had to go to my boss and tell him everything about my past. My tragic, haunting past. Plus, I had to tell him I needed time off. Could I do it? I didn't think so. I didn't even know if I wanted to go back to trial. How long would Michael's murder weigh me down? When would I finally get the chance to draw a line and say, "Now it's time to work on my life?"

Even as I thought otherwise, I knew I would go through with the trial. I could never have forgiven myself, if I didn't do everything in my power to put his killers away. I didn't care if that guy hadn't pulled the trigger, he was going to pay for Michael's murder.

With the experience of the first trial, I was stronger through the second. I was honest with my boss, and he allowed me to work around the trial schedule. My life didn't come to a stop. The guy was found guilty again, and another five years were added to his sentence. It doesn't sound like much, but seeing him in court again, I could tell it was like a life sentence to him. After spending a few months in jail, he wasn't so cocky. Wasn't so smug. He was scared to death. Like a stray dog. I could see in his eyes that he was living in hell, and I was happy. Now, instead of two years of it, he got seven. He was just a kid, but I didn't feel sorry for him in the least. This time, I was the one scoffing at him, and he was the one who was fearful and tortured.

I was getting stronger, and it wasn't just from my trial experience. I could feel it. I was becoming someone. I was beginning to realize who I was and, more importantly, who I could be. Joel and Devin had a whole world of opportunity open to them. Everything was finally falling into place.

The parking lot was overflowing with SUVs, all open at the back and all packed with hockey gear. Boys—young men, really—were suiting up, putting on pads, taping their sticks, flipping pucks, while their parents sipped coffee and gossiped about which scouts were there and which scouts weren't. I parked my little compact between two giant Suburban gas-guzzlers, locked the door and turned around to the glass-enclosed hockey arena, glittering under the cold New England sun like the Stanley Cup. It wasn't a pro arena, but everything about it felt like a pro game—the barbeques in the parking lot, the painted faces, the thrill of the crowd and, mostly, the exuberance of players and fans certain that victory was here. Only these were high school kids and parents, and victory didn't mean winning the game, it meant playing at the top of your game and hoping that somehow, someway, you do something to impress an NHL scout. It didn't have to be much, just a great play, a high-scoring game, a brutal block. As long as they made a note. As long as they took notice. Of course, what really drove the energy was the unspoken hope that your kid or kids would get noticed or maybe even drafted right from the tournament. It didn't happen often, but it had happened enough to keep the dream alive.

I didn't have an SUV, and I didn't have a car full of gear. Joel and Devin got a ride in from school, and we planned to meet after the first game. I didn't have coffee, I didn't have a tailgate, much less a tailgate party, but I was here because this is what the boys want. Their hopes and dreams were here. They were hoping that maybe they would have the game of their lives. After all we had been through, it was time for a turn of events, for some balance. Deep down, I had a feeling it would happen. My intuition was telling me something good was going to happen here.

Armed with excitement, hope and no face paint, I took my seat in the arena and settled in for the first of seven consecutive days of hockey. There was nowhere I was happier. Watching the boys do what they love, not having a worry in the world, the sound of their blades cutting the ice, the shaking of the boards. It was true joy.

The boys played on the same team, but not on the same line. They were never on the ice together, which made it a little easier for cheering. The first game was a rout. Joel played very well. At least, that was my impression. If anyone had been getting the scout's attention in this game, it was Joel.

"Don't exaggerate, Mom," Devin said outside the arena after the game.

"I'm not! I'd tell you if you sucked. You worked hard out there and did a great job. Both of you," I said, giving them both a hug.

"It felt good, anyway," Joel said, "But there are a lot more games and a lot of great players here."

"Let's check into the hotel so you can take a shower before the next game."

"What's the point of taking a shower if we're just going to end up stinking again later?" Joel asked.

"The point is to be the best. You have to feel your best. Besides, it was a long drive here for me. I need to relax little."

"You mean hockey isn't relaxing?" Devin joked.

In a way, he was right. Hockey was relaxing. It's a

total escape.

The hotel was like the movie "Animal House." All the hockey players and their parents were staying there, and it was more like a giant party than a place to sleep. Every door was open, players and parents are shuffling back and forth between rooms, drinking beer, dancing to blaring music, skinny-dipping in the pool. Girls everywhere. Friends of players, sisters of players, wannabe NHL mothers, they were everywhere. I had to admit, it was pretty fun, and Joel and Devin turned out to be very popular players on their team, so our room was party central. Some of the boys, whose parents didn't come, took showers in our room. Some even slept on our floor. I couldn't walk from the door to the bathroom without climbing through a maze of giant hockey bags, pads, suitcases, skates and ice chests. It was good to see Devin and Joel having so much fun, so carefree. I just hoped they were getting enough rest for the games. I knew I wasn't.

The second day was even better. Joel and Devin's team was still undefeated, which was critical. In a single elimination tournament, it was one loss and you were out. And not only was the team doing well, but Joel was leading the tournament in points. The lack of sleep and the girls hanging out didn't seem to faze them. I admired the boys' dedication, determination and guts, but even with all the validation, even with the certainty that my boys were playing well, even with all the hope I had allowed myself to feel for their future, I was taken aback by the man who came up to me in the stands and sat down right next to me.

"Mrs. Rubin," he said. "Tex Walters. I'm an NHL scout." He whispered the last part so none of the parents around me can hear.

"Hi," I said, not knowing what else to say. "I'm …"

"Sunny Rubin. I know."

"Great game here, don't you think?" I was at a lost for words. I didn't want to be obvious and ask if he was scouting Joel, but why else would he have approached me? Better to be discreet. Let him take the lead.

"Joel's skating very well today," Tex said, "In the whole tournament, truth be told."

"Well, he and his brother Devin sure do love hockey."

"Lots of kids love hockey. Heck, lots of kids are good at hockey. Not too many are great at it."

I felt a surge of pride inside, combined with the heat of excitement. This was starting to sound good.

"Of course, I've always thought they were great hockey players, but I'm their mother."

"I've got a conference call with the office in ten minutes. Can we have lunch later? I'd like to discuss Joel's future, and what he can do. We have a lot to talk about."

"Yes. Of course. Should I meet you?"

"I'll pick you up out front. Say one o'clock."

"I'll be there."

Back at the hotel room, I tried hard to contain my excitement. I still hadn't decided if I would tell the boys about the meeting or not. I didn't want to get Joel's hopes too high. After all, it was only a meeting, a first step, and I didn't know what he was going to say, or how Devin would feel. He was only 15, but he had hopes and dreams just like his older brother Joel. On the other hand, it was a meeting with an NHL scout! He wouldn't have been taking the time to meet if he didn't think Joel had talent.

"What's up?" Devin asked as he popped out of the bathroom.

"Nothing," I said, wondering how to broach the subject.

Joel, lying on the bed, looked up from the TV. "That smile on your face. Something's up."

"I'm just proud of the way you're both playing. That's all."

"No," Devin pressed. "Proud is this smile." Devin curved his lips and crossed his eyes as Joel laughed. "This smile is more like," Devin smiled wide and opened his eyes like a goggle-eyed baby.

"All right, you clowns," I said. "If you must know, Tex Walters is taking me to lunch."

"Tex Walters!" Joel jumped up. "The NHL scout? What'd he say?"

"He said he had a call he had to make, and we'd talk more at lunch."

"Well, what are you doing here?" Joel yelled. "Get going!"

"I'm not meeting him until one."

"So be early," Devin said. "This is huge."

"An hour early?"

"Mom!" Joel yelled. "Don't mess this up."

"How could I mess it up? He wouldn't even be talking to us if he wasn't interested."

Joel fell back onto the bed. "Tex Walters!"

"Don't get too excited," I cautioned. "He just wants to talk."

"But Tex Walters!" Devin said.

"Let's just see what he says and take it from there. Even if he's interested, it could be a few years down the road."

"Just go, Ma. You'll be late."

"All right, all right. I'll go. You've got a game at two. I'll be late, but I'll be there. Make sure you keep this to yourselves, and don't get too cocky out there."

Chapter 17
Alone Again, Unnaturally

I was on time for my lunch appointment with Tex, which was unusual, because for almost everything else, I was late. As other parents walked in and out of the arena, I reveled in my secret—an NHL scout was watching Joel. I was anxious and unsure where this would lead, but for the moment, all their SUVs, BBQs and cliques didn't matter. What mattered was that my boys were at the top of their game.

Tex pulled up in a blue Cadillac. As soon as I got in, he sped away.

"Sorry I didn't open the door for you," he said. "Better that no one sees us leaving together."

"No problem with me."

"Parents can be pretty determined when it comes to their kids. Once they see us talking to one family, they start hounding us to pay closer attention to their kids."

"I've always felt if the kids didn't have it on the ice, there wasn't anything anyone could do to change it."

"I admire that, but you're in the minority. I've had parents show up at my house at three in the morning. I've had hate mail, death threats, even a letter bomb once."

"My God, you're kidding."

"The bomb didn't go off, but I'm telling you, parents become beasts when it comes to getting their kids into the league. Like you say, though, none of it matters if it's not on the ice."

We merged onto the turnpike and drove out of town.

"Where's this restaurant?"

"Oh hell, I'm sorry. I forgot to tell you. I'd like to take you to Gunnery. A school in Connecticut, great hockey. I think this is the place for Joel. I want to show you the rink."

"Will we be back for part of the two o'clock game?"

"Should make it by the third period."

I hated missing that much of the game, but what was I going to say? Missing one game was nothing compared to an opportunity like this.

Tex said little of substance on the drive, mostly small talk. Finally, we pulled onto the grounds of an empty prep school. New England prep schools were all on winter break, and the school looked pretty deserted. Tex turned his Cadillac toward the track and pulled behind a building that looked like a gym or locker room, though it probably was the hockey coach's office.

"Pretty dedicated coach to be working on winter break," I said.

Tex parked in a gated area with green mesh screens attached to the surrounding chain link fence. It was a parking lot with ten or so places, but there were no cars here today.

"Come inside with me," Tex said. "I want you to meet this guy." He walked around to my side of the car and opened the door for me. As I got out, I noticed a heavy chain wrapped around the handles of the double doors. The building was padlocked.

"Are you sure he's here?" I asked, feeling a twinge of anxiety.

"He said I'd have to pound on the door. I guess he wasn't kidding," Tex said. He closed my car door, then put his arm on the roof of the car and leaned toward me. He was close enough for me to smell his bad breath. "Listen," Tex said. "I didn't give you much information on why I'm interested."

"I figured you'd get around to it," I said, stepping back a few inches until my back was against the car.

"Truth is, I think Joel needs better competition to step up his game."

"I know he's got the talent," I offered.

"To make it in the NHL," Tex said, leaning closer, "it takes more than talent."

"What do you mean?" I was drawing a blank. Suddenly, I felt Tex's lips on mine. They were cold, rough and forceful. A sick feeling burnt in my stomach. I pulled away.

"What was that?" I shouted.

"What's the problem?" Tex said calmly. "We're both single adults."

I was horrified. I realized Tex had a full profile on Joel. He knew I was a widow, and he was taking advantage of that.

"Let's just keep this about Joel," I said from a safe distance. "Can we do that?"

"This is about Joel," Tex said. "If you want him to have a chance at all "

"What are you saying?"

"It's no big deal," Tex said, moving closer. "It happens all the time."

"Not to me, it doesn't," I said, moving back. Tex grabbed my arm to stop me.

"Listen," he said. "We can do this the easy way, or we can do it the hard way."

I felt like vomiting. I looked around and finally

realized there was no prep school hockey coach. There was no one at this school. There wasn't another soul around. And even if there had been, we were completely secluded in this gated parking lot. No one would have seen us even if they were driving right by. This wasn't about the NHL.

I tried to kick him in the balls but missed, hitting him in the leg. Running as fast as I could, I headed for the entry gate, the only way out. Just as I was about to reach the opening, I felt Tex's hand on my shoulder. He jerked me back and threw me against the fence. I screamed as loud as I could, but it was muffled as Tex's mouth pressed hard against mine, suffocating me with rough skin and foul breath. Heart racing with terror, I was kicking, swinging, but he was too big. His body weight pressed against me, keeping me pinned hard against the fence. I felt tears burn down my cheeks as his hand lifts my skirt and tugged my panties down. I wanted to die. I wanted to close my eyes and disappear. My back was in pain, cut open by a broken wire in the fence. My legs were throbbing from Tex kicking them to hold me in place. My head ached from the horror of this beast overpowering me, but nothing came close to the pain of him fumbling around and finally entering me. I was dying. That was my only thought. Shame and death. This horrific act was ripping the last shreds of emotion from me. I saw flashes of red, glimpses of his unshaven cheeks, and smelled the sickening smells of his body odor and breath.

Then it was over. I crumbled to the ground sobbing. I didn't want to look up. I didn't want to see him.

"Let's go," he said.

I couldn't answer. I couldn't believe he was still there. Did he have no shame? Had he given all his shame to me?

Why wouldn't he run? What else did he want from me?

"Come on," he said. "I'll drop you back at the rink."

Didn't he know what just happened? He raped me, and now he wanted to give me a lift back.

"Get the fuck in the car," he said. "And if you ever say anything about this to anybody, your boys will never skate again. I'll make their lives a fuckin' horror story."

Shit. I was in the middle of nowhere. Not a soul around. I didn't even know how we got here. I wasn't really paying attention. How could I have gotten into the car with this guy?

"They'll be finished with hockey forever," he said. "You think I don't pull that kind of weight?"

I know he did. He could do it. I could never say a word about this to anyone. Not to the police, not to the boys, not to my friends. He wanted this to go away, and I had no choice. I had to pretend this never happened. The shame, the humiliation, the powerlessness, the loss of my humanity would never go away.

I pictured Joel and Devin, imagined their joy at suiting up for games, their smiles on the ice. I couldn't risk taking away their love for hockey. It was the only thing that had held them together since Michael's death. It had given them a goal, a purpose.

I stood up, waved off Tex's helping hand and got in the car.

I told Tex to drop me off at the hotel. I couldn't face the boys looking like this.

"We have an understanding?" he asked.

I nodded and softly closed the car door. I showered, changed and made up my face. I could not allow this to destroy me. I had to guard against the fear rising within me. I couldn't allow that fear to convince me that I was weak. My love for the boys gave me courage and strength. I refused to give in. I couldn't let myself cry. The boys would be back soon.

The phone rang. I didn't want to talk to anyone ever again, but I thought the sooner I got my life back to normal, the easier this would be for the boys. Maybe a friendly conversation would help.

"Hello," I meekly answered.

"Sunny, it's Nancy. Thank God you're there. Becca is cleaning out Mom's house. She's taking TVs, dishes. She's not asking anyone. She just thinks it's all hers. Cara needs dishes. She doesn't have any. Becca has two sets, but she wants a third for outside entertaining. Cara should have those dishes, don't you think, Sunny? ... Sunny?"

I slowly hung up the phone.

Chapter 18
Fighting for Our Lives

In 1996, before I had even heard of the Gigante Family, Vincent Gigante and I found ourselves in surprisingly similar situations. We were both fighting for our lives.

As the old, Chinese woman stood on the sidewalk near her family's newsstand, she watched the man who everyone said was crazy. She watched him shuffle down the side of the street toward her. She shook her head, and with a disgusted look, turned away.

The large man continued his shuffle-walk toward the newsstand. He was noticeable because of his size, but if by chance, someone had not noticed his imposing physical stature, certainly his attire, or lack there of, would have been a clue that this man was different. This day, the man was dressed only in a bathrobe, and slippers. He appeared disheveled. His black, curly hair needed a trim, and stuck out in an unruly manner. He also looked as if he needed a shave. He talked as he walked, to no one in particular, a non-stop soliloquy on a private stage. The man's name: Vincent Gigante, and he was known to everyone on this street as "The Chin".

This was Sullivan Street, the same street on which this man had lived as a boy. The old tenement, where he had been raised, had been renovated and now housed a trendy bar and café. His mother still lived on this street, and that is where he would tell people he lived as well, if they had asked. Yolanda Gigante, mother of Vincent, lived at 225 Sullivan St., and at ninety-something years old, would still defend her boy to anyone who dared bad-mouth him in front of her.

As the man in the bathrobe shuffled to the newsstand, the old woman said something to a young boy in Chinese. For the boys' ears only, she said, "Wait on this vermin and get him away from here quickly. I don't want his blackness casting a shadow over our day."

The boy, eleven-year-old Zhong Woo was her grandson. The woman was Ying Woo, and together they ran the corner newsstand that Vincent "The Chin" Gigante visited almost every day.

While "The Chin" purchased a newspaper and cigarettes, and continued to mumble incoherently to himself, Ying fought the urge to scream out,

"I know you're not crazy! I only pretend to not understand your English. I hear every word you say, everyday. I hear you talk to the bad men. I hear you tell them to do bad things." Instead, Ying stood silently in the shadows of the stand and watched the man make his purchase and continue down Sullivan Street.

"Someday," she thought. "Karma will see you roam the earth in your death, searching for peace in your soul but finding none. Someday."

As Gigante continued his walk, someone else was watching as well. Ying saw the men, trying to look nondescript, trying to blend. Men in casual clothes, walking their dogs, buying cigarettes, playing checkers on the stoop, all watching. She saw them everyday. Some days the same men, some days different, but she could always tell which ones were FBI. She could always spot the one's that were watching Gigante, and she knew when he noticed them watching as well. His shuffle would get more intense, his crazy ranting louder. His lips would quiver and his arms shake, all the while, Ying was sure, Gigante must have been laughing inside. Thinking he was fooling them all. Well, maybe the rest were fooled, but Ying was no fool. Her name meant "Clever Eagle" in Chinese, and that's what she was. An eagle hovering over Sullivan Street, watching, waiting, hoping that the man who wanted everyone to believe he was crazy would soon get caught, and get what was coming to him.

Not long after that day that Ying had been watching Gigante on Sullivan Street, Jerry Capeci, America's foremost expert on organized crime, watched from the gallery in Brooklyn Federal Court while Vincent Gigante delivered a masterful performance. Prosecutors were trying to revoke the reputed Mafia don's $1 million bail that would keep him behind bars.

Looking sloppy with a three-day-old beard and a blue windbreaker over a white T-shirt, Gigante stumbled into court. He held onto the left arm of his heart specialist, Dr. Bernard Wechsler.

Capeci said Gigante's gray hair was mussed, his legs trembled, and his eyes looked everywhere but where he was going. The murderous crime kingpin was led past Judge Nickerson to the defense table, where Gigante plopped into his chair, mumbling and staring.

As Jerry Capeci wrote on his website, www. gangland.com, "For 12-spellbinding minutes, Vincent Gigante showed a standing-room-only courtroom why psychiatrists have been saying he's crazy for 30 years. He twitched and he trembled. His lips quivered and his arms shook. He played with his ear, he rubbed his chest. He shook his head, stroked his chin and scratched himself.

And as the judge and opposing lawyers spoke to each other, Gigante talked to himself."

The crowded courtroom was filled with Gigante Family members, including Yolanda, Father Louis Gigante (wearing his Roman collar), plus about 20 other relatives. Gigante's attorney, James LaRossa, played up the insanity angle.

"I have not had a discussion in which I think we were communicating in any meaningful fashion," LaRossa told the judge. "Just getting Mr. Gigante here was an incredible task."

The judge watched Gigante's actions intently, then ordered him to return to court in one month for a status conference and scheduled trial.

For the moment, at least, Gigante's crazy act had bought him a little more time.

Ying Woo made a huffing noise as she read this news in the morning paper. Cursing under her breath in Chinese she said aloud to her Grandson, Zhong, "That man is as crazy as I am. Crazy like a fox!"

Gigante's trial was the nation's biggest Mafia trial since John Gotti had his career-ender in the same courthouse five years earlier,

The trial of Michael's killer wasn't anything like the spectacle Gigante had going. At my legal battlefront, there were no standing-only courtroom scenes. Only I cared that I was fighting for my life, fighting for my reputation, my dignity and my livelihood.

After a succession of low-paying jobs, I had managed to re-invent myself as an insurance agent. It hadn't been easy. I worked days at a men's clothing store and attended school at night to learn the insurance business. After a grueling year of no sleep, fueled by caffeine and desperation, I passed several licensing exams. Now, finally, I could have a career—instead of just a job.

I was ecstatic when I got hired by a large, respected insurance firm. I was earning a decent salary—certainly not enough money to make me rich, but enough to pay the mortgage. There were commissions to be earned, in addition to the salary, and I was hungry to make those sales.

Almost immediately, my chance of a lifetime, my entrance into the fast track corporate life, was soured. Scott, the General Manager, was a big, fat, sloppy, jolly dirt bag. Picture Santa Claus—with his genitals hanging out. His idea of a joke was to verbally degrade women, blacks, and Jews. He had me on two out of three.

Married five times, he was now sleeping with one of the women who worked in the cafeteria. His pet nickname for her was the "mere," as in, she was a "mere" woman. Every Tuesday we would have a meeting. Instead of conducting any meaningful business, Scott would tell filthy jokes. After throwing in a few about niggers and Jew boys, he would end the meeting by ringing the bell and announcing he was going to the cafeteria to cop a feel with the "mere."

Scott steadily demeaned and demoralized every woman in the office. He would return to the office from the local strip bar, drunk and horny, and demand sexual favors from the women agents in return for sales leads. His flagrant disrespect for women permeated the entire office like an offensive odor, setting the tone for how all the other men treated the women in the office. One repulsive 60-year-old man repeatedly fell to his hands and knees in my cubicle and begged for sex. Since he stood only 4'9", the floor was not far for him to go. I would demand that he leave my cubicle and resist the temptation to slam a garbage pail over his head.

Nowadays a sexually charged atmosphere is taboo in the workplace. Everyone is too afraid of a sexual harassment suit, but this was the early 90's. The term "sexual harassment" was not part of everyone's vocabulary. Evidently, Scott had never heard of it at the time. He harassed and belittled the women in the office until they quit, most of them in tears.

I did not have the luxury of quitting. I needed this job, and he knew it. I didn't have a husband whose shoulder I could cry on, who would pat me consolingly and tell me to leave that toxic atmosphere. Besides, I had been toughened by tragedy. Death was a more formidable adversary than a low-life boss, drunk on middle-management power. I maintained my dignity but had no problem fighting back when provoked.

So I continued to work there, despite the abuse, the constant unwanted advances, the cocaine that was passed around as openly as Kleenex. Why should I quit? I was a top producer, without ever compromising my integrity. Unfortunately, I stood up for myself one too many times. My outspokenness landed me a spot right in the unemployment line.

I wasn't the only one to get fired. Two other women had also been fired, and I found out that they had gone to see a lawyer. Out of pure curiosity, I consulted the same attorney. He informed me that The Civil Rights Act of 1991 had expanded the rights of women to sue and collect punitive damages for sexual discrimination or harassment.

He also told me that in 1991, a famous lawsuit became the first sexual harassment case to be given class action status, paving the way for others.

Turns out, we had a case.

For five years this company fought me, tooth and nail. They pried into every detail of my private life. Repeatedly, they brought me in for depositions, trying to shatter my composure and get me to admit things that weren't true. They hired detectives to trail my every move, to prove that I was a wanton woman who had invited this behavior. My life, like Vincent Gigante's, was put under a microscope and dissected. Unlike Gigante's, there was nothing to be found.

After five draining years, the company finally offered up a small settlement. It wasn't even big enough to consider it as a consolation prize. It certainly didn't begin to cover the humiliation and outrage I had suffered, but my attorney no longer wanted to continue, and I was out of options.

Is the justice system really just? With enough money, even the most heinous of criminals can drool, twitch and mumble, and then beat the charges with a "get out of jail free" card. Ordinary citizens like me, without the unlimited resources of an organized crime Family, have to settle. Literally.

Chapter 19
A Nice Italian Family

Joel and Devin graduated from prep school and went on to play college hockey at two different SUNY colleges. At times they played against each other. College hockey was pure fun.

The team always had parties with their parents and yes, the girl groupies would be there, too. Billy came for some games and in typical Billy fashion, since he couldn't offer money for a victory, he offered one night with his girlfriend Denise for the player who scored the winning goal. The entire team called him Uncle Billy, and he took the whole team for drinks after the game. Joel actually scored the last goal, but the team lost. Denise was disappointed; she had wanted to be Joel's prize.

When we were in Plattsburg for a tournament with Devin's team, Billy had reserved a suite for all of us. We had this amazing suite with a living room, two bedrooms and a giant hot tub.

That's when Billy decided to take Devin for a real man's drinking experience. Devin wanted beer, but Billy insisted he should be a real man and drink Wild Turkey with him. Denise was downing Wild Turkeys with Billy. Devin was having a hard time drinking the Wild Turkey. Billy made fun of him by holding his nose and telling him, "C'mon, kid, be a real man. Real men don't have to hold their noses."

S   oon Billy had everyone in the bar joining him and encouraging Devin to drink. Finally Devin finished the drink and was immediately sick to his stomach. Billy decided he needed another Wild Turkey, this time without ice. Devin was gagging and shaking his head back and forth. "No, no I can't..." Finally Billy bought him a beer, because he said Devin wasn't a real man yet. Billy had his flaws.

Until their graduations, my life was always geared to what was best for my boys. In those days, I never imagined that my relationship with my boys could ever be challenged or destroyed. I had expected them to be loyal and loving. We had many hard times, and both boys knew the struggles I had being a single attractive widow.

Devin still plays hockey for fun on a men's league, and is now teaching little Jack Michael how to skate. When Joel graduated from college, I wept profoundly, because Mike was not there to see him. I was overwhelmed with emotions. Devin sat by my side. Mike would have been very proud that both boys played college hockey. As a young boy, Mike was a gifted athlete, but his family never encouraged or watched him play any sports. His family thought sports were a waste of time and useless. He was told he was not college material, and he would be an electrician. It was his dream to make sure, if the boys were talented athletically, they could reach for the stars. I took that dream and reached for the stars for both boys.

During his senior year, Devin tore his rotary cuff and his AC/LC, so he never skated in his senior year. The abrupt end to his amateur career marked another passage in our lives.

Bittersweet. I missed the fun of watching the boys play hockey, but, I watched the graduation ceremonies of our youngest son with pride and a sense of accomplishment. After college, Joel went to Sweden to play on a Division 1 professional Swedish team. During his prep school years, Joel skated with the two Swedish boys who introduced him to their Swedish team. After that, he returned to the States to run a youth hockey league.

Devin works for a very well known pharmaceutical company. He is the executive who creates marketing materials for certain drugs the company is promoting...

"Bitter, Skunkie...bitter, bitter, bitter. You are so very bitter."

My brother Billy's rough voice crackled over the speaker phone, but his tone was clear enough. It was a mixture of goading and warm brotherly love, a strange but familiar brew. Even his use of the childhood nickname he had christened me with so many years ago—a name I despised now as much as I did then—was intended to provoke me. So I took the same approach now, as I did when we were kids. I ignored him.

"Billy, when are you going to quit smoking?"

He coughed into the phone dramatically, and I chuckled. I took a second to check out my appearance in the hallway mirror. Let's see, I had to adjust the purple beret on my head, tilting it at a more rakish angle. There.

"Well?"

"The day after I quit drinking." That was Billy. A lovable rogue.

"So, Skunkie."

"Oops, gotta run, Billy!" I strode quickly through my bright family room decorated in African Jungle prints towards the speaker phone.

"You ever stop to wonder what you're running from, Skunkie?"

"I love you too, Billy!" I clicked off the phone and

without slowing my pace, headed back into the kitchen. Koho, my Siberian husky, looked up expectantly. "You don't think I'm bitter, do you, Koho?" I could have sworn she shook her head. I rewarded her with a kiss, and she wagged her tail and slurped my face. I gave her another kiss and stood up, brushing dog hair off my black pantsuit. I stirred the pot of French onion soup and, blowing on the spoon, tried a bit. Delicious. I peeked at the filet mignon cuts marinating in teriyaki and Worcestershire sauces, and, since nothing earth shattering had happened to them since my last peek 10 minutes ago, I tossed homemade dressing into a Portobello mushroom salad.

I went to freshen my makeup. I took another look at the mirror in the hallway, this time lingering a bit. The purple beret was a great color against my blonde hair. Most of my makeup was still intact, despite Koho's enthusiastic slurps. I pursed my lips and moved in closer for another coat of lipstick. My skin was nice and smooth; almost totally wrinkle free. High cheekbones, a small, delicate nose, big blue eyes—I looked damn good. Maybe I didn't look 30 any more, but I certainly didn't look 50, either.

"Bitter." I said it out loud into the mirror. I was comfortable talking out loud when no one else was present in the room. Twelve years of living alone does that to you. Did Billy really think I was bitter? Or did he use that word because he couldn't bear to say "tragic?" In his strange way, he was trying to cheer me up. I guess he must have thought I needed cheering up. Ah, hell, nobody lives the life they expect, anyway.

I was heading into dangerous territory. Better go check on dinner. Rosemary garlic rolls? Heating in the over. Almond butter? Dolloped into crystal finger bowls, softening on the table. Spring tulips? Buy tomorrow at the nursery and plant in the color garden. Buy 10 pounds of enriched soil, too.

"Bitter."

I stared at the kitchen table, smartly set for three. Mauve cloth napkins, sparkling silverware lined up under crystal wine and water glasses, flowery china salad plates centered on matching dinner plates. Martha Stewart had met her match in Cream Ridge, New Jersey. My table looked amazing. So why did my insides feel so empty? The feeling rippled from my stomach to my chest. I gazed at the table, remembering Billy once telling me that I was like a shark—If I stopped moving, I would die.

Billy and I were so alike. He was always on the move too, running from city to city, casino to casino, chasing the next big win. My travels were not so exotic. I ran from one business appointment to the next, from the gym to home to the mall then home again. I collapsed at night, too exhausted to think. I preferred it that way.

The doorbell rang. Koho barked. Candles! I scrambled to a cupboard and rifled past phonebooks and insurance papers, finally grabbing two long, lavender candles and jamming them into sterling silver holders.

The doorbell rang again.

"It's open!" I called, over Koho's excited barks. I placed the candles on the table, then inched them back and forth in search of perfect center.

"Did you miss me, baby, huh? Did you miss me?" Devin, my charming, quick-witted 26-year-old son stepped into the kitchen and bent down to exchange licks with Koho.

I turned my attention nonchalantly back to the

soup. "Nice. You kiss the dog before you kiss your mother?"

Devin gave Koho a final smooch, then approached me with puckered lips. "You're my sweetheart, Mom, you know that." He planted a quick kiss on my lips. I relished it a second, then pulled back.

"Where's your brother?"

"How should I know?"

"I don't know, I thought maybe you might have spoken to him."

"He'll be here, Mom."

"He'd better get here on time. I've got a gourmet meal going here, and timing is everything."

"Mom, its quarter to six. He's not even due for another fifteen minutes."

I checked on the marinating steaks and gave the salad another toss. "So, why have you graced me with your presence so early?

"I took off early to spend a little extra time with you."

"Well, thanks. How about you go out on the deck and light the grill? I never can get that fire going right, you know."

Devin cracked open a beer from the refrigerator and took a long gulp. "How was your date Saturday, Mom?"
I glanced up from the salad and gave Devin a sly smile. "I got lucky."

"Mom! Ugh! I don't need to hear that!"

"What? I'm a healthy woman. I get horny, just like you."

My son spewed a mouthful of beer. "Mom! Change the subject!"

I turned away and smiled to myself. It might not be

chores, homework and curfews, but I could still push my son's buttons. What was that expression? Nobody pushes your buttons like your parents. After all, they were the ones who sewed them on.

"Your Uncle Billy just called." I handed a pitcher of water to Devin, who dutifully filled the three water glasses on the table.

"Winning or losing?"

"He wouldn't have left the tables to call if he was winning."

"How much?"

"Eighty thousand."

Devin groaned.

"He'll get it back. I've seen him come back eighty thousand in one game."

"Does he ever lose?"

I paused a moment. "Everyone loses sooner or later".

The doorbell rang again. It was a repeat performance of 10 minutes ago, with Koho barking and me yelling "it's open!" I thrust out questioning palms at Devin. "What kind of sons ring at their own mother's home?"

"The kind who don't want to walk in on their Mom getting action on the couch."

Joel, my older son, stopped in the kitchen doorway. He was smaller and more reserved than Devin. "Mom's getting action on the couch?"

I stirred the pot, and said offhandedly, "Ravaged is more like it, honey."

Joel shot me a stern look. He was only two years older than Devin, but by now he seemed almost paternal.

"What? Don't tell me you thought I was frigid? You

two are just going to have to face the fact that I'm a sexual being with sexual needs."

"Oh, great, Joel, here she goes with the 'sexual being' speech," Devin interjected.

"Mom, please, not in mixed company." Joel stepped further into the kitchen. Behind him, a young, beautiful girl with fine Mediterranean features followed shyly.

"Mom, this is Andrea."

I stood, momentarily at a loss for words. Joel had never mentioned that he was bringing a girl to dinner. We'd been having dinner together, just the three of us, once a month for years. After the boys lost their father, it was important to me to preserve whatever sense of family I could. Years later, our monthly date still was important to me, and somewhere in the back of my mind, I always assumed my boys would eventually bring a girl home to dinner. I just wished I had had advance notice.

"   Joel, why didn't you tell me you were bringing someone?"

Andrea cringed. "I shouldn't have come."

My manners took over. "No, of course you should've come. "I quickly moved to shake her hand. "Joel just should've called."

"Aw, Mom."

I took her hand and pulled her into the kitchen. "I'm Sunny." She was a knockout, this Andrea. She had long brown hair with the kind of shiny, rich luster that can only come from being under 21; perfect, rounded breasts sweetly suspended over an impossibly thin waist, washed-out, tight, jeans and a lace top that might as well have been lingerie. If she wasn't a Victoria Secret model, she certainly modeled herself after one.

"Come in, Andrea. It's a pleasure having you in our home."

Devin, half polite and half flirting, took Andrea's hand from Sunny. "I'm Devin. The sexy one."

"Oh, I don't know about that." Andrea looked over her shoulder and smiled seductively at Joel.

I winked playfully at Andrea. "My sisters always said Devin was the sexy one, but I guess a Mom isn't supposed to say that. They're both handsome, that's for sure. So tell me, Andrea, how did you two meet?"

Andrea finally relaxed, but her demeanor was still timid. "Well, it was at the hockey rink …"

I suddenly remembered the table was only set for three. "Wait a minute, sweetie, hold that thought. We have to set another place." I started scrambling through the cupboards, trying to find place settings and listen to Andrea at the same time. "Go ahead, I'm listening."

Devin handed Joel a beer. "What can I get for you, Andrea?"

"Water's fine."

I dug through napkins and placemats. "Get her one of my Snapples. They're delicious."

Joel rolled his eyes. "She said water, Mom."

"Snapple has water in it."

"It also has other things in it, like …"

"High fructose corn syrup," said Andrea, stealing his recitation, "citric acid, juice concentrate."

Devin, having already poured a glass of water, handed it to Andrea. "One Snapple light," he retorted.

The three of them laughed, and as I started setting another place at the table, Devin elbowed Joel. "Mom's acting a little strange. I think she's finally snappled."

Andrea, Joel and Devin laughed again. That was Devin, always with the witty remarks. If you can't beat 'em, join 'em.

I waved a fork menacingly at Devin. "Shame on you. This is the respect I get, after I've been slaving over a hot stove all day?"

"Mom, how hot could it be? You just asked me to light the grill!"

I looked towards Andrea. "Can you believe these two jokers? Good boys though, both of them."
Andrea, looking a bit more comfortable, smiled at me. "So, I was telling you how we met."

"Yes, you were, weren't you?"

"It was at the hockey rink …"

I took Andrea's arm, and led her towards the table. "I want to hear all about it, sweetie. Over dinner. You sit here."

"Andrea has a great family," Joel said casually as he took his customary seat. "You'd like 'em, Mom. They're good people. A real, old-fashioned, tight-knit Italian family."

Chapter 20
The Family

For all their accuracy in depicting life inside a Mafia Family, *The Godfather* films got a lot of it wrong. The head of a Family, for example, was never really called "Godfather," at least, not until the movies became popular among Mafiosi. A certain amount of life-imitating-art took place, and some of the rituals depicted by author Mario Puzo and director Francis Ford Coppola eventually found their way into the real-life Mafia.

Until then, the don or leader of a Mafia Family would simply be called "Father." He played a patriarchal role for the captains or Caporégimes along with crews of "buttons," who were soldiers or hit-men who worked under the umbrella of the don's power and intimidation.

Vincent "Chin" Gigante was a father of many stripes. He fathered five children with his wife Olympia, and fathered three more with a mistress who, oddly enough, was also named Olympia.

Gigante's brother, and one of his most vocal advocates was also called "Father," but for quite a different reason. Louis Gigante was a priest, as well as a New York City Councilman.

Ying Woo often saw Louis Gigante, at or near her stand, talking to his brother, Vincenzo Gigante who was wearing nothing except his old, striped pajamas, ratty blue robe and slippers, and a an old cap pulled down over his eyes. Father Louis would be in a dark suit, or a clergy shirt, depending on the weather, but always in his clerical collar. This was another point of contention with Ying.

"A priest!" she would say to Zhong. She could tell by the way Chin and his brother spoke that they were very close. Louis was vocal about defending Vincent as well. He would often point at his brother's pathetic, hulking figure and say things like, "I know my brother very well. My brother was a street kid, but to label him as a boss of a conglomerate that extorts is ridiculous." The priest had once said. "He doesn't run anything because he couldn't run anything. My brother's warped, but not crooked."

"Why does a priest not see through his act?" she would wonder aloud to her grandson. "Why can a priest not see or feel the evil that oozes from that man's soul?"

"Grandma," Zhong asked, "Why do you hate the Italian man so?"

Ying looked at the boy with sadness in her eyes.

"Xiao Zhong," she began, "come sit with me and I will tell you a story."

Zhong knew Grandma only used the term of endearment "Xiao" which meant "little" in Chinese, when she was feeling very sad and thinking about his mother, Jing. He went to her, and sat at the foot of her chair.

"Do you remember all of the things I've told you about your mother? My beautiful daughter, Jing?"

Zhong nodded slowly as the old woman continued,

"We named her Jing, her father and I, because in our language it means 'essence perfect', and perfect she was. She was born beautiful, Zhong. Even as a baby, her beauty took people by surprise. If we had stayed in Hong Kong. If, if, if … "

Ying stopped her story for a moment, gazing into the distance. Zhong looked in the same direction, but was unsure what his grandmother saw.

She took a deep breath and started again. "My Jing was just a girl, when we came here. So innocent and excited to be in this new place. Her father, your grandfather, died just a short time after we came here to America. I worked so hard every day to make a home for us to be proud of. Jing went to school. At first she was so excited to learn the new language and the ways of America. After school, she would come here to help me at the stand, as you do. I do not know exactly when it happened, or if it had been happening all along, but she began to have a very hard time at school. The kids teased her about her poor English. Humph! Kids of Italians and Jews and Irish who had barely learned the English themselves! They laughed at her accent, our customs, they made fun of her cheongsam's that I sewed for her with my own hands. They were ignorant, but your mother, Xiao Zhong, she took it all into her heart."

Ying paused here, and wrapping Zhong in a rare, grandmotherly hug, she wiped a stray tear from her cheek.

"You ask, my grandson, why I hate this man so? I will tell you, it is men like this one who prey on the young and weak. Men like him who eat away at the innocence of children like Jing. She wasn't strong enough to stand up to these people who mistreated her. She allowed the wrong people to lead her, and she turned to drugs."

Zhong sat silently as his grandmother shuddered, and took a sip of her tea. He knew she would continue when she was ready.

"Jing was only sixteen. She had stopped showing up for work after school. At first she would make up excuses. I would believe her, even when my eyes could see the signs, my heart did not want to believe. She had gotten to where she would barely speak to me. As I struggled to learn

English, she would refuse to speak to me in Mandarin. She treated me as if I were a fool, an embarrassment. She started to dress in clothing that made her look cheap, and wear way too much make-up. In time, she stopped coming home at all. Through all of this, I would wonder, if Jing didn't have any money, where would she be getting drugs?"

"Then, one day, that man came by. He stopped here like he always does, in his ratty old robe, acting like a fool. Another man came over to him, that one was dressed in a suit that could have paid our rent for a year. The big, 'pretend crazy' one said something to him about the suit, angry that he was 'being as flashy as Gotti'. The man in the suit looked ashamed, and afraid. Then they began to talk about other things. They didn't think I could understand them, but by that time my English was much improved. I heard the big one, this "Chin," tell the other one that he 'owned' this neighborhood, and everyone in it. They talked about pimps and whores, and even though they didn't use their real names, these so-called 'nick-names' that American's use are self-explanatory. They were calling her 'Jade', and I knew it was my beautiful Jing they were talking about. The crazy fox told this other man that even the pregnant whores had to work to pay for their dope. It was a few weeks later, my Jing dropped you off here. You were wrapped in a dirty towel, a cheap motel towel. Her eyes were dead, Xiao Zhong. The street and organized crime had already killed her. It was only two months later that her soul was finally released. She took too many drugs, or someone gave her too many drugs, and she was gone. The police found her body in an alley, dumped like yesterday's trash."

Ying had to stop again, her grandson thought she was

finished, and then she added, "I wonder what this "Chin" would feel like, if his own daughter, the fat one they call Yolanda had been tossed aside that way."

Named after Vincent's dear, sweet mother, Yolanda grew up in a lifestyle not unlike that of Mafia princess Victoria Gotti, who would later star in her own reality-based television show called *Growing Up Gotti*. The paths of Yolanda Gigante and Victoria Gotti crossed in ways remarkably similar to those of their infamous fathers—both started as bitter enemies and eventually learned to work together.

The big difference was that, as far as we know, Yolanda Gigante never tried to have Victoria Gotti killed, whereas Vincent, well, let's just say that John "The Dapper Don" Gotti was lucky to die a natural death in prison.

As he moved into his senior years, Vincent Gigante found himself closely protected by his family, being cared for by two women named Olympia (his wife and his mistress), plus two women named Yolanda (his mother and daughter).

The FBI was closing in.

Vincent's stocky, black-haired daughter Yolanda helped Daddy with administrative and personal chores; his frail, white-haired mother Yolanda took Vincent into her home. She claimed her son was too ill to survive without her care.

The old lady insisted her son had nothing to do with the Mafia.

"Boss? No boss," said mother Yolanda, then a feisty 94 years old. "He's boss of the toilet. My son is sick. Boss of shit. Six years he lives here with me. Every day I care for him. I feed him, I wash him, I cry over him."

It was the elder Yolanda who gave Vincent his nickname. Many figured "The Chin" referred to Gigante's prominent jaw or had something to do with his boxing career, but it was actually a term of endearment from his mom.

She'd named him Vincenzo, pronounced Vin-CHEN-zo in Italian, and the boy soon became "Chinzo" for short, and then just "Chin."

The bonds of family are strong among Italians. Nothing could be more sacred. Old Yolanda Gigante and her sons Vincent and Louis understood this well. Those bonds came from the blood of their forebears, who had to stick together through centuries of conquest by foreigners in Sicily and Italy. Through it all, there was always family, only family. That was all you could trust. Vincent passed this heirloom to his children.

Little Yolanda, as the eldest daughter of "The Chin's" five children with his wife, carried far more than her grandmother's first name. She was also a chalice for Family, with a capital F.

When she became a mother herself, Yolanda hoped that same absolute loyalty would burn inside her pretty young daughter, Andrea.

I would soon learn that it most certainly did.

Chapter 21
You Can Decide to Change

Forks clinked against plates, punctuating a conversation of chewing and very few words.

"Great steak," Devin mumbled.

I smiled, then took a petite bite of filet mignon and let it water in my mouth, slowly savoring the burst of flavor each new chew released. The marinade was just right, and the steaks had been grilled to perfection.

I eyed Devin's plate. He was eating about as slowly as I was. Good boy. Joel was gobbling, but obviously enjoying his food. I peeked at Andrea. She was picking bits of onion and cheese out of her soup and scraping them onto her untouched steak. The sweet flavor in my mouth turned a bit sour.

"Andrea, sweetie, you don't eat meat? I can heat up some pasta for you."

Andrea guiltily dropped her fork, trying to hide the beached onions. "No, it's delicious."

I couldn't help myself. I looked pointedly at her plate, where my expensive filet mignon sat neglected. She shrugged politely. "It looks … delicious."

Maybe she was a vegetarian and too polite to say anything, but there was something strange about the way she rearranged the food on her plate. It was almost as if she hoped she could make my meal disappear by using dishware Feng Shui. She reminded me of Devin, hiding vegetables in his napkin when he was six years old.

I wiped my mouth and got up. "I'm heating some pasta."

"No! Really, Mrs. Rubin, I'm just not that hungry."

"Please, call me Sunny. Are you sure?"

"She's fine, Mom," Joel said, stuffing another bite into his mouth.

"I'm fine, really." Andrea seemed uncomfortably self-conscious.

I slowly sat down. I just wasn't used to someone not eating my food. "It's no problem to make something else."

"Please, Mrs. …"

"Sunny."

"Sunny, just enjoy your dinner."

"You're sure you're okay?"

"I'm fine."

I paused a minute, almost ready to continue eating, then jumped up. "I'll make you a sandwich."

Joel, Andrea and Devin yelled in unison: "No!"

"Mom, she said she's fine," Joel said.

"Well, she has to eat something!"

Andrea picked up her fork and used the edge to cut a watercress leaf in half from the Portobello salad. I watched, amazed, as she scraped whatever dressing she could off the watercress leaf and cautiously slid the smaller half into her mouth.

Was I the only one that found this behavior bizarre? I'm not a shrink, but since Andrea weighed 90 pounds soaking wet and just gagged on half a watercress leaf, I began to think—eating disorder.

Not Joel. He smiled. "There, she's eating."

I sat down and took a bite of steak. Now it was cold, chewy and held the distinct bitter aftertaste of Andrea's performance.

"Compliments to the chef," Devin smiled.

"It's great, Mom," Joel assured. I appreciated that.

Andrea daintily set the other half of the watercress leaf into her mouth. "Really great."

Before I could unleash again, Devin steered the train away from a potential wreck. "So how's Uncle Billy, Mom?"

"Don't talk with your mouthful, sweetie," I scolded.

"Mom!" Joel yelled. "We're grown men!"

"I'm sorry," I said to Andrea, suddenly aware that I was probably embarrassing my sons in front of the pretty guest. "It's just habit. Once a mother, always a mother."

Andrea's face brightened. "It's OK. I tell Joel the same thing all the time."

Now, what did that mean? I wondered if Andrea was already acting like Joel's mother. I wondered if Andrea's mother, like myself, like my own mother, had to move heaven and earth to make ends meet, never losing sight of the fact that nothing was ever more important than taking care of your family.

My mind flashed through my own years of joy, sorrow, rejoice and regret. Joel was right. The boys were men now. My own youth was slipping away. Everything was slipping away. Motherhood. Family. Control. Years. My life seemed to be running away from me, and every time I reached out to pull it back, it sprinted farther into the distance.

"Mom? You still with us?" Devin asked. "You got a funny look on your face."

"Just thinking," I said softly.

"About what?" Andrea was trying to reach out.

"Life," I whispered involuntarily.

"Pretty broad subject," Devin said. He saw my eyes grow distant again and tried to needle me back. "Can you be more specific?"

"My life. Life in general, I guess..."

I drifted even further, my mind racing through a well-worn groove of pictures from the past. I had learned not only to survive, but to thrive. Yes, life brings tragedy, but it's how we deal with that tragedy that makes the difference. I learned how to deal with tragedy the hard way, losing a father, mother and husband within a three-year period. And still I embraced life, always moving toward happiness and fulfillment.

"No matter what happens to you in life, no matter where you live, no matter how old you are, you can always decide to change your life."

I looked around the table, seeing all eyes upon me, and realized I had spoken those final words aloud. I cleared my throat.

"Well, who needs another beer?" I asked cheerily.

"Smartest thing you've said all night, Mom." Devin handed me his empty bottle.

"Make that two." Joel handed over his empty, too.

"Andrea?"

"No thanks, my water's fine."

As I opened the refrigerator, I heard the boys and Andrea laughing and joking, and a sense of warmth and lightness filled me. I wasn't losing my family; in fact, it was growing. Joel had brought home a girl.

This was a milestone. There would be weddings, for both my boys, and eventually grandchildren. I felt happy realizing that there were many memories and feelings yet to come, and for the first time in years, I was ready to meet them. I was standing at the edge of a cliff, ready to jump, and it felt good.

Chapter 22
Meet the Parents

"Bitter, Skunkie. You're always so bitter." Billy coughed through the speakerphone, and then took a drink of something on the rocks.

"Is that Wild Turkey?" I knew the answer before he gave it.

"Would it be anything else?"

"It's eight in the morning. You can't drink at eight in the morning."

"That rule only applies if you actually went to sleep the night before."

I sat at the kitchen table, working on insurance policy changes. "Billy, am I going to have to come out there and straighten you out again?"

The sound of slurping and ice cubes clinking against glass prefaced Billy's reply. "Definitely. Come out here, but I'm the one who'll be straightening you out, Skunkie."

"And how do you plan on doing that?"

"You need to let your kids go, Sunny. Like I do."

"Billy. You didn't see your daughters for ten years."

"OK, maybe not that much."

Billy's attempt at humor only partially covered up the pain in his voice. There was a pause while he took a long swig of his drink.

"Look, you know I love those girls more than anything in the world."

"I know you do, Billy. And I love my boys."

"You have to give them some room to breathe."

"I just don't think Joel's ready to settle down yet."

"He's twenty-seven, Skunkie. He's not trying to settle down. He's trying to get laid, and even if it does get serious, people get married. Look at me."

"You didn't see your wife for 10 years, either."

"But I am married, aren't I?"

"I don't want Joel sending cabbies to deliver bags of guilt cash to the wife and children he never sees."

"Well, not everyone has to do it my way. I wish it could be different. I just can't live the life Deanne wants me to live." Billy could be heard sucking on a cigarette and blowing out smoke. "So, how'd they meet?"

I dropped one stack of files on the floor and started another. "Joel was giving Andrea's kid brother skating lessons. She says it was love at first sight."

"Kids."

"Joel thought she was too young. Smart boy, but her dad started tipping Joel a hundred and twenty bucks a lesson. Can you believe it? A hundred-and-twenty-dollar tip for a sixty-buck lesson?"

"I've taught that boy well."

"Well, it sure got his attention, and then the gifts started. Gold watches. Armani suits. Her whole family's very persuasive, very strong and very Italian."

"Sounds like Mafia to me. But I always say … "

"I know, Billy. Marry for money."

"No, I say don't get married at all, but if you're going to make the mistake, do it for money."

"And with Andrea's dad taking Joel to play golf at every exclusive country club in town … "

Billy took another gulp. "The Wild Turkey's speaking to me, Skunkie, giving me the answers."

"What?"

"You're worried about Andrea's dad taking Michael's place."

"No, I'm not." Nobody could ever take the place of my children's father. My children know that better than anyone.

"Taking your place?"

"Not at all. I'm just worried about who this girl is, and who her mystery family really is." Just saying it out loud agitated me. There was something strange about the way this family showered my son with wretchedly expensive gifts. Were they trying to buy him? Was it working?

"Listen, Skunkie, first off, I'm the boys' father figure."

"God help 'em."

"Let him go. You're far too busy being the Tragedy Queen to be spending time worrying about Joel."

"Gotta go, Billy. Someone's beeping in."

I clicked over and heard, "Mom?"

"Joel, I had Billy on the other line. Were your ears burning?"

"Andrea's family invited you to the *Star Wars* premiere. We're all getting together at their place."

"*Star Wars*? That came out twenty years ago. Before Andrea was born."

"This is the new *Star Wars*, Mom. The prequel."

"Premiere, huh? Very nice. Well, it's been three months. I suppose it's about time I met the parents, don't ya think?"

"Promise to behave, Mom."

"Have I ever done anything else?"

Chapter 23
Knockout

Ying smiled as she read the morning paper. Sitting there, with the early morning summer sun shining down on her, Zhong could almost see the young woman she had been, long before he had come into her life. She had been smiling a lot lately. Her shoulders didn't seem to sag as much as they used to, as if an invisible weight had been removed from them.

"Grandma," Zhong asked, "What are you reading about that makes you smile so?"

Lying the paper down at her feet, Ying patted the stool next to her and said,

"Xiao Zhong, come sit with me."

Zhong sat, and smiling, again, Ying rested the palm of her hand on Zhong's face.

"Karma is about to get him, Zhong, finally, after all of these years!"

Zhong knew whom she was talking about without asking. Her obsession with the "crazy" Italian man had only grown over the years.

"This reporter, Mr. Fried from the Times, says that yesterday, during The Chin's trial, the F.B.I. showed over seventy pictures of him with people they either believed to be, or had already been convicted of being mobsters. The pictures were all taken right here, on Sullivan Street. They even had phone conversations they taped of the fancy one, what is his name? Gotcha, or Gott-me?"

Ying picked up the paper,

"Gotti, that is it! The one who used to come by all gussied up in suits and ties and shoes that could feed all the hungry children in China. They have tapes of him talking about things that make them believe even more that this big Italian is not only not crazy, but the boss of the mafia!"

Ying laughed softly and said,

"They should have only asked me, Zhong, I could have told them all that."

Laughing again, she said,

"I was reading in the paper, not too long ago, about this Gotti character's trial. He got sent away, back in '92, I think it was. One of his good friends was the most damning witness against him, but what I really remember, was reading about what that man, I think they called him "The Bull" told a reporter about the Chin. He told him that one of the most important meetings he had ever attended was among the bosses of the various New York crime families. He said the Chin was there, even though he was supposed to have been too mentally deranged to find his way there. He said this Gotti character was bragging, that his son, John Jr. had 'just been made'. To these gangsters, 'made' means that they are a full member of the mafia. This Bull said that the Chin looked at Gotti and said 'I'm sorry to hear that' and that made this Bull person think, 'here was the Chin who had not allowed any of his son's to be made, and Gotti, who was boasting about it.' He said it made him think, 'Who is really the crazy one here?'"

Chuckling again, as if to a private joke, Ying said,

"A cunning old fox, that Chin, I could have told them that."

That summer, Zhong saw his grandmother smile many times. Vincenzo "Chin" Gigante was convicted of racketeering and unsuccessful plots to kill other mafia members, most notably, John Gotti in the late 1980's. He was sentenced to twelve years in federal prison. Although

Ying would have liked to see him convicted of the murders the prosecution had tried to blame him for, twelve years was a good start.

"Vincent Gigante's trained and savage fist cut through the air. He pulled the punch, stepped back, feinted to his left, and then fired a deadly right uppercut, followed by three sharp left jabs.

The compact boxer breathed through his mouth, danced on his toes, and then delivered a left-right combination to the head of his imaginary foe. In his mind, Vincent saw his opponent wobble and fall backward to the floor. A devastating knockout.

Shadowboxing cleared his mind and kept him alert. At 71, Vincent was still in remarkable shape. Inside his cell at Butera Federal Correctional Institution in North Carolina, he didn't have much else to do.

Just a few weeks before the 1999 release of Star Wars, Episode I, The Phantom Menace, Vincent was facing the toughest legal battle of his life. His daughter Yolanda and her family would enjoy the movie's premiere screening up in New Jersey, but Vincent's luck appeared to have run out. A federal jury had found him guilty of labor racketeering and masterminding a sophisticated bid-rigging and kickback scheme.

His appeal wasn't going so well. Prosecutors now said Gigante had hired "a sexy female operative" who was trying to compromise one of the jurors. Plus, Vincent's 30-year history of always appearing insane was starting to unravel.

The Feds had secretly taped some of his phone conversations with his wife, Olympia. He sounded lucid. And some of the prison guards who Vincent befriended were now reporting their star inmate acted more like a

Mafia boss than an Alzheimer's patient.

Christopher Sexton, a correctional officer stationed next to Vincent's cell, said Gigante was a respected leader among the inmates. He groomed himself, made his own bed, showered regularly, ate by himself, shadowboxed and maintained cordial relations with employees at the facility.

"He was very charismatic," Sexton testified. "The way he carried himself and the way he did speak - he was soft-spoken, he was respectful - he just kind of commanded respect."

One day, another inmate tried to harass Sexton while Gigante watched from his cell.

"I wanted to come out to help you so bad," Gigante later told the guard, "but there was nothing I could do. The cell was locked."

They developed a friendship, and Sexton once asked Gigante if the other inmates were bothering him.

Vincent looked Sexton in the eye and said, "Nobody fucks with me."

His inner strength seemed completely at odds with the frail-looking Vincent Gigante who appeared unshaven in court, wearing sweatpants and a white T-shirt. Sometimes Vincent was pushed in a wheelchair, other days he would wobble into court on his own feet, grasping tables to keep his balance. Often a doctor would hover at Vincent's elbow, holding a black medical bag while trying to steady his patient.

Once in a while, Vincent would greet every individual he saw in the courtroom with a loud "Good morning!" Other days he would tremble, stare at walls and mumble to himself.

For two years, Vincent's lawyers fought the

conviction in court, but on January 22, 1999, "Chin" absorbed a vicious knockout punch from a trio of judges: The Honorable Whitman Knapp, United States District Court, and United States Circuit Judges James L. Oakes and John M. Walker, Jr. They ruled that Gigante had been malingering, was competent to stand trial, and found him guilty as charged of conspiracy to murder, extortion conspiracy and labor payoff conspiracy. He was in violation of the Racketeer-Influenced and Corrupt Organizations Act, a law written specifically to attack Mafia bosses.

The gavel came down hard: Gigante was fined $1.25 million and sentenced to 12 years in federal prison.

Vincent would not be attending any movie premieres with Yolanda's family. He would not be meeting the family of his granddaughter Andrea's new boyfriend, Joel.

Chapter 24
Spock's Ears

I felt out of place as we drove through a neighborhood of Mercedes, BMWs, enormous homes and perfectly landscaped estates. I wondered what my date, Jack, thought about all this—arriving in this neighborhood in my Honda *Accord*.

I couldn't prepare him, because I didn't know what to expect myself. I knew almost nothing about Andrea's family. Jack's presence was a comfort. We had been friends, through the insurance business, for quite some time now. Jack had been asking me to go out with him since we met. He was attractive, but since he was closer to Joel's age than to mine, I managed to stave him off while remaining friends. Too bad. He had such a sweet personality. He knew I was nervous about meeting Andrea's family, and offered to accompany me as my "date."

As we drove through the affluent neighborhood I wondered, how do these people do it? Why does money come easily for some people, while I have to struggle for the mortgage every single month? Why are some people blessed with easy lives, while others suffer through crises and tragedies? Okay, I really didn't know if Andrea's family has had an easy life. For all I knew, her father may have worked like a dog to live this lifestyle. All I was thinking was that I work just as hard, and I certainly didn't have a house like this to show for it. All I had was survival.

I checked the address, pointed and Jack pulled into the driveway of the big house right smack in the middle of the cul-de-sac. Prime location. I couldn't help it—I felt envy creeping through my bloodstream.

Not for myself, but for all the things I couldn't give the boys when they were growing up. Hockey equipment that wasn't second-hand. Clothes that didn't scream "I have a single mother who's seriously considering selling the house and moving to an apartment." Maybe a vacation once every few years. For the boys. OK, maybe a little for me.

Jack parked the car in front of the double oak door. I dug under a stack of papers on the back seat, pulled out two plastic, *Star Trek*, Mr. Spock ears and slid them onto my ears. I checked my look in the mirror and had to smile. All the hype over *Star Wars*, let's see if this family has a sense of humor.

"Well," Jack said, smiling at the pointy ears, "this ought to be an interesting evening."

A large, overweight woman opened the double oak doors. I smiled and hoped it covered my shock. I was standing in standing in front of a dowdy middle-aged woman who looked like she was wearing her black, frizzy hair the same way she did in high school. This woman needed celebrity boot camp. She had three chins and cheeks like water balloons. How did beautiful Andrea come from this?

The woman opened her arms and smiled with the kind of radiant happiness that can't possibly be faked. She pulled me in for a big, warm hug.

"You must be Sunny," the woman said. "I'm Yolanda. Andrea's mother. Welcome. Welcome to our home."

"I've heard so much about you," I said, though it wasn't true.

"And Joel never stops talking about you."

"Really? He's barely called me in three months."

"Well, you know how children are. Never want to let their mothers know what a good job we did raising them."

That certainly was an insightful remark. She might not be attractive, but I liked the way she articulated one of the more ironic facets of motherhood. If you do a great job raising your kids, you may rarely see them. "This is my date, Jack. Is Joel here? I didn't see his car."

"He called to say he'd be a few minutes late. Good boy, that Joel."

Yolanda pulled me inside, Jack in tow, and closed the door. "Come in. Meet the family."

The home was nicely decorated, but not in a grandiose way – Native American artifacts, a few paintings. Perversely enough, I was almost hoping it wouldn't be my taste—less to envy them for—but I couldn't find a thing about it I didn't like. Yolanda guided me and Jack into the dining room.

"Dick, Sunny's here."

Dick, in a grey sweat suit and sneakers, got up from a leather chair and turned off an overwhelming, 90-inch TV. "How are you, Sunny? Glad you could make it."

"Well, it's nice to finally meet you both," I said. "This is Jack." I eyed Dick, a balding, slightly overweight guy who'd be more at home on a construction site than a corporate boardroom. Yolanda and Dick didn't fit here, I thought to myself. They don't fit the home, the neighborhood.

Andrea glided in. I hadn't seen her since the night we first met. She was even prettier than I remembered.

"Hi, Sunny." Andrea smiled, perky and much more confident, now that she had the home-court advantage. It was obvious the way the others in the room deferred to her, almost as if royalty had entered into the scene.

I wished I hadn't worn the ears, because suddenly I felt self-conscious. I felt like an idiot. Yolanda and Dick hadn't even noticed them, or worse, they had noticed them and thought they were real.

"And this is Gino," Yolanda said.

A husky, 12-year-old boy wearing jeans, a Polo Shirt and a walkman had rolled into the room on inline skates. "Hey" was all he said as he continued skating past and into the kitchen.

I waved back and waited for Yolanda to chastise her son for his lack of manners, but Yolanda didn't seem to think he was impolite. Instead, Yolanda, Dick and Andrea were oddly eyeing my ears.

"I had some earring trouble this morning." I winked, hoping they'd get the joke.

Yolanda burst in a hearty laugh, while Andrea giggled approval, and Dick belted out a grunt before heading back to his chair.

"That's hilarious," Yolanda laughed. "They'll be perfect for the premiere."

"Listen," I whispered. "Don't say anything to Joel. See how long it takes him to notice."

"Sunny," Dick said, "do you need another drink? Jack?"

Jack shook his head. I took the last sip of my wine and smiled at Joel, who was on the couch with his arms crossed. "Why not?"

Dick, still in his chair, motioned to Yolanda, who took my glass and headed for the bar.

"Joel." I smiled. "You're being so quiet."

"Yeah," Andrea said, rubbing Joel's leg, "And you

seem kind of tense."

"Bad day at work?" Dick asked.

"I'm fine," Joel said under his breath.

I could feel Joel seething at me.

Is he mad because I'm getting along with everyone? That wouldn't make sense. Is he embarrassed because Andrea's family dresses like a bunch of slobs, and I chose to dress up? Is it the ears? He's been here twenty minutes and hasn't said a word. I know he's seen them.

Yolanda handed me another glass of wine. "To your health." Yolanda held her own glass in a toast.

"Salud," I replied, although I didn't know why. I took a drink and winked at Joel, who shook his head.

"What are you wearing, Sunny?"

I blanched at my son. Sunny? Joel's never called me Sunny before. I wasn't "Mom" anymore?

"It's a pantsuit, sweetie. Chanel." Then, almost instinctively, I turned to Yolanda and mouthed, "Knockoff." I wondered if Yolanda would recognize a Chanel suit if she saw one. For all their money, Dick and Yolanda certainly didn't seem to care about fashion. Here they were, going out for a night on the town, and he was in sweats, and she was wearing a cheap sweater over shapeless pants.

"I'm not talking about your outfit, Mother. What are those things on your ears?"

Mother? Who is this boy?

"I don't know what you mean, Joel. Is something on my ears?"

Yolanda and Andrea suddenly burst out laughing. Dick was right behind. Finally, I joined in. Joel looked around, realized everyone was in on the joke, and started laughing himself. I was pretty sure he was still mad and laughing just to smooth things over, but no one else seemed to notice.

Andrea gave Joel a kiss. "We got ya, Joel."

Joel blushed. "Yeah, you did." He uncrossed his arms and kissed Andrea back.

"All right, you lovebirds," Dick said. "We better get going."

As everyone got up and headed for the front door, I thought to myself, it feels good. Being here. Laughing. Seeing Joel happy, comfortable with another family. It's not so bad. Not so threatening after all. I'm still his mother. The circle's just getting a little bigger. I could get used to this. I had forgotten what it felt like to be with family. It's natural. Normal. Being at home alone all the time isn't natural or normal, although over the past 10 years, it sure got to feel that way. This is better, I thought. I like this better.

Even so, something about this family seemed odd. I couldn't quite put my finger on it, so I chased it from my mind.

"Listen," I said as I grabbed my coat. "We won't all fit in one car, so if someone wants to drive with us ..."

Dick helped me with my coat. "Drive? What drive? We're taking a limo."

Yolanda opened the door. In the driveway was a glistening, black stretch limo, complete with a driver in tuxedo and cap, opening the door with his white gloved hands and motioning for everyone to step in.

I like this a lot better, I thought. A lot better.

"We use limos all the time," Dick said, waving his hand as if it were nothing. "One of the guys in our Family owns a limo service."

This family seems unusually large, I thought. Ah,

well. *Star Wars* waited.

Chapter 25
One Big Happy Family?

I opened my front door and walked into the dark, empty house. I flicked on a green light saber to find my way to the hall switch.

"Koho?"

After flipping on the light, one by one I pulled souvenirs out of my purse – a champagne flute from the limo, engraved Star Wars premiere ticket, and finally a picture of myself surrounded by R2D2, C3PO, Yolanda, Dick, Joel, Andrea and Gino. I stared at the picture, wondering why I looked so good. Then it hit me. I was smiling. Laughing, actually. Having fun. Spending time with "family."

I headed upstairs, smiling to myself. I could see why Joel had been spending so much time with Andrea. He was part of a real family again. They weren't broken. It doesn't mean he loves me any less, it just means he has the chance to be even happier, and he's taking it. And I'm going to take the chance too, I thought. Why not? I'm his mother. If he and Andrea are that serious, we can all be one big, happy family.

1200 miles away, in Springfield, Missouri, the inmates of the U.S. Medical Center for Federal Prisoners were decidedly not one big happy family.

At the corner of Wabash and Sunshine Street, the prison medical buildings arose out of a placid park setting, forming a large circle around manicured lawns. The brick complex in Springfield had been caring for sick inmates since the Depression era. The Birdman of Alcatraz once walked its halls, as did sheik Omar Abdel Rahman, the terrorist who plotted the 1993 bombing of New York's World Trade Center.

Now it also held Vincent "Chin" Gigante.

Yolanda traveled from New Jersey to visit her father in prison every Thursday and Friday. It didn't matter whether he was confined in Jersey, North Carolina or Missouri; Yolanda made the trek every week.

The FBI believed she was exchanging information with the "Boss of All Bosses" and helping her father maintain control of his vast illegal empire from behind bars.

The Feds also suspected Yolanda was running a real estate company for the Gigante Family, and that she was looking after various Family business duties. They had no evidence, however, that she had broken any laws. Yolanda always insisted she was just running a few personal errands for her dad.

But the FBI's interest in the Gigante situation heated up when "the Chin" was transferred to the U.S. Medical Center for Federal Prisoners.

That's because another high-profile inmate also happened to incarcerated at the same Missouri medical facility:

John Gotti, "the Dapper Don," head of the Gambino crime Family.

Gigante was being treated for heart ailments, dementia and various other psychological conditions, real or imagined. Gotti, at 58, had been diagnosed with throat cancer and was undergoing radiation treatments.

The Feds didn't know if the two Mafia dons would try to hatch plots together or kill each other. They just knew they had to be separated.

"They can't have any contact," Yolanda told a reporter from the New York Post. "They can't even be in the same room together."

Gigante and Gotti took their meals privately, in separate rooms, while the rest of the inmate population ate in the dining hall. The Gotti and Gigante families weren't even allowed to use the visiting room at the same time.

Yolanda actually gloated that Gotti's family was forced to wait outside while she visited with her dad. "The Gotti's couldn't come in," she told a reporter, "because we were there."   For a woman who claimed that her life was legitimate and non-Mafia, she was awfully proud that her daddy was a bigger slime ball than John Gotti. You can take a Mafia princess out of the gutter, but you can't take the gutter out of the Mafia princess.

Ying read this quote as she sat in her newsstand on Sullivan Street.

"Bái ch ,"

She spat this as she threw the paper aside.

Zhong came towards her after finishing up with a sale.

"Who is mentally retarded, Grandma?" he asked, once again sure it had something to do with Vincenzo Gigante.

"That fèi wù daughter of The Chin! She is so stupid, she brags about that ridiculous man! If it were me, I would have buried my head in the sand from the shame!"

Zhong smiled. His grandmother rarely ever used expletives, and two in one sitting was extremely rare. She had referred to Yolanda as a 'good for nothing' in the second one. Although for most people, these were not strong terms, they had rarely passed through Ying's lips. For all of her hate of the Gigante's, Ying had always otherwise had a positive outlook on life and people. Losing Jing had dampened her spirit, but knowing the man that she believed responsible for her child's downfall was locked away, lifted them once again, but she too longed to once again be one big, happy family.

Ying had come from a strong family in China. Her father had been a businessman and her mother a Cáiféng, or in English, a dressmaker. Ying was an only child, born during a time when China had imposed limits on its population. but she had been surrounded by grandparents, aunts, uncles, cousins and mostly of all, two parents who had loved her dearly. She had a good life there, and when she met her husband, Wei Woo, she knew their life together would be great, as his name had implied in their native language. They had lived in Hong Kong for quite a few years after they were married, and that is where Jing had been born. Ying could still feel the sweet softness of Jing's hair, or the gentle touch of her small hand when she tried. She closed her eyes sometimes and recalled the memory of rocking her in the chair her own mother had used to rock Ying, and singing to her at night.

Sighing loudly she chastised herself for allowing the memories to flood. She tried to shake them off and get back to work, but once the gates were open...

Ying remembered everything about her little girl. Her first smile when she was only a week old, and no, she did not believe it was Qi, or in English, gas, as her mother-in-law had said. She remembered waking up sometimes at night, and finding her husband, the traditional Chinese man no less, in the rocking chair, staring at their lovely Jing as he rocked and cooed to her. She remembered her first steps when she was barely a year old. Her Wei, having to hold Ying back from grabbing her, afraid she would fall and get hurt. There were shopping trips and vacations, long, winter days when they read together by the hearth. Ying's eyes filled with tears, because, unfortunately our minds kept the good memories stored right next to the bad. Ying had not told Zhong the whole story. A boy did not need to hear every detail of his mother's spiral down into the abyss. But Ying was there for most of it, and she couldn't erase those ugly memories that had etched themselves into her brain.

During those first days, the days when Ying was still in denial that her beautiful Jing would ever knowingly put anything into her body that would harm her, or warp her mind, there were many signs that she chose to ignore.

The school called often to say that Jing had not shown up for classes. When she would come home, Ying would confront her about this. At first, Jing would appear to be hurt that her mother would not trust her. Ying would try to discipline her, giving her more chores to do, and tightening her curfew. Eventually though, Jing would not even try to make excuses. She wouldn't try to appear hurt or sad. She would get angry, and turn her anger towards her mother. Calling Ying an "old Chinese fool" and telling her she did not fit in America. Jing said that her mother just did not understand how things were done here, and she should just go back to the old country where she belonged. After a while, Jing wouldn't come home sometimes for days. Ying would walk the neighborhood, looking for her everywhere she thought she might try to hide. She would lie awake at night, sometimes crying, sometimes angry, waiting for the knock at the door that every mother fears. When Jing would finally resurface, she would look worse and be harder to talk to each time. They would fight, and Jing would say things that no mother should have to hear come from the mouth of the child she had born and raised.

Ultimately, Ying could no longer live in denial. She had to know the truth about what Jing was taking, and where she was getting the money to buy it, and most frightening of all, where she was staying on those days and nights that she would disappear. Ying had lain awake one entire night, working up her nerve to approach the subject with Jing, and trying to formulate exactly how she would ask. She also spent time that night practicing those words in English, because her daughter, who had been raised in the Chinese culture, refused to speak to her mother in Mandarin.

It was the second worse day of Ying's life.

Jing was defensive at first, trying to make excuses, and turn things around to make Ying feel as if the problems were hers. Ying wouldn't relent, and when Jing finally gave up and decided to tell the truth, Ying felt as if the gates of Hell had opened up, and all of the demons had unleashed at once upon her world.

"You want to know the truth?" Jing had spat at her, her once silky long hair now laying limp across her shoulders and falling across her face into her eyes.

"Yes, Jing." Ying had answered, "I need to know the truth. What has become of you? I don't recognize your behavior I don't recognize you. I feel as if my own child is a stranger to me."

"I am not your child! I am a woman, and that is our first problem, you don't see me as such! I am an American woman! I can live my own life; I do not need you pushing me to work in that silly newsstand. I don't need you trying to get me to wear those silly cheongsam's that you sew for me. We are not in Hong Kong anymore, Mother!" In that single instant, the word mother went from a term of endearment that Jing had been so proud to call Ying when she was first learning English, to sounding like a curse word.

"Okay," Ying told her, trying still to keep the situation in hand, "tell me what the second problem is."

"It's all you, mother, first, second, all! You bring me to this place, this foreign world, and tell me to fit in. When I try, you tell me I should be more Chinese. I started taking pills to drown out your nonsense in my head! I would be right there watching your lips move, but my head was in a completely different place, someplace nice, without your nagging!"

"Pills?" Ying asked, "Is that all that you've been taking?"

Jing laughed. It wasn't a joyous sound. It was almost pitiful, sad and lonely and sarcastic all at the same time.

"The pills stopped working. I started smoking it then, Mama. Your little "perfect essence" put a little white powder on a piece of tinfoil, rolled up a piece of paper, and ran a lighter underneath. The first time I inhaled those fumes, let me tell you, there are no words in English or Mandarin to describe it. Ecstasy, Mother, that is the word that comes closest. Pure, ecstasy, I had no troubles and no worries. I eventually bought a glass pipe, that worked better." She smiled a little at this, and Ying had to shudder as she realized her daughter was actually reliving that moment a little. She was looking at her daughter, hearing her words, and trying desperately to block it all out. She wanted so badly for Jing to tell her this was all a horrible trick someone was playing on her. Better yet, she wanted Jing to shake her awake, take her in her arms like she had done on those long, awful nights when she had cried in her sleep after her Wei had died, and say "it's okay, Mama. It was just a bad dream. Your Jing is here."

But instead, she heard her daughter say,

"And then I learned how to use a needle. It works so much faster that way."

Ying thought surely she had heard wrong. Did Jing really just say she was using needles? And then, she really looked at her daughter. The once creamy, pale, flawless skin, now a sickly yellow, dotted in places with ugly red splotches that Ying had tried to convince herself were just a case of normal adolescent acne. The stringy, dry hair that Ying used to love to brush out like a silky mane. The collarbones protruding from underneath the cheap, dirty halter Jing now wore. The thin, almost bird-like legs showing from beneath her very short skirt. Nails painted what Ying had heard people on American television refer to as "hooker red", but broken and cracked in places.

No, she couldn't see any visible places where the needle had gone in, "tracks" she thought they were called, but all of the other signs were there, staring her boldly in the face. Her "perfect essence", her gorgeous, sweet Jing was a drug addict, and from the sound of it, a proud one at that.

"We can get you help..." Ying began, before she was interrupted by more of Jing's laughter.

"My pimp gets me help when I need it, Mother. I don't think I'll be needing any from you, thanks." Jing laughed again, and as Ying watched, Jing walked out the door, and except to steal money or food, never returned to their home again. One big, happy family they were not.

Back in Springfield, no big happy family there either, Gotti had good reason to fear Gigante.

In 1985, Gotti seized control of the Gambino Family by allegedly ordering the murder of its boss, "Big Paul" Castellano. This infamous hit was carried out in front of a Manhattan steakhouse called Sparks, with Castellano and his bodyguard gunned down in broad daylight. Photos of their bloody bodies were splashed all over the New York tabloids the next morning.

Gigante and some of the old-style bosses weren't pleased. They thought Gotti's flashy clothes, his taste for the media spotlight, and his loose lips would draw unwanted attention to their operations.

Besides, Gotti never received approval for his assassination plans from the Commission, a ruling board of national crime bosses that included Gigante.

So "the Chin" personally ordered a hit on this overly talkative "Dapper Don." The scheme called for using a bomb to make Gotti's murder look like it was the work of the Sicilian Mafia, according to testimony from Mob informer Alphonso "Little Al" D'Arco.

Gigante denied all that in court, but the United States Court of Appeals for the Second Circuit affirmed that Gigante was boss of the Genovese Family, that the Genovese Family had conspired to murder John Gotti, and that Gigante, as boss, had to have been involved in this conspiracy.

The judge who wrote those words was careful to adhere to the letter of the law, but the Feds were prepared to use far more damaging testimony to nail Gigante.

A former under boss of the Lucchese crime Family named Anthony "Gas Pipe" Casso agreed to tell the whole story. He would testify that he was part of Gigante's plot to kill Gotti, and that he very nearly pulled it off.

Casso told the FBI that on April 13, 1986; a powerful bomb was fashioned out of C4 plastic explosives and a remote-controlled toy car. It was detonated outside a social club in Benson Hurst, Brooklyn, where Gotti was supposed to meet his under boss, Frank DeCicco.

Gotti changed his plans at the last minute, so when the bomb exploded, only DeCicco was killed.

As Gigante stewed in the U.S. Medical Facility for Federal Prisoners, it must have enraged him to know that Gotti resided in the same building. Not only had Gotti eluded assassination, but he also helped put Gigante behind bars.

A federal surveillance tape had recorded Gotti planning a hit on Corky Vastola, a high-profile New Jersey mobster who was part owner of Roulette Records and used to hang around with Sammy Davis Jr. In a conversation with Sammy "the Bull" Gravano and another associate, Gotti said he wanted to use a particular hit man for the job, but that he needed to get permission first from Vincent Gigante.

As far as the Feds were concerned, this testimony unquestionably established Gigante's position as a kingpin of organized crime.

Chapter 26
Love and Joy and Loyalty

Dressed in a dark purple business suit, I walked quickly into Marino's Restaurant and spotted Yolanda at a table in the center of the dining room. Yolanda bit into a breadstick and waved at me, while I made my way to the table and into the empty seat.

"Sorry I'm late." I smiled apologetically.

"What's five minutes?" Yolanda smiled back, the breadstick still in her mouth.

"I have a presentation this afternoon and needed to make a few last-minute arrangements."

"Insurance?"

"No, it's for The Right Stuff, my marketing business."

Yolanda took another chunk out of the breadstick. "I thought you sold insurance."

"I do sell insurance, but I have my own company as well. I offer incentive programs for companies to offer their sales teams."

"Smart."

"Well, I saw how lousy the incentives were that the insurance industry offered. Always geared to men. Golf. Steaks. Tires. So I thought to myself, why not incentives that appeal to women and men? Since no one offered it, I started my own company to do it myself."

"I can't keep up with you." Yolanda flagged the waiter. "Should we order?"

I smiled at the waiter. "Salad Niçoise for me."

Yolanda eyed me over the menu. "And what about for lunch?"

"That's plenty for me." I winked.

"Why don't you eat something? You're skin and bones."

The waiter grinned at me flirtatiously. "Whatever you're doing, keep it up."

Yolanda cleared her throat. "I'll have the Salad Niçoise as well."

"Very well, madam."

"And the Gnocchi Bolognese." Yolanda handed the menu to the waiter. "With a stuffed pork chop."

As the waiter nodded, Yolanda nudged me. "Red or white?"

"Iced tea for me," I said. "I've got the presentation."

"So add a little color to it." Yolanda nodded to the waiter. "Tenori Chianti. Two glasses."

The waiter left with a nod. Yolanda took the last breadstick out of the basket and bit off the tip. "You're coming to New Year's."

"What?"

"We have a big Family party every year. You're Family now. You're coming."

"I'd love to, I guess." A big New Year's Eve party sounded exciting, but I was a little taken aback by being called "family" so soon.

"It's at my brother Andrew's this year. Big party. We know how to celebrate, I'll tell ya that much."

"It'll be good to meet everyone."

"Not Frankie and his wife. They're not coming. Can you imagine? My own son? Frankie tells his wife, Doris, how we have a party every year on New Year's Eve. That woman wouldn't listen to Frankie if he told her the house was on fire. Can you believe she didn't come to my Mother's

Day dinner?"

I opted for diplomacy. "Maybe she spent the day with her own mother."

"You'll meet Angelo and his wife. She's a wet noodle. Does what Angelo says. She's a good wife. Not like Doris."

A wet noodle was Yolanda's idea of a good wife? I didn't know how to respond to that, and was happy when the waiter arrived with the salads and wine. Without tasting it, Yolanda motioned for the waiter to fill the glass.

"Do you know," Yolanda pointed with her fork, "Doris pulled me aside one night and told me she decides what she and Frankie do, and if I try to pressure Frankie into coming to Family parties she doesn't want to come to, well then I'll never see my grandchildren again."

"Whoa. Had she been drinking?"

"She's been drunk her whole life. Drunk on selfishness. Poor Frankie, stuck with a wife like that. Breaks my heart. You're coming, right?"

I smiled. "It'd mean a lot to me."

"Then it's done. Our best Family party ever."

I took a sip of wine. It warmed me inside, almost as much as "Yo" calling me family. As much as I had to admit I felt like I was losing Joel a little bit, I was happy he was becoming part of a family that cared so much about being together. A family that understood what it meant to be family. They stuck together. They enjoyed each other. They were full of love and joy and loyalty. How could that be anything but good for Joel, and for me?

Holding a giant gift-wrapped box, I walked into the boardroom of the insurance company, smiling at the men gathered around the table. I felt a little tipsy but, as Yolanda said, it just might help the presentation. I set the box down in the center of the conference table and shook hands with the man at the head of the table.

"Martin, good to meet you. I appreciate that you are taking the time to learn about my company. I promise you won't be disappointed."

Another man smiled. "No chance of that."

I walked over and shook his hand. "Sunny Rubin."

The man, a Dennis Quaid look alike in a business suit, held my hand a bit too long. "You can call me Ted."

"Well, Ted, you're in for a real treat here."

"You read my mind."

I pulled back, eying the room full of men.

Martin glanced at his watch. "So, tell us about your company."

I handed Martin and Ted my business cards. "For your best salespeople, you need the Right Stuff. I have an insurance background myself, gentlemen. I understand what agents want, and I know the incentives most companies offer either don't work or don't measure up, especially for women."

Ted looked at me warmly, and now I was certain this guy was flirting with me. Keep it all business, I told myself. Be professional, dignified, above-board.

"Well, speaking from experience," I said without missing a beat, "I can tell you that if you want your sales team to be motivated, productive and loyal, the incentives you're offering better be worth the effort."

"So what's in the box?" Ted asked.

"That's a surprise, Ted."

"I like surprises, as long as they're worth the effort."

Martin shifted in his chair. "What kind of tracking

results do you have for your incentives, Sunny?"

"My tracking comes from experience. From being on the other side of the table. Your good agents will sell regardless of what you offer them. The question is, who will they sell for? Your company or the competition? I can tell you, it's the company that offers the better pay, the better benefits and the better incentives."

"But what are the numbers?" Martin asked.

"That's what we're going to find out," Sunny answered.

"So you don't have any track record?" Martin sounded skeptical.

"She looks like she's got a track record to me." Ted smiled.

I realized I needed to wrap it up. Martin was restless, Ted amorous. I had given it my best shot. I flipped off the lid of the giant gift box, and out popped several helium balloons, each with an empowering message – You're Fantastic! You're a Winner! Congratulations!

As the balloons floated to the ceiling, I grabbed a few and handed them to Martin and Ted. At the same time, I scooped a handful of confetti from the box and threw it on all the men. "Congratulations! Salesmen of the Year!"

Ted enjoyed every minute of it, but Martin didn't look exactly amused. I let go of the last balloons.

"Of course, this is just a token. We have a vacation trip destination, lots of other incentives. We're creating competitive energy with rewards and recognition."

"We'll think it over and get back to you, Martin said.

Certain I'd hit a dead end, I looked to Ted, the friendliest face in the room, for some kind of sign.

"May I walk you to your car?" he asked.

Ted placed his open palm on the small of my back as we walked through the parking lot.

"So where are you from?" His friendly banter distracted me from my disappointment that Martin would almost certainly torpedo my proposal. Ted's rugged good looks were disarming, but I was here for business, and I'd failed.

"I'm living in Cream Ridge."

"What's your husband do?"

"My husband passed away."

"Sorry to hear that." Ted sounded sincere and compassionate, but his intentions were obvious and his mood brightened. "Listen, here's my card."

I looked at the job title.

"President?" I had thought Martin was the key person I had to impress during the meeting. Now I wasn't so sure.

"I'm a partner with the company, and I'll be the one making any decisions with our incentive plan," Ted said. "I like your enthusiasm. I like your spark. I think we should talk."

Chapter 27
Living between the Cracks

In a three-piece, black-and-white pajama ensemble, I sat at my dressing table brushing my hair. "It's about my life, Billy, not yours."

Billy's voice rasped through the speakerphone. "And I'm not part of your life?"

"Well, of course you're in it ... "

"No paper trail, Skunkie. How many times have I told you? The government can't get you. The IRS can't get you. If you're not on paper, you don't exist."

"It's not so bad, existing, Billy."

"Yeah, it's done wonders for you."

"You can't live your entire life between the cracks."

"I have so far."

"And what's it gotten you? What good is all that money you're winning if you don't have family?"

"I saw my girls two weeks ago, and I have you."

I smiled. "When's the last time you saw me?"

"It's Vegas, Skunkie. It's not like you need an invitation."

"Why don't you come out here for once?"

Billy wasn't biting. "Do you know how hard it is to travel without leaving a paper trail? Plane tickets, hotels ..."

"You used to come out all the time."

On the speakerphone, I could hear Billy take a gulp of Wild Turkey. "It used to be easier."

I heard a deep sadness in his voice and didn't know what to say. After a few seconds of silence, I changed the subject.

"So, did I tell you I got invited to the Family's big New Year's Eve party?"

"Are you going?"

"Of course. Why wouldn't I?"

"Last time we talked, you said they were coming on a little strong with Joel. Expensive gifts, fancy golf outings …"

"I might have been too hard on them. There's nothing wrong with being a little generous."

"A little generous is a bottle of aftershave, not an Armani suit."

"Joel seems really happy, and if he's happy, I'm happy."

There was a pause while Billy dragged on his cigarette. It sounded like he blew the smoke right into the phone. "All right, what's his name?"

"What are you talking about?"

"Don't try and bamboozle me, Skunkie. I invented that crap."

I had to smile. Billy was a professional gambler. He could read me as easily as if I was sitting opposite him at a poker table.

"His name is Ted."

"And where'd you meet him?"

"Work."

"A co-worker? Not a good idea, Skunkie."

"He doesn't work with me. I did a presentation at his company."

"A client? Even worse, but I like it."

"Well, he's technically not a client. Hasn't bought anything yet, but I have a feeling he will."

"Yeah." Billy grunted knowingly. "So do I."

"It's not like that, Billy, at least not yet. We haven't even gone out yet."

"Sounds like my kind of relationship. No commitment."

"But he emails me every day."

"Everyone's finding love on the Internet. I'll have to get me one."

"You do that, Billy. Talk to you tomorrow."

"You're going to meet him right now, aren't you?"

"Bye!" I hung up the speakerphone and smiled in the mirror. I started to turn off the light, and then noticed a shoebox on the shelf of my closet. I opened the box and took out black men's dress shoes, dusting them off with my hands. Slowly, I lifted the shoes to my face and took a long, deep breath, closing my eyes as images flooded my mind.

It's Becca's wedding reception. Her second marriage, after she had divorced the no-good Aaron. Becca is an accomplished ballroom dancer, and most of her friends are, too. The couples gliding elegantly and effortlessly around the dance floor look like professional dancers. They move so adroitly that the rest of the guests are intimidated. No one else is dancing.

The band begins to play a tango, sensual and evocative. Becca's ballroom friends move across the dance floor, intertwined dramatically. They move across the dance floor slowly, almost slithering, punctuating the music with a quick flick of the foot or a sharp snap of the head. Their movements are calculated and theatrical. All of a sudden, Michael stands and pulls me to my feet.

"C'mon, beautiful, let's tango."

"No way, Michael! We're going to look like idiots next to these people!"

"You think I care about them? Besides, you look gorgeous in that dress. I want to show you off."

I am wearing a ruby-red off-the-shoulder dress. It is stunning—iridescent satin organza, slit up the front, and trimmed with just a touch of black and red feathers. I have on red spike heels to match. I love my dress. As much as I love it, Becca hates it twice that much. She is clearly the center of attention in her regal wedding gown, but she doesn't' want anyone else looking pretty, at all. That is the epitome of Becca.

Michael is determined. "I'm not taking no for an answer!"

I try and protest, laughingly, but Michael pulls me onto the dance floor. "Ah, hell," I think. "Why can't we have a little fun." Michael grabs me around the waist with one arm, and raises the other in the air.

"En garde!"

"Michael, that's French. Tango is Spanish."

"Who cares?"

He pushes his face next to mine in a parody of the other dancers and slides me across the floor. Around us, the couples seriously dancing the tango look disgusted. Two by two, they leave the floor.

"Michael, they're leaving the dance floor."

" 'F' 'em if they can't take a joke."

Michael's right. Becca's wedding guests are laughing and enjoying our show. I throw caution to the wind and kick it up a notch, lifting my leg in the air when Michael dips me back. He pretends to almost drop me, then lifts me up and spins me. He picks up roses from the dance floor and places the stems in my clenched teeth. One more time, he drags me across dance floor as my spike heels scrape across the floor. The song ends. Friends and family cheer Michael's sense of humor.

We get back to the table, and my mother and Nancy are laughing so hard, there are tears in their eyes. Nancy applauds us, and my mother tells me our little show made the party. Michael thanks them, telling them he owes it all to years of dance training. He does his best Elvis impersonation.

"Thank you, thank you very much."

I'm flushed and excited and thirsty. I reach for my glass of punch and look over at Becca. She is definitely not amused. Oh well, when is she ever?

I had such conflicting emotions, as I put Michael's shoes back in their box. Pleasure at the memory, pain at the reality and everything else between. I closed the lid on the box. I'd gotten rid of most of Michael's things, but I had to hold on to a few pieces of our life together. Maybe it wasn't such a good idea. The memory of him is so wonderful that it only makes the reality of him being gone that much more painful.

Chapter 28
Life's a Party

"I'll never find a parking place," I thought to myself, as I slowly drove through the exclusive neighborhood of mansions and gated estates. Someone else must be having a New Year's Eve party. because I'm two blocks from Andrew's house, and the curb is packed with luxury imports.

"Maybe I'll get lucky," I said to myself as I drove the two blocks and found Andrew's to be the biggest house on the street. It was illuminated by floodlights. Tiny white lights, thousands of them, glowed in the trees lining the quarter-mile long driveway.

"Valet parking? For a family party?" I watched as a dozen , beefy men in business suits—big, bouncer-type guys—scrambled to park the cars of arriving guests. I pulled into the driveway and stopped at the back of a six-car line. Two men in black suits, each with two Doberman Pinschers on leashes, spoke into two-way radios as they walked past my car. I rolled down my window. "Is the president here?"

The men didn't even acknowledge my joke. The line moved quickly, and I found myself at the entrance. A man opened my car door.

"Good evening, ma'am."

Yolanda walked toward me with open arms and a wide smile.

"Yo, how are you?" I felt a little funny calling her that, but Yolanda insisted. In a few seconds, I was whisked inside by the large woman.

I stood there in amazement. It was like a castle. Vaulted ceilings, spiral staircases, Roman columns, marble floors, Oriental rugs, Persian vases, original paintings. "My God," I said. "It's beautiful."

"Andrew has good taste," Yolanda laughed.

"It's like a museum," I said.

"The Family loves the holidays."

Stepping into a backyard the size of a football field, I saw three giant, white tents holding hundreds of guests, all in suits and evening gowns. Servers peppered the crowd, offering hors d'oeuvres on silver trays. A band played on a stage in the middle of the three tents. As 'That's Amore' belted from the speakers, I eyed the singer and realized he was a Dean Martin look-alike. Standing just offstage, snapping to the music, were Frank Sinatra, Tony Bennett and Bobby Darin look-alikes.

"I've never seen anything like this," I said.

"It's just a Family party," Yolanda smiled.

Two more black-suited men with Doberman Pinschers walked by. I turned to Yolanda, who had disappeared. I scanned all directions and saw Yolanda being pulled away by another couple. Yolanda mouthed "sorry" to me, and I smiled back, letting her know it was all right. I headed toward the first tent and found my way to the bar. "A cosmopolitan, please."

As the bartender quickly spun out bottles of vodka and triple sec, Joel and Andrea suddenly appeared. "Happy New Year, Mom," Joel said.

"Yeah, Happy New Year," Andrea chimed in, a little tentatively.

I hugged them both, noticing how nice Joel looked in his suit, and how pretty Andrea looked in her strapless, silver gown. "You look stunning," I told the waif-thin girl.

"Good genes, Mrs. Rubin," Andrea smiled. I thought

of tubby Yolanda and wondered whose genes she was referring to.

"Please, call me Sunny. And you two look just like the perfect couple tonight. I'm very happy for you both."

Andrea grabbed Joel by the hand. "Let's dance."

"Anything you say." Joel smiled at me, and the two disappeared into the crowd.

The evening flew by. It was a blur of drinks, caviar on ice, wandering minstrels, dancing, Dick belting out "New York, New York" with Yolanda and Frank Sinatra, surveillance cameras, pasta, Doberman Pinschers and a hundred handshakes. I also got the impression that our little Andrea was everyone's favorite princess. No Family member I met failed to let me know just how lucky my Joel was to be with her. At the time, I thought it was a good thing that they all thought so well of her. I didn't really put it together in my mind until much later, that the guests, although speaking to me, would look in Dick or Yolanda's direction when they mentioned Andrea, almost as if to make sure they were being heard.

My head was still spinning when I locked my front door behind me and headed upstairs. I was tipsy and exhausted, and collapsed on my bed without even taking off my shoes.

I was sipping coffee in the kitchen, reading email off my laptop, when my eyes suddenly lit up. "Listen to this, Koho."

Koho barked from her bed.

"That's right," I answered, "It's from Ted. He says 'Bright Sunny day' – I love when he calls me that – 'you haven't replied to my job application, so I'll ask again: Handsome, successful president of his own company seeks entry level position to your heart. Romance available upon request.' So what should I do?"

Koho barked again. The phone rang. I pushed my breakfast cereal away and picked up the phone to hear, "Sunny, it's Ted."

I beamed at the sound of his voice. "Ted, I was just reading today's email."

"And still no response? I've written every day for three months. I'm either going to get a date or carpal tunnel syndrome."

I laughed. I had to admit, I adored the attention. "Well, if you do get carpal tunnel, I've got a great health insurance policy to sell you."

"I have to see you, Sunny. You can't just walk into a man's life, shower him with confetti, and then walk out."

"Well, if you hired my company, you'd see me a lot more often."

"I'm working on that. But I think we need a few more face-to-face meetings."

"Great, I'll call Martin."

"I meant without Martin. Just you and me."

"Sounds fishy."

"That's because it is. I can't get you out of my mind, Sunny. Ever since that meeting, all I can think about is your amazing smile, your sexy body, your magnetic personality. I'm in pain here! I've never felt anything like this before. It's like love at first sight."

"I don't know anything about you."

"Then find out."

"I don't know ..."

"At least have lunch with me."

I couldn't help myself. I toyed with him just a bit. "I

just don't know if I want to get involved."

"It's lunch, Sunny. We can talk business."

I was nervous, but I knew this could be interesting. It had been awhile since a man was this persistent.

The doorbell rang, an unwelcome intrusion. Just when I was having fun. "That's the door, I gotta go."

"Not until we set a date."

I started for the door and saw Yolanda and Andrea through the window. I had invited Andrea for a day of pampered beauty treatment at a spa. It was time to cut to the chase. "All right, Ted, lunch, tomorrow. I'll meet you at your office."

"Great. There's a hotel nearby—"

"Hotel!" I yelped indignantly.

"With an Italian restaurant. We can eat there."

"No, I'll bring a picnic."

"Picnic?"

"It's the first week of spring. It'll be fun."

"I don't see how it can be anything else."

I opened the door. "Gotta go!" As I clicked off the cordless, Yolanda and Andrea walked in.

"Hotel?" Yolanda asked. "Are you going somewhere?"

"Just a client," I said. "Setting up business meetings."

In the living room, I poured coffee for Yolanda and Andrea, and then set out a tray of pastries.

"You shouldn't have," Yolanda said as she scooped up a bear claw in her napkin.

"It looks great, Mrs. Rubin." Andrea smiled, not taking a bite.

"Andrea, I admire your manners, but please call me Sunny. I don't feel nearly as old as 'Mrs. Rubin' makes me sound."

Andrea smiled and eyed the pastry.

"What'll you have, Andrea?" I asked. "Croissant? Danish?"

Andrea tapped her stomach. "Nothing for me, thanks. I had a late breakfast."

"It's nine A.M.," I said.

"She's a pencil," Yolanda said, biting into her bear claw. "I don't know how the both of you do it."

I turned to Yolanda. "So what brings you here, Yo? Coming with us to spa?"

"No," Yolanda answered, crumbs and icing clung to her lower lip before sliding to her chin on their way to her lap. "This is girl talk." She took a swipe at her mouth with the paper napkin clutched in her pudgy, gilded fingers tipped in bright red nail polish.

"Well, I'm always up for that." I chuckled.

"You see, Sunny, Andrea here is a good girl." Yolanda smiled, revealing yellow teeth between scarlet lips.

"She's great," I said, as Andrea looked away.

"What I mean, though, is that she's a good girl. That way. Like, you know?" She reached over to pat Andrea's knee.

I felt confused and knew my face showed it.

"She's a virgin," Yolanda whispered.

Andrea glanced back for my reaction, which was something like a double shot of espresso—full of energy, but not sure where to direct it. I stared at both Yolanda and Andrea, then suddenly blurted, "Oh my God, is Joel pressuring you?"

"No," Yolanda laughed. "Joel's a perfect gentleman. But Andrea and I have been talking."

It didn't sound like Andrea was doing a whole lot of

talking.

"We've decided that Joel will be the one."

I couldn't help but wonder why my days tended to take these strange twists. Did I invite it in? What could have possibly occurred in a former life to attract these incidents into this one? "What do you mean, the one?" I asked, looking at Andrea.

"The first one," Yolanda answered. "The one to take Andrea's virginity."

OK, are there actually mothers and daughters in the world who have these discussions? How do I respond to that? What does a mother of "the one" say to a statement like that?

"Well." I grasped for something to say and found only air. "Lucky for Joel." I instantly knew that wasn't right, but hell, what kind of response were these people looking for?

"He's a gentleman, he's kind," Yolanda said, apparently not offended, "and we think he'd be perfect."

"You know," I said, deciding that maybe I had to be as blunt as they were, "I think he would be good. When Joel was 21, he dated a flight attendant who was 28. I always thought it was great that he was with someone older, more experienced. I think he really learned how a woman wants to be treated."

I took a sip of coffee, hoping I'd hit the mark they were seeking. Andrea bolted out of her chair, glared at us and ran upstairs. Oops, I guess not. I looked to Yolanda, who smiled.

"She's nervous."

"I should apologize," I said, rising. What the hell was acceptable in this conversation?

Heading upstairs, I heard rustling in Joel's room and

peeked through the door. Andrea was at Joel's desk, rooting through the drawers. I couldn't believe it! I felt violated, but decided to leave it alone. I didn't want to make things worse. Without Andrea seeing me, I slipped away and headed back downstairs.

After a few more awkward minutes of bear claw, crumbs and sex talk with Yolanda, I saw Andrea heading down the stairs carrying a stack of letters. She also held a framed picture of Joel and another woman, which she brandished at me.

"Is this her?"

"Excuse me?" I said.

"Is this the flight attendant?" Andrea was turning red.

"Andrea, I really don't think you should be going through Joel's things."

"And these are her letters, right?"

I looked to Yolanda, who ducked the conversation by studying the pastry tray. No rescue would be coming from her.

"Those are Joel's things, Andrea. I'm sure he'd share them with you if you asked." I wanted to jump up and rip the picture and letters out of Andrea's hands, but this family had been so good to me, and now it seemed Andrea and Joel were getting serious. Andrea marched toward the front door.

"He'll share them with me, all right. Let's go, Ma."

Yolanda grabbed an éclair for the road and gave me a hug. "I'll talk to her. She's just a bit upset."

"Well, I hope I haven't offended anyone, but they are Joel's things."

"Of course they are," Yolanda said, giving no indication that she was going to stop Andrea from taking them. It was one of my first indications that little miss Andrea got whatever little miss Andrea wanted from her family.

"Listen, Sunny, next Friday night. We're all going to see *Cats*. You're joining us."

"*Cats*? That'd be great. I'm probably the only person on the East Coast who hasn't seen it."

"We'll meet at my house. Take a limo. Have dinner. It'll be fun."

"Sounds like a wonderful evening," I said, happy to have the conversation on a comfortable tack again.

"And maybe that'll be Joel's lucky night." Yolanda winked at me before she followed Andrea out the door.

Was Joel lucky to be involved with this girl? I wasn't so sure anymore...

Chapter 29
Wow!

Ted and I walked through the green, tree-lined park until we found a quiet spot near a brook. I laid out a large blanket, then took the picnic basket from Ted and started setting out plates, wine glasses, imported cheeses, strawberries, finger sandwiches, marinated artichokes, olives and flatbread.

"Well, I thought I had found the perfect woman, but now I know for sure," Ted said.

"The question is do you deserve her?" I smiled.

"I hope to prove I do." Ted reached out and touched my hand. I instinctively pulled back.

"Not yet."

"You're driving me crazy, Sunny. Here I finally found a beautiful, sexy woman I'm nuts about, and I still don't know what you think of me, except that you won't let me touch you!"

I needed to delay things with Ted. Yes, I was enjoying the attention. Yes, I thought he was sexy. Yes, I was dying to kiss him as much as he was dying to kiss me. But I didn't want to rush into sex. As clichéd as it was, I needed him to respect me. "Let's just take it slow," I said, handing him a slice of Gouda on flatbread.

"Isn't that what we've been doing the past three months?"

"Has it been that long?" I knew it had.

"I'm not usually like this, but there's something about you. I want you. There's no other way to say it. I want you in my life. I want you sexually. You're all I can think about.

I've never felt this way about any woman."

Those words were music to my ears. I wanted to feel special, not just be some woman he was trying to bed "I'll tell you what, I've got a game we can play."

"Now you're talking." Ted grinned.

"It's called Truth or Dare."

"I know that game!"

"You have to answer a question honestly to get points. And when you get 25 points, you can kiss me, but you can't touch any part of my body."

"And when I get a hundred points, we make love?"

"I didn't say that. Let's see. A hundred points, and you get to…kiss me again. But no touching. And if I think you're lying, you lose points."

"How will you know if I'm lying?"

"Oh, I'll know."

"How many points is each answer?"

"I'll make that up as I go."

"So you're in control?"

"Complete control."

Ted smiled. "Sounds like fun. What's the first question?"

I sipped my wine and took the plunge. "Why did you and your wife separate?" It was something I'd wanted to ask him for a while.

Ted looked away, realizing this wasn't going the way he'd hoped. "It's complicated."

With a dozen more questions, Ted told the story of marrying his pregnant girlfriend right out of high school, and her getting pregnant again right after their first child was born. After two more children, the marriage was more about convenience. He didn't love his wife. She didn't take care of herself, and she didn't take care of him. She didn't want sex, and on the rare occasions she agreed to sex, she didn't participate. She would just lay there, waiting for it to be over.

I wondered how a marriage could be so devoid of passion. With Michael, my marriage had always been exciting. Not just sexually, although that was great too, but with the boys, with friends, with life itself. It was a dream world.

Ted interrupted Sunny's daydream. "That has to be 25 points by now."

I really wanted him to kiss me. "Yes," I said. "That's 25 points."

Softly, gently, Ted leaned into me and kissed me. Feeling an electric pulse vibrate through me, I leaned deeper into the kiss. I knew I was attracted to him, but I didn't realize how much. I knew right away that I hadn't felt anything this good since Michael. I continued the kiss, hoping Ted would take me into his arms. I wanted to feel his hands run up and down my body but, like a gentleman, he obeyed the rules of the game and didn't touch me. That impressed me almost as much as the kiss.

Together, instinctively, both Ted and I pulled back and whispered, "Wow."

As we laughed at the synchronicity, it began to rain. We quickly gathered up the picnic and ran for shelter. By the time we got to the street, it had become a downpour. We ducked into the lobby of a hotel.

"How convenient," Ted said.

"It's not going to happen." I said it with a smile.

"Well, we can at least get a room and finish the game."

"I don't know if I can trust you," I said playfully.

"Hey, I followed the rules," Ted pleaded.

I couldn't argue with that.

With the picnic laid out on a queen-size bed in the governor's suite, I playfully fed Ted a strawberry, and he returned the favor.

"So, what's my next question?" Ted asked.

I wanted another kiss, and even more. I was tired of the game and yet…there was something so delicious about the anticipation.

"OK." I decided to move things in a sexier direction. "What's your favorite part of a woman's body?"

"Not just one part," Ted said. "All of it. I love the soft cheeks with the proud cheekbones, the blue, sparkling eyes, the petite nose. I love the tender neck that feels like velvet to the touch. I love the luscious, blond hair, the strong, firm shoulders and the ripe, apple breasts."

I realized two things. One, he wasn't describing women in general—he was talking about me. And two, he was very good.

"I love running my hands softly down a creamy back, then around to a thin waist and curved hips. I love the slim legs and the way they make the tight butt wiggle when they walk."

I was leaning closer and closer, drawn to Ted like a flower toward the sunlight.

"I love nibbling every inch of buttery skin, slowly making my way to … "

"That's another 25 points," I gasped.

We kissed passionately, I wrapped my arms around Ted, and he did the same. I melted as his strong hands slid up and down my back, then caressed my breasts. We fell flat on the bed as Ted's knee slipped softly between my legs, pushing up my dress. His hand followed, warmly touching my bare thigh, then bravely moving up my leg. I started unbuckling Ted's belt as his hands slipped inside my panties. I surrendered completely. I'd been with other men, but nothing had ever felt like this. It was like twin sparks of the universe having found each other after thousands of years apart. Our bodies blended into each other so easily, our hunger for each other such a perfect match.

We made love into the evening. After a candlelight dinner at the hotel, we returned to the room for more. My body felt alive. It had been dead for so long. Finally, at midnight, Ted walked me to my car, kissed me goodnight, and I drove home, knowing that he was trouble. With a capital 'T'. And that I was definitely seeing him again.

Chapter 30
60 Minutes

"Two dozen red roses!" Billy's voice scratched through the hands-free speaker in my car.

"Two dozen a day." I smiled as I pulled off the turnpike.

"Every day?" Billy's voice asked.

"For two weeks." I stopped at the off ramp's red light.

"And the sex is good?"

I smelled the fresh, long-stemmed roses on the seat next to me. "Unbelievable."

"It always is with the married ones. That's why women love me so much."

"I'm telling Denise you said that."

"As long as you don't tell my wife."

Hidden under Billy's playful banter was the pain he felt at having a wife he was not able to live with. He'd only been married to Deanne a short while when it became obvious that his lifestyle would never be acceptable to her. Denise, his longtime girlfriend, was a different story. She was the quintessential party girl; never wanted marriage or children, didn't care that he wandered like a nomad and made his living in casinos. She was his partner in crime, the Bonnie to his Clyde.

The light went green, and I turned left. "He's not married, Billy. He's separated. Not quite divorced yet."

"Who cares? Have fun. Enjoy it. Carpe diem."

"I'm not like you, Billy. I can't live moment to moment. I want more. I want ... "

"Skunkie, are you falling in love?"

"No!" I shouted it, but followed with a much softer truth. "Yes."

"Well, don't confuse sex with love."

"With the boys gone, I just feel like something's missing."

"Hey, just because they don't live with you, doesn't mean they won't be there for you. They're family. Always will be."

"That's all I want."

"And with Joel and Andrea getting serious, you have a bigger family. Think of the parties, the holidays. You'll always have family to fall back on."

He was right. My boys were doing great. And with Joel bringing a whole new family into the picture, I would finally have what I'd wanted all my life—a big, happy, healthy family. "You're smarter than you think, Billy," I said.

"And I think I'm pretty smart." Billy could be heard taking a gulp of his drink, something with clinking ice cubes in it.

I pulled my car into Yolanda's driveway. "I'm here, Billy. I'll call you tomorrow."

Before I could knock on the front door, Yolanda swung it wide open and pulled me into a bear hug. "Sunny, so good to see you!"

I returned the hug, then pulled back and handed Yolanda a single rose. "A belated Happy Mother's Day. I have roses for everyone."

Yolanda took the rose, then pulled me inside, whispering, "Is it from lover boy?"

I winked at her—two girlfriends talking boy talk. "My house is like a flower shop!" I looked around and noticed there was no one else there. "So, Yo, where's everyone else? Shouldn't we be leaving soon?"

"We'll leave at 7:00 P.M. Go straight to the theatre and get dinner after the show. If you're hungry, I can get you something here."

"I just hope we get to our seats before the curtain." I was looking forward to *Cats.*

"It'll be close, but I have something on a DVD I want to show you first."

What DVD could possibly be more important than getting to a big Broadway show on time? And what happened to the limos? The rest of the family? Where were Dick and Gino? Where were Joel and Andrea? Even if we were leaving late, why was I the only one here? Yolanda slipped in a disc and pressed 'play' on the remote, bringing up the familiar ticking of the watch on *60 Minutes.* The first segment was something about the trial of a New York Mob boss. "Yo, why did you tape this?"

"Sunny," Yolanda said, "I need you to watch it."

I looked at Yolanda, whose eyes were fixed on the screen.

The authoritative veteran reporter Ed Bradley was speaking to the camera.

"Can a seventy-year-old man who mumbled incoherently to himself and wandered the streets of New York's Greenwich Village in a bathrobe and slippers also be the most powerful Mafia boss in America? His Family says no, that Vincent Gigante is just a poor, bedraggled old man who, for as long as they can remember, has been crazy. According to federal prosecutors, Gigante is crazy like a fox..."

Footage of The Oddfather appeared on the screen.

"...and has been faking his mental illness for the past three decades to conceal his real-life role as the shrewd and ruthless leader of the Genovese Family, the nation's largest criminal organization."

Yolanda squared her shoulders, drawing her big body up proudly.

"What is this all about?" I asked.

"Sssshhh!" Yolanda pressed the remote several times, turning up the volume.

"Yolanda and Sal Gigante are Vincent Gigante's children," Bradley told a nation of television watchers.

Yolanda's face appeared on the screen. Stunned, I let out a gasp.

"I would hear him speaking to himself in the middle of the night," said the woman on TV, who was sitting right next to me. "It was frightening."

"What did you think when you would hear this going on?" Bradley asked.

"My father's crazy."

My head began to spin. My mouthed dropped as I watched the story of Yolanda's father.

"Prosecutors say Gigante concocted this crazy act after he got a taste of prison in the nineteen-sixties, serving four years for heroin trafficking," the narrator said. "Shown here being booked, Gigante's rap sheet back then included arrests for weapons possession, gambling and attempted murder. According to the government, Vincent Gigante's ruse was so successful, he eluded the law for the next thirty years, while one after another of his fellow mobsters, including his better-dressed nemesis John Gotti, went to prison."

Yolanda let out a little chuckle.

"But the strongest evidence against Gigante," Bradley's voice said, "came from those six mob informants who named Gigante as a Mafia godfather, the man who ordered whether people lived or died. The star witness was Sammy 'The Bull' Gravano, an admitted killer who cooperated with the government in exchange for a reduced sentence."

Yolanda's face appeared on the TV again. She was denying she ever met a man named "Sammy the Bull."

The segment ended with footage of a Catholic priest—Father Louis Gigante—insisting that his brother wasn't faking insanity.

"God will judge," Father Gigante said. "God will judge everything."

"That priest is your uncle?" I asked.

"Yes." Yolanda said.

"And Vincent Gigante is your father?"

"Yes."

Nervously, I leaned forward on the couch, ready to leave on a moment's notice. I'm in trouble here, I thought. This family ... this Family ... is part of the most powerful crime organization in the world. And Joel? He's getting involved in this? Where's Joel? Did they whack him? Are they going to whack me? You don't step out of line with these kinds of people. You do what you're told. My heart was racing and I felt sick to my stomach. I had to conceal my terror from everyone in the room. They seemed so proud of themselves and I was just terrified.

Yolanda clicked off the TV. "Sunny."

I jumped from the couch. "Where's Joel?"

"He'll meet us at the theatre, Sunny."

"I want to talk to him now."

"Relax, Sunny," Yolanda stood. "It's not true."

"That was you, Yo! That was you on the TV."

"It's true that Vincent Gigante is my father. But that's the end of it."

I looked at Yolanda, unable to speak.

"People believe my father's a mobster, Sunny. There's nothing I can do about that. But he's not. And neither am I. None of the family is. We're just regular people living regular lives."

"Does Joel know?"

"We've talked to him about it, and he understands."

I churned at this. I was beginning to feel that Joel was closer to the Family than he was to me. For God's sake, he's already living in their house. Why didn't Joel tell me? Why didn't he bring it up? Is this some secret Mafia code?

Yolanda put her arm around me. "There's really nothing to it, Sunny."

"It sure looks like there's something to it."

"Look, I'm not disowning my father. I love him. Do I know friends of his? Yes. Do I look after his medical care and legal fees? Yes. But it's not my life. I'm sure when your father was sick you did the same things for him. Joel has told me how you were always at his side until he died. Family is everything, Sunny, I know you believe that as much as we do. My Andrea, she gives her blood to her grandfather. His illness, sometimes leaves him needing transfusions. Andrea's blood works like magic in his veins. He's like a young man again for a little while after he gets a transfusion. The whole Family is so grateful to her. Her precious blood is keeping our father alive, and no matter what people say, Sunny, he is my father, and Andrea's grandfather, and we will always be there for him. Dick and I have our own family, and it's not that kind of Family. We're not involved in anything illegal. Never have been."

The look in Yolanda's eyes was enough for me to want to believe it. We had become close over the past few months, and I felt I could trust Yolanda. "What about the real estate management company you told me about? Wasn't that your father's?"

"That's a legitimate company. Always has been. It has nothing to do with any of those criminal charges against my father. I run it for my family, that's all.

It didn't make sense to me. Even if the real estate was legitimate, the money had to come from somewhere. But I didn't feel it was important to press the point. Better to come to a resolution. I turned to thinking about Joel. I wasn't ready to accept what might happen to my new Family if I pushed this too hard.

"Well," I said, moving closer to Yolanda, "I trust you."

"Family, right?"

I couldn't help but smile at the irony. "Family." I hugged Yolanda.

I sat in the theatre while rubber-limbed cats pranced around the Broadway stage, but I just couldn't stop my swirling thoughts. Was Joel in danger? Was he getting in too deep? I'm his mother, I should warn him about this. Who knows what they said to him. I want to believe Yolanda ... I do believe her, but she is the daughter of the boss of one of New York's biggest crime Families. She can't be completely clean ... can she?

The musical cats continued to dance onstage and through the audience. Music blared, lights flashed. I began to get hooked into the show. My questions of the Mob were drowned by the rhythm and melody of singing, dancing cats. Before I knew it, I was standing in the lobby, listening to an excited crowd buzz about the show.

I found myself surrounded by Yolanda and Andrea, both as excited as can be. Yolanda put her familiar arm around me.

"What'd you think, was it wonderful?"

I was still in a bit of a *Cats*-induced daze. "You know, it was a marvelous production. Fantastic lighting, staging, costumes. But the play itself wasn't much...."

The smile on Andrea's face fell like a curtain. Yolanda's smile followed. I realized I'd said something wrong. But what? Was it impolite? After all, they invited me, treated me to a fabulous night. But I said it was a marvelous production, didn't I? What did I say? I traced back for my exact words. My mind reeled. Offending these people was definitely not like offending just anybody. Not anymore. Not since I'd seen *60 Minutes*. People who offended the Family sometimes woke up with bloody horse heads in their beds, right?

"Let's go," Yolanda said. "We got dinner reservations."

I was grateful. I didn't know if Yolanda was cutting me short or moving the night forward, but it didn't matter. I was out of the spotlight. Hopefully my comment would get lost in the excitement and music of the night.

Chapter 30
What You Don't Know

"Billy, what am I going to do?" I paced around my family room, wishing I smoked. Billy's cocktail, ice clinking over the speakerphone, sounded good to me. I wished I were one of those people who drank in the afternoon.

"There's nothing you can do, Skunkie. Not everything is in your control. Especially not this. Don't mess with this."

"You're scaring me even more, Billy. Are they going to try and kill me?"

Billy chuckled. "Not unless you try and set up a drug operation in their territory."

"But Yolanda says they're not Mafia anymore. Shouldn't I believe her?"

"Believe what you need to believe, Skunkie. Look, Joel's not in any danger. And neither are you. But once Mafia, always Mafia. Didn't I tell you they weren't legit? The Gigante family, huh? They're big time. The biggest." The head of the Mafia Food Chain.

"I've never even heard of them."

"How many Mafia guys have you heard of?"

He was right. Not that many. John Gotti. And Michael Corleone, if you count movies.

"So, what do you know about them. About the grandfather?"

"Well, the "Chin," is the famous Mafia guy who used to walk right down Sullivan Street in Greenwich Village, shuffling his feet and muttering to himself. In his pajamas. That was his whole thing. He pretended to be crazy for years."

"Pretended? Yolanda says he really is suffering from dementia."

"What's she going to say? That her father is a ruthless thug? All I know is, the FBI spent years following him around, until they finally nailed him."

"How? How did they get him?"

"I don't know all the details, Skunkie. But if I know you, you'll find out."

Had I ever crossed paths with Ying Woo, my research on the Gigante family could have ended there. While I was scrolling the internet archives, Ying sat in her front room, sipping her favorite tea and spinning a tale for Zhong out of all the stories she had heard over the years, when people didn't know she was listening, and all of the articles she had read in the papers that she sold every day.

Zhong had asked her to tell him more about the mafia, and astoundingly, Ying had remembered everything she had read and heard.

"First, my grandson, know that even though the stories people tell of these men sometimes make them sound exciting and glamorous, they are plain and simple Fú zh !" In Chinese, Fú zh loosely translates to scum. Continuing with her story, Ying said,

"In the old country, these gangsters ruled only in Italy, but like the rest of us, they too saw opportunity here in America. From what I have heard, there are at least five major 'families' in power. The Genovese Crime Family, the one the police are sure that the 'crazy' Italian is the boss of, came about over a hundred years ago in the 1890's."

Ying snorted as she told Zhong,

"These people, murderers and thieves, were called 'The Ivy League of Organized Crime' by one writer. What he meant, I suppose, was that they became the most famous. Or, I think, in this case we would say infamous? Anyways, I am sure that in the American movies you have watched, you might have heard of some of them. Joe Masseria, Lucky Luciano, Bugsy Siegel, Meyer Lansky, these were all bosses of this family at one time or another. This 'lucky' one, Luciano, he got sent to prison for 30 to 50 years back in the 30's for prostitution. I'm not sure that 'Lucky' was the right name for him! Anyways, I read that he still ran the family, making the major decisions and such from prison. These families have 'acting bosses' and there was a man by the name of Vito Genovese who 'acted' under this Lucky character. Eventually, that one, Vito, left this country and went home to Italy to keep from being sent to prison on a murder charge. I'm sure Italy was as pleased to have him as the American's were."

Ying smiled at her small joke, and continued.

"There's another guy, they call him a 'Consigliore' it means advisor. Frank Costello was the 'Consigliore' under Vito, and after that one left the country, Frank was made acting boss. This is where the 'crazy' one started coming into the picture. It was way back in 1957. My Wei and I were still in Hong Kong, and I did not know a thing of this nonsense then."

Sighing again, Ying said,

"We should have stayed in our home, Zhong. Bad guys are easier to spot among your own people, I think. Anyhow, on May 2, 1957, Vincenzo 'Chin' Gigante, who was a young gunman and protégé then, made an assassination attempt on Frank Costello. The older man was in the lobby of his apartment in Manhattan and The Chin shot him."

Rolling her eyes, Ying said,

"He couldn't even kill someone right, Zhong.. He only gave the man a minor head wound. I suppose it scared him though, because they say he retired soon after that. Vito Genovese was able to keep running the family, even out of the country, and the family was even named after him then. The 'Chin' was only what they called a soldier back then, but for some reason, about twenty-five years later, even though he didn't know how to shoot straight, they made him boss."

The headline of the article was "Strolls in Robe Notwithstanding, Mob Figure Must Stand Trial."

Ying was reading this one out loud to Zhong, looking as pleased as if she had written the report herself,

The writer, Joseph P. Fried, had this to say:

"Vincent Gigante, considered the most powerful Mafia boss in America but perhaps best known for walking through his Greenwich Village neighborhood in a bathrobe and pajamas, was declared mentally competent to stand trial on murder and racketeering charges yesterday by a judge who called his odd behavior an "elaborate deception."

Judge Eugene H. Nickerson of Federal District Court in Brooklyn found that the reputed head of the Genovese crime family "has feigned illness for over 20 years" in an attempt to skirt prosecution. Mr. Gigante's organization is considered the wealthiest Mafia group in the nation, until recently having major influence on lucrative industries and operations like garbage hauling, the docks in New Jersey, the Fulton Fish Market and the Jacob K. Javits Convention Center."

"There it is, Zhong, in black and white. The most powerful Mafia boss in America, AND NOT CRAZY!"

Zhong looked puzzled and said,

" But, Grandma, what led the judge to decide that "the Chin" was faking being crazy?"

Ying took another sip of her tea, and leaning back in her chair said,

''According to what I have heard on the street, and read in the papers, Gigante's lawyers tried to say that he now leads a very narrow existence, lives at home with his mother, sees only a small group of friends and family and rarely leaves his mother's apartment. His mother is the old Yolanda, the one that lives here, in the village. But, the judge in his case said that people, some of them police officers who followed him all the time, said that he would travel in the middle of the night to the Upper East Side. His 'mistress' lived in a town house there. He had several illegitimate children with her; they had been together for a long time. The judge also said that there was testimony that this 'Chin' was driven quickly through the streets at night, trying to avoid the police who were always following him. They also had evidence that he had attended meetings with his co-horts in organized crime, and was still making important decisions involving large sums of money and the fate of certain people."

With a harrumph, Ying said,

"Not only was this man a gangster, but he was a cheater on his wife. It figures, his soul is black, Zhong, I could see it through his eyes every time he came here to buy his papers."

"So, Grandma," Zhong asked, "If he was this great big boss, of this great big family, why didn't he want any one to know? Why live like a crazy man and not a prince?"

"Well, from what I understand, Zhong, Vito

Genovese finally went to prison in 1959. The family took an oath; the Mafia people call it a vow of secrecy, or omerta, to new levels. I read something once, about these mafia people, wanting to understand it all more. It was written by a man named Jerry Capeci. It was called The Complete Idiot's Guide to the Mafia. He said that the family had bosses that they used "up front" to take the suspicion off of the real boss. He also believed that sometimes the Genovese family would go out of its way to appear they couldn't shoot straight. I think, personally, this was probably true of the 'crazy one'. But Mr. Capeci said it was an act as well. He said the Genovese family was a money-machine, and arguably, the top Mafia family in America. He said that Gigante took secrecy to new levels, and that he managed to rule the largest Mafia family in America for many years before it was generally known that he was the boss."

Ying got up from her chair to stretch her legs, and Zhong asked,

"What exactly does that mean, Grandma, the boss?"

"Well, Zhong, from what I know, the Boss controls everything that happens in the family. This is why I blame this Chin for my beautiful Jing's death. He controlled the drugs and the pimps and the prostitutes then. No one did anything without his ultimate blessing. So, even if he never put a needle in her beautiful arm, or even if he did not lay his eyes on her, it was his evil that brought her down into the depths that ultimately took her from us."

Ying wiped a tear away, and sitting once again continued,

"The Boss, my grandson, decides everything. Who joins the family, who lives and who dies, whose life they will ruin next. It is all his choice. There is the under boss, who actually takes those decisions back to the members of the family who will carry them out. He will become the boss when the big one dies. Then there is the advisor we talked about earlier. He is important to the big boss, and the under boss, but he is nobody's boss. He just gives advice. Like that lady in the paper, Dear Abby."

Zhong looked at Ying and she was smiling. Her attempt at humor was to lighten the dark story she was telling, not just for Zhong, but for herself as well.

"The next highest position in a Mafia family is the Captain, or in Italian, the Caporegime, or Capo. There are several Caporegimes in every family, sometimes as many as 20, depending on the size of the family. These Captains are each in charge of a group of workers, and report to the Under boss. One of the primary jobs of the Captains is to collect money from the workers and make sure the Boss, Under boss and Consigliore receives their cut from everyone. Then, Zhong, there are the Soldiers. These are the actual workers in each family. Like you and I, they get their hands dirty. Unlike us, they do whatever the boss tells them to do. No matter how heinous the job. They must do whatever job is asked of them by the Boss or the Under boss. Some families have as many as 300 Soldiers."

Zhong, trying to absorb all of this, asked,

"So, Grandma, what about this Gotti? Was he a boss? He dressed so fancy, and was always in a fancy car with a driver. He looked like a boss, but Mr. Chin does not. He may not be crazy, but he looks crazy.

"Yes, Zhong, I do have to admit, the Chin was very good at looking and acting crazy. John Gotti was very good at showing off. I've read he was one of the most famous Mafia figures since that Al Capone person. You know, the one that Geraldo opened his vault? Anyways, Gotti started out as a Captain in the Gambino family. That family was ruled by a man named Carlo Gambino from the late 60's to the late '70's. He died of a heart attack while he was asleep. To me, Zhong, that seems too easy, but hopefully the afterlife finds him wandering the earth in misery. After he died, his brother-in-law took over. His name was Paul Castellano, and he was boss for nine years until, in 1985, he was killed, the newspapers called it 'gunned down' in front of a restaurant in Manhattan called Sparks. Believe it or not, the restaurant got famous for it. The rumors were, that this Gotti, was behind the killing, and shortly after, he was elected boss of the Gambino family. The way he dressed and flaunted himself earned him the name "Dapper Don" in the magazines and papers. After he died, not in a three thousand dollar suit, but in prison garb, his son 'Junior' took over as acting boss. In 1999, Junior was arrested for racketeering, and his uncle Peter Gotti took over as Acting Boss. According to police and news reports, the current street Boss of the Gambino Family is John "Jackie Nose" D'Amico."

Ying laughed sardonically,

"These nick-names, no class these people."

"So, Grandma," Zhong said, "you said there were five families? That is only two, the Genovese and Gambino families. What about the other three? And if it's all so secret, how do so many people know all of this?"

"Well, these vermin eventually get arrested for one thing or another, and like common rats, turn on each other. Way back in 1959, a man named Joe Valachi, just a peon in one of the families, testified about the five families and who the bosses were at that time. The Lucchese family was named for Gaetano "Thomas" Luchese, who headed the family from 1953 to 1967. His main area of interest was the garment industry, and he had worked closely with Carlo Gambino and his family in this area. He headed the family during its most powerful days. Henry Hill, another mobster they made a movie out of, called it 'Goodfellas' I think, was an associate of the Lucchese's. That one, Lucchese died of Cancer in 1967. That is better that heart attack in his sleep, but still not good enough, I think. Anyways, there were quite a few bosses after that. First, a man named Anthony Corallo was boss until 1986. He handpicked the next boss, Vittorio 'Little Vic' Amuso. His under boss was a man named Anthony Casso. It is said that the reign of these two men was considered one of the bloodiest in the history of this family. Amuso was eventually arrested. They convicted him of racketeering. I think, Zhong that is something they use often to get these scum off of the streets. You hear it more often than arrested for murder, which, I am sure, most of them are guilty of as well. But he is serving a life sentence in prison. It's a Federal prison, and I hear those are not as tough as say, our Riker's Island. But better than on the street, maybe, even though he is in prison for life, I've read that he is still reputed to be the official boss of the family. Who knows, really, except for those inside the family? Then, there is the Columbo family. It was originally called the Profaci family after Joe Profaci, the first boss. He was the boss for over thirty years, from 1930-1963. When Joe Columbo took over, he became well known to the city. He was shot at an Italian-American Day rally which he had helped to plan in 1971. The rumors were, that Carlo Gambino had arranged that hit, because he was angry with Columbo for attracting so much press.

Another Persico was boss after that, Carmine Persico. He was known also as 'Junior' and the media called him 'the Snake', because of all the situations he seemed to be able to get out of. He was finally convicted of, guess what? Yes, racketeering and, sentenced to one hundred years in prison. In the 1980's the family was split in two. There was one side for the imprisoned Persico, and the other for the acting boss, Vic Orena. Orena was convicted of racketeering as well, in 1992. That started a civil war of sorts within the family. Each side was killing the other. Finally, Persico won out and was allowed to appoint his nephew, Andrew Russo as acting boss. It is believed that Persico really intends to have his son Alphonse, a longtime Capo in the crime family, take over the family eventually. But that one too, will soon end up in prison. The Bonanno Family was considered the closest knit of the Five Families because it was made up of mostly Sicilians from the seaside town where Joe Bonanno was born. Does it do your heart good to hear of families sticking together, Zhong?"

Ying asked with a sarcastic tone and a smile.

"In 1931, Bonanno was the youngest of the bosses of the Five Families – just 26 years old. I'm sure his mother was proud."

Ying said with a dark edge to her voice, and then continued,

"Early in his reign, Bonanno played a part in the creation of the Commission. This board of directors was composed of seven Bosses whose goal was to negotiate disputes between families in the hopes of avoiding bloodshed. For the next thirty years, from 1931 to 1961, Bonanno and his family prospered. Bonanno's strength began to wane in the late 1950's. Many men in Bonanno's family were discontented, complaining that he was never around. Eventually, the commission decided that he no longer deserved to be boss, naming Bonanno Caporegime Gaspar DiGregorio the new boss. Although he fought this decision for many years, after suffering a heart attack Bonanno retired to Arizona in 1968. The Commission he helped create had proved to be his undoing. Imagine, welcoming your new neighbor, the boss of a crime family for over thirty years to your retirement village, disgusting, isn't it my grandson? I wonder if he tried to take over the bingo games?" Ying smiled grimly, patted Zhong on the back and said,

"Enough stories for one day let us get back to work."

Meanwhile, after I had spent several hours on the computer, I had to take a break. I dialed Billy's cell phone. I wanted to share all my newfound Mafioso expertise with someone who I thought might appreciate all the sordid details.

"Look, Skunkie, I'm on my way to Atlantic City. Why don't you come with me, and we can talk all about it there?"

"I have to work, Billy. Some of us have to work, remember? Besides, there's tons of stuff about this "Chin" guy on the Internet. I'm not going anywhere until I read all about the Family my son is getting involved with."

Chapter 32
Because the Night

I stood in high heels and a black lace dress and stirred steaming pots on the stove with one hand, while dialing my cordless phone with the other. Multi-tasking. I was famous for it. I could talk on the phone, go over insurance paperwork and touch up a pedicure all at the same time. Never waste a moment. I scooped some marinara sauce onto a wooden spoon and held it to my mouth, blowing on it, then slowly tasted it as I held the phone to my ear. All I heard was the recorded message I'd been hearing for days now. I straightened the two elegant, linen table settings, moving crystal and china into their proper places. The beep pierced my ear.

"Yo, it's Sunny. Are you out of town? Haven't heard from you in days. I've been leaving messages. Is everything OK? Give me a call. I may have some gossip for you in the morning!" I hung up and shook my head. I hadn't spoken to Yolanda since Cats, and this sudden freeze unnerved me. After all, I didn't want to piss off the family of the girl my son was dating—given who that Family was.

"Gossip?" The man's voice came from behind me.

I jumped, startled. I spun around to see Ted, holding a bouquet of roses and a bottle of wine. "My God, you scared me. When did you start inviting yourself in?" I said it warmly.

"Wasn't that you inviting me in at the hotel?" Ted pressed his body against mine, and I wrapped my arms around him.

"And you thought that was an open invitation?"

Ted kissed me softly. "Wasn't it?"

"I hope so." I kissed him back.

We kissed again, pressing hard against each other. The flowers dropped to the floor. Ted reached to set the bottle of wine on the table, but it fell over and rolled toward the edge, finally stopped by clinking against a salad plate. As we kissed, Ted dropped his hands to the back of my thighs, then slid them up my legs, lifting my dress to my waist. With a moan, I pulled him back until I was leaning against the kitchen wall. I unbuckled Ted's belt, unzipped his pants and pushed them to his ankles. I reached into his briefs and slid them down, while Ted yanked my panties down to my knees. His hands gripped the back of my thighs, lifting me slightly off the ground. I wrapped my legs around his waist, gently guiding Ted inside me. With pots steaming on the stove, Koho barking from the backyard and the wine bottle hanging precariously over the edge of the table, we made love like two lonely souls desperately trying to become one.

We sat at the candlelit table, dressed again, but with our clothes slightly wrinkled and disheveled. We gazed at each other with a spark that cut right through the darkness and made the candlelight pale by comparison. Ted poured the last drop of red wine into my glass, then set the empty bottle on the table between plates of half-eaten rigatoni marinara, garlic bread and veal cutlets. "Next weekend, we're going away," Ted said.

"What?" I sipped her wine. "You didn't like my cooking?"

"Best Italian I've ever had. But you shouldn't have to work so hard for me. Besides, I have other plans for you than cooking."

I wondered how I'd gone so long without this. Having a man to share dinner with. Having a man want me, care about me. This wasn't just dating, this was more. Maybe it wouldn't go further, but right now, in this moment, it was more. "So what'd you have in mind?"

Ted reached out and took my hand in his. "Virginia. There's a nice hotel ... "

"A hotel?" I feigned shock.

"Separate rooms of course." Ted played along. "There's a restaurant nearby, in an old mansion. Music, great food, in the middle of nowhere."

"Sounds dangerous."

"Yes, but the right kind of danger."

I giggled, then took the last bite of pasta on my plate. I didn't want to break the mood, but I had to ask. "Don't you take your kids on the weekends?"

Ted looked down, pushing some pasta around on his plate. "I don't always...sometimes I have to travel for work, and..." His voice trailed off.

"I'm sorry," I said. "I shouldn't have said anything."

"No, it's just ... "

"You don't have to say anything."

"It's just that, we haven't really set up any visitation terms yet. Technically, we're only separated, and until we file for divorce ... "

My blood felt hot, then cold. "You haven't filed for divorce yet?"

"Sunny, it's a big mess right now. We were married for so long, and the kids, especially my little guy, don't understand what's going on."

I felt terrible. He has kids, for God's sake. I never thought I'd be this person. I was torn between guilt for being the reason he would push for a quick divorce and wishing he had one already. I'd never had this kind of lust for anyone, not even Michael. We fit together so well. The great conversations, the playfulness, the sex. I suddenly realized I was in deeper than I'd thought. It's one thing to have a fling, it's another to attempt to develop the relationship.

"Ted. Is this just sex for you? I know we haven't been dating that long, but I have to tell you. It's more than that for me."

"Can't you tell that it's more than that for me, too?"

"I don't want to rush into anything, but I'm not interested in casual sex. That's not me."

"There's no way you can call this kind of sex casual."

"You know what I mean."

"Sunny, being with you has brought me back to life again. I was dying in that marriage. Kathryn never liked sex. It was always me who initiated it ... not to mention that I did all the work."

"I can't imagine that," I said. "Michael and I always had great sex." I immediately thought I shouldn't have brought up Michael, but I desperately wanted the freedom and comfort level to be able to say anything to Ted. Now was as good a time as any to test it.

"Sounds like you had a great marriage," Ted said sincerely.

"We were best friends." I felt relieved. "Nothing came between us. He was playful, loving, protective." I glanced away. I almost felt like I was cheating on Michael.

"And great sex to boot!" Ted said.

I turned back and whispered, "Yeah. Great sex."

"Kathryn would just as soon do laundry. We maybe had sex once every six months."

I felt torn again, this time between jealousy of Kathryn

and wanting to know everything about his marriage. Maybe it was voyeuristic, or maybe it was to convince myself I was doing the right thing. Either way, I let him continue.

"And I couldn't even really call it sex." Ted's face showed strain. "That would imply that she was involved. I got the feeling it was more like she was just letting me use her body to masturbate."

I felt heartbroken for him. No one should have to live without sex. I wanted him to know that I wasn't like Kathryn. That if he let me, I could make him the happiest man in the world.

I slid onto his lap and wrapped my arms around his neck, pulling him closer for a long, wine-inspired kiss. I whispered softly into his ear, "Stay the night with me?"

Ted whispered back, "That would be incredible."

I imagined waking up next to a man I had such passion for, making love in the morning, and then off for breakfast in a quaint café. Taking a drive along the coast, maybe going into the city for dinner, and doing it all over again that night.

"But I have a breakfast meeting in the morning, and if I stay, we'll never get any sleep."

The romantic movie in my mind transformed into a horror flick, complete with a gut-wrenching pit in my stomach and, internally at least, a blood-curdling scream. I scrambled for damage control, careful not to let go of the dream too quickly.

"I promise not to keep you up all night. I'm a working girl too, remember? I need my sleep, too."

"Sunny, I really can't tonight. My company is going through a lot of changes right now, and I have to be at the top of my game. There will be other nights for us, I promise."

My face fell. I nibbled Ted's ear. "Just one night?"

Ted started to pull away and get up. "I'm sorry, Sunny. I really am. In fact, I should probably get going before it gets too late. I don't want to be too tired driving home."

The rejection was new to me, more bitter because I cared about him so much. I'd send any other man walking, if he treated me like this, but Ted was different. I was falling in love with him. I'd never felt this submissive, not even with Michael. "Why don't we take a shower together? That should wake you up."

Ted smiled. "Now that sounds better than dessert."

Feeling empowered yet helpless, confident yet fearful, sexy yet tawdry, I led Ted upstairs, where we undressed and showered together. As we sensually massaged each other with body wash and made love in the steamy cascades of water, I couldn't help convincing myself I'd never had it so good.

Chapter 33
On the Outside Looking In

I rolled over in bed and unconsciously reached over to the pillow next to me. I jumped up and surveyed the bed. No Michael. No Ted. Nobody.

I checked the clock—8 A.M.—and headed downstairs to the kitchen, where the dirty dinner dishes still sat on the table, covered in cold, gelled food. Scummy pots covered the stove, next to dirty glasses and serving trays on the counter. A fly landed on the serving dish, then moved on to the table.

"How could something so romantic become so disgusting?"

Koho barked, then wagged his tongue as I took two plates from the table and set them down for Koho to lick clean.

After starting a pot of coffee, double strength, I waded through the dirty dishes. In a routine honed from years of repetition, I rinsed and washed the stack of dishes, cleared and cleaned the counters and, by the time the coffee was brewed, had the kitchen looking sparkling clean. I took a clean mug from the cupboard and poured a cup of steaming, hot coffee, then sat at the table and relished my first sip of brew.

As the taste of coffee invigorated me, I wondered at how good I was feeling, how comfortable my situation with Ted was. "I don't need to set up house with him," I thought, surprising herself. "I'm content having him come and go, living my own life. It's the best of both worlds. Great romance, great sex, and the freedom to live my life. How did I get to this point? How did I come to value my independence so much?" Ted was the perfect relationship for me. He cared for me deeply, but didn't expect me to do his laundry and clean up after him. It had been a long time since I was in one, but maybe this was what serious relationships were like today. The phone rang. "Speak of the devil."

Taking another sip of coffee, I reached for the phone on the counter, smiled and answered with speakerphone.

"Good morning, sweetie-pie," I chimed. "You're a little early today."

"It's me," Joel's voice answered.

"Joel, I was expecting … "

"I don't want to know, Mom."

"You should be happy for me. I'm having fun."

"I am happy for you. I just don't need to know every detail."

"Well, then tell me about your love life. I never get enough details."

"I'm getting married."

I banged my coffee cup down, sending a small black wave over the rim and down the side of the cup. "Married! What?"

"Well, actually, I'm going to get engaged."

The tension with Yolanda and the whole Mafia thing ran quickly through my mind, but those thoughts were drowned out by jubilation. "Joel, that's fantastic!" A sense of pride overcame me. Accomplishment, really. The boys had been on their own and doing well for years now, but getting married? A stable, settled life? What mother wouldn't want that for her son?

"I need your help, Mom. Picking out a ring."

A tear begin to slide down my cheek. As many times

as I'd cried in the last ten years, it felt good to finally have tears of joy.

"Joel." I choked up. "There's nothing I'd love more." I realized this was not just a defining moment in my relationship with Joel, it was also the very thing needed to mend the fence with Yolanda. Far from being worried about the way Yolanda had been acting toward me, I felt certain that Joel and Andrea getting married would make everything right again. After all, we were going to be family for real now.

"Can you meet us at Fortunoff's at noon?"

"I'll be there with bells on."

I walked into Fortunoff's a half hour early, hoping to get a jumpstart on the ring shopping. I was so excited. This was a time-honored tradition, and one I felt proud to finally participate in. A mother helping her son pick out a ring for his intended. With a deep breath and an ear-to-ear smile, I pushed through the door of the legendary jeweler and stepped into a roomful of diamond ring showcases.

"Sunny, what are you doing here?"

I turned my head and saw Yolanda, standing in front of three diamond rings on a black velvet pillow. Next to her was Andrea, who rolled her eyes. My swell of excitement deflated like a pin-pricked balloon.

"Yolanda!" I tried to hide my confusion. Why is Andrea here? Isn't Joel going to surprise her? Are Andrea and Yolanda here for something else?

"I'm supposed to meet Joel here," I finally said, as noncommittal as possible. "What are you two ladies doing?"

Andrea sighed loudly, and then stepped away, pretending to be interested in another display. Cubic

Zirconia? No way is Andrea looking at those. She's avoiding me.

"Do you remember that crystal flower vase I loaned you?" Yolanda curtly asked.

What? I wondered what this could be about. Something was definitely wrong. Better to make the peace, though. For Joel's sake.

"No, but it's great to see you," I said. "You must be swamped. I've left you a dozen messages."

"It's the one with the engraving?"

Why were we standing in the middle of Fortunoff's, talking about vases? Time to stop pulling punches. "Yo, what's this all about? Are you mad at me about something?"

"No, why would I be mad?"

"I don't know, but ever since *Cats*, you've been avoiding me. And now … "

"I'm sorry you didn't enjoy yourself at the play, Sunny. But I need the vase for a party. That's all."

I knew I struck a chord. So that's what this was all about. I had somehow offended the girl with the magical blood, and now I had to pay. "Yo, I had a terrific time. I enjoyed the production. The evening was fantastic. I just made a small comment that the play didn't have all that much of a story."

As Andrea let out a disgusted sigh behind me, Yolanda whispered sternly, "It's just that *Cats* is Andrea's favorite play, Sunny. Your comment belittled her."

Did she just say that? Could they have taken it that seriously? "Yolanda," I said, "if I offended Andrea … "

"She's a big girl. She'll be fine."

Really? So why was she acting like a spoiled 10-year-old? Was it because that was the way she was treated by her entire family? She was the only girl with three brothers to look out for her, and adore her. The whole family believed Andrea was special, and they expected everyone else to see her that way as well.

Still, I pressed forward. "So how about lunch today? I was with Ted last weekend. You and I have a lot of catching up to do."

"I'd love to Sunny, but I'm really quite busy."

"Tomorrow then?"

"The next year is going to be crazy. Really crazy."

"The whole next year? What's going on?"

"Andrea and Joel are engaged. I've got a wedding to plan."

I stepped back, not sure if I should feign surprise or let on that I was baffled at why they already knew this. "Engaged?" As soon as I said it, I felt stupid.

"Oh, didn't Joel tell you?"

Of course Joel told me. What else would I be doing in Fortunoff's? Buying patio furniture? I whispered, "I thought it was a surprise. You know, for Andrea?"

Yolanda waved her hand. "What surprise? I'm getting ready for the engagement party as we speak."

"Well, we should have lunch and plan it together."

"No need. But can you drop off the vase?"

"Of course, Yo. Should I get you an invitation list?"

"Actually, the party's just for our side of the family. Andrea wanted to keep it small. Of course, you and Devin can come if you want."

We can come if we want? This is my son we're talking about, right? What kind of invitation is that? No one else from my side of the family? I was about to speak up when Joel walked in. He started to move toward me, but Andrea cut him off with a big hug and kiss. "I found the perfect ring," Andrea chimed.

Joel, smitten, looked at me but didn't say a word.

I shook my head, then headed for the door. Joel pulled away from Andrea, who not-so-gently pulled him back. "Where are you going? Mom?"

"Just to get some air. I'll be back in a sec." I stepped outside and reached for my cell phone like a cigarette. I stared at the sky, noticing the gray clouds of early winter slowly creeping in. I hit speed dial and waited for the ring.

"This is Ted," his modulated voice said in the phone.

"Ted, I'm glad you're there. I need someone to talk to."

"Can we do it later, Sunny? I'm swamped right now."

"I don't need to talk later, Ted, I need to talk now."

"I know, it's just ... " Ted's voice drifted off. I heard a muffled conversation on the other end of the line. "Sunny," Ted said. "I'm sorry, I have to run."

"Call me later?"

"If I can. Things are really busy here."

"When you get a min ... "

The phone clicked, and a dial tone pierced my ear. Peering through the window, I saw Andrea excitedly showing Joel rings, while Yolanda negotiated with the jeweler. "On the outside looking in," I whispered to myself, then slid into my car and drove off.

I raced down the highway, hands gripping the wheel so tightly my knuckles were white. On edge, I changed lanes to pass a truck, then cut back in a little too closely. The truck blasted its horn. I jumped and then pressed the gas harder. A few turns, eight stop lights and one stop sign, which I ran. Finally, I was at the hockey rink. I sat tapping the steering wheel for half an hour, and then walked inside.

The cold blast from the ice invigorated me, reminding me of the boys growing up. How many hours did I spend in ice rinks? I took a seat in the stands and watched a junior hockey class in session, remembering when Joel first started as a hockey coach, and how his boss was so impressed they made him director of the entire youth program. It's not pro hockey, but it's something. We don't all realize our dreams, but Joel came damn close. And it's not like he didn't give it everything he had. He played in all the right leagues, caught the attention of all the right people. But for all of my justification, for all of my acceptance, I still couldn't help blaming myself for Joel not making the NHL. As wrong as I knew it was, I couldn't help thinking if it weren't for that one trip, that one pro scout, that one afternoon ...

"Mom! What are you doing here?" Joel walked up behind me.

"I can't visit my son at work?"

"Where'd you go? You said you'd be right back."

"You had your hands full."

"Mom, we didn't buy a ring."

"Why not? I thought Andrea had one picked out?"

"They wanted sixty-five hundred for it. I want to take some time, learn about diamonds, then pick a ring and match the setting Andrea likes."

"That's my boy." I smiled, my disappointment drifting away in a cloud of beaming pride. What a man Joel had become. My son. Working, responsibilities, and now this. "And Andrea was OK with this?"

"Not really. She's pretty pissed. But she'll live."

"Just do it fast. Now that she knows, you can't waste any time."

Joel nodded. "We're engaged, Mom."

I wrapped my arms around him. "I couldn't be happier for you." I stood back and smiled at Joel, then swatted him playfully. "But why were Yolanda and Andrea there? The ring is something you should get on your own. And what about surprising her?"

"Andrea doesn't like surprises, Mom. And we've been talking about it for a while, so I figured, why not let her pick the ring?"

"Well, you still need to ask her properly."

Joel nodded, then eyed the lesson on the rink.

"Your father would be proud, sweetie."

Joel changed the subject. "How about some coffee?"

I scoured the photographs in Joel's office—hockey teams, classes, tournaments—all with Joel at the center of the action. A skiing picture of Joel and Andrea sat on his desk next to a picture of Joel, Andrea, Yolanda and Dick at some country club.

"It's just a small party, Mom. Family only." He studied the look on my face. "Immediate family."

That made my expression worse. "Their immediate 'Family' numbers about two hundred, according to the FBI," I said.

"You know what I mean, Mom. It's just their side of the family. Not friends, not anyone from my side. It's almost not even a real engagement party. It's more of a Family party."

"It's just not right, Joel. Marriage is the uniting of families, not the exclusion of one family."

"You and Devin are invited."

"But not Billy? Nancy? Cara? Your cousins? Your friends?"

"I just don't want to do anything to upset Andrea."

"Why would it upset her? It's a party."

Joel looked away, shrinking in his chair.

"You need to say something, Joel. It's your marriage, too."

"I know. I just don't want to rock the boat. Not now."

I could see how uncomfortable Joel was. It bothered me that he was letting this go, but maybe he knew what was best. Besides, it was just an engagement party. It's not like we wouldn't all be together for the wedding. For the sake of the Family, for the sake of not starting out the marriage with a big, fat black mark, I decided to let it go too. Joel's a good boy. He knows when to stand up and when to give in. This is one of the times to give in.

"Well, let them have their little party."

"Are you sure, Mom?"

"Yes, I'm sure. But just so you know, I'm planning on having an engagement party for our side of the family, too. And you and Andrea need to be there."

"We will, Mom. Don't worry." Joel was visibly relieved, and it made me feel good. Somehow, despite everything I'd been through, I had learned to be a good parent. I knew how to help my boys, how to push them through their obstacles, how to guide them through their challenges. I knew how to make them feel good about themselves. I was, I thought to myself, much like Michael as a parent.

"So who else is invited?" Joel asked, trying to be nonchalant.

I smiled. "Yes, Andrea's immediate family is invited. It wouldn't be a family party without them." I couldn't resist that last dig, although Joel pretended not to hear. I liked the idea that he knew his mother was taking the high road. How do I teach my children? By setting an example. I have to live the way I want them to live. I have to lead the way.

Chapter 34
The Boss of the Ring

Yolanda opened her front door and didn't say a word. I handed her the vase. "Isn't it exciting, Yo?"

Yolanda took the vase without expression. "Thanks." She started to close the door, but I held my hand out.

"Yo, you said we could talk."

"I changed my mind."

I felt the anger burning beneath my skin but tried to hide it. "We need to talk, Yo. Things have been strange between us."

"Come in if you want. I'm doing dishes anyway. I guess I can listen to you at the same time."

I walked through the door, remembering the first time I came to the house. A bear hug from Yolanda, who didn't even know me at the time. A welcome into their house, drinks, talk, limos, Broadway shows. How could things have changed so much? And why?

"Yo, tell me what I did wrong. With the kids getting married …"

"Married? I thought Joel changed his mind."

"What?" I was taken by surprise.

"Well, we haven't seen a ring yet. How can they get married without a ring?"

I realized these were just more dramatics. "Joel just wants to make sure it's the perfect ring."

"I had the perfect ring picked out," Andrea curtly said, walking toward me and scowling. "You talked him out of it."

"Me? Joel wanted to shop around, that's all. It's a big step. He wants to make sure he does it right."

"Well, who the fuck made you boss of the ring?" Angelo, Yolanda's oldest son, took the right flank beside me. I was surrounded.

"No one. Joel made the decision by himself. He'll get the ring. He just wants to find the right one."

"Well, I got a guy," Angelo said, scratching his unshaven face, then running fingers through his greasy, unwashed, sandy hair. "A friend of the Family. He's bringing some rocks. Joel can pick one from there."

"If that's what Joel wants," I said, "its fine with me."

Picking his teeth with a toothpick, Angelo sneered before turning his back on me and leaving the room. Glancing at her brother, Andrea's drawn face pinched as her eyes threw darts at me. A sniff, and she walked away.

I took a deep breath and turned back to Yolanda. "What's going on, Yo? It's me here. You can talk to me."

"I really gotta get these dishes done, Sunny." Yolanda walked away, leaving me alone in the foyer. I turned to leave, when Joel walked in the front door, followed by an unwashed, fatter version of Angelo.

"Hey, Mom," Joel says. "I didn't know you'd be here. This is The Turk, a friend …"

"Of Angelo's. I know."

The Turk walked into the living room and dropped a dozen diamonds on the coffee table. "Take your pick. Not a dud in the batch."

Andrea, attracted by the glitter of jewelry, re-entered the room. She pounced on the diamonds, admiring each in rapid succession. Joel, on the other hand, picked them up one at a time, holding them up to the light and examining them like a pro. He'd been doing his homework.

Angelo elbowed The Turk, "A regular DeBeers, this

one."

I could tell that nobody in the Family wanted me involved, so I tried to stay out of it, but from where I sat, they looked like junk stones. Oversized and inauthentic, just like the mother of the bride-to-be.

"They're all so beautiful," Andrea chimed.

"I don't know," Joel said. "They're a little cloudy."

"Cloudy?" said The Turk. "These are grade-A diamonds."

"Diamonds aren't graded by letters," Joel said.

"It's an expression," Angelo said. "Give me a break, here."

"What'd ya want for three grand?" The Turk started to pick up his diamonds. "You can do better? Be my guest."

"Joel," Andrea begged.

"Don't worry, I'll find the right diamond. I saw one at Fortunoff's." He leaned over to kiss Andrea, but she pushed him away and stormed out of the room. Angelo gave me a look so vicious it chilled me.

Yolanda placed an arm around her son's shoulders, matching his look, "A shame you can't stay for dinner, Sunny."

I set plates of spaghetti on the table for Joel and Devin, then served one for myself and joined them at the kitchen table.

"How could you let them talk to me like that?" I asked.

"Mom!" Joel rolled his eyes. "That was two weeks ago. Why are you bringing it up now?"

"Because I haven't talked to you for two weeks. You don't call, you don't come by."

"I'm here now."

"So am I," Devin said, "if anyone wants to hear about my life."

"I'd love to," Joel said.

"When are you going to ask her to marry you, anyway?" I asked Joel.

"I love you, too, Mom," Devin smiled.

"I need a ring," Joel said.

"Well, get it already. You're going to drive that girl crazy. And they're going to blame me for it!"

"Mom," Joel said, "you're being paranoid."

"Paranoid? You were there, Joel. You saw the way they treated me. Yolanda pushed me out the door! And before you got there, that Angelo actually asked me 'who da fuck mayd'ju da boss udda ring'!" Try as I might, I still could not quite capture his Neanderthal inflection. "By the way, I don't appreciate being called a Jew Bitch.

Devin looked at Joel, who shook his head 'no.' I saw it and swallowed my anger, along with a bite of spaghetti. I just wanted to have a nice dinner with my sons. In silence, we ate.

"I did get a ring," Joel finally said.

"So give it to her," Devin said.

"I don't know how. It has to be perfect. Angelo says he asked his wife under a bridge at the river."

"Forget Cro-Magnon man." I set down my fork. "Why don't you give it to her at the hockey rink? After all, you did meet her there. It has to be special for you two, not some loudmouthed Mafia wannabe."

"Take it easy on the Family," Joel countered. "We all need to get along."

I shoved a forkful of spaghetti into my mouth,

although my appetite was gone. It stopped me from blurting out my disbelief that Joel would defend them over a tiny comment I had made, yet he didn't seem at all disturbed by their treatment of me. What was happening to my son?

Chapter 35
Rules of Engagement

The engagement party I threw for Joel and Andrea was an elegant vision in silver and white. Huge heart-shaped, silver Mylar balloons were tied together with plush white velvet ribbon. Silver candelabras held 16-inch pearlescent white taper candles. Outside, I had draped rented tables with white paisley table cloths and covered the chairs in matching fabric. Each chair had been draped in a sash tied in the back into an elaborate bow. Every table had silver bud vases holding miniature white roses; white floating candles in the shape of roses floated in silver, mosaic bowls. The food tables were strewn with tiny, heart-shaped silver confetti and faux silver rings. For party favors, I had purchased exquisite white embossed boxes, filled them with silver Jordan almonds and tied each one with ribbon topped with a flower. An enormous white banner, inscribed with "Congratulations Joel and Andrea" in flowing silver letters, was draped from tree to tree in the backyard. While a DJ blasted music over a rented dance floor on the lawn, the Family mingled with my family. All except Angelo, who was alone in the dark living room watching football from Michael's old chair.

Outside, Nancy handed Joel and Andrea glasses of champagne. "An ice skate?" Nancy asked Joel. "You put the ring in an ice skate?"

"It was romantic," Joel said, putting his arm around Andrea to pull her closer. "When she tried to put the skate on, she found the ring."

"That's great!" Nancy said. Nudging Joel with a kidding gesture, she asked, "Did it smell like feet?"

Andrea pulled slightly away from Joel and eyed me at the bar. "It was his mom's idea," Andrea said curtly.

"It was my idea," Joel protested. "And it was a brand new skate."

Andrea sipped champagne. "Your mom gave you the idea."

"My mom told me to ask at the ice rink, because we met there. The rest was my idea."

"Well," Nancy said, realizing her kidding was getting Joel in trouble, "I think it's romantic. And I'm really happy for you both."

"Where'd your mom get this DJ?" Andrea asked "He doesn't play anything good."

"He's a DJ," Joel said. "He'll play whatever you want." Nancy gave Joel a dirty look, but he pretended not to see it.

"We're having karaoke later," Joel said. "That'll be fun."

"I'm not singing." Andrea rolled her eyes disgustedly.

At the bar, Yolanda and Dick stepped on either side of me, and Dick ordered a whiskey from the bartender.

"Enjoying the party?" I asked, immediately regretting it.

"I've been to better," Dick grunted.

"It's nice," Yolanda said politely. "Shame Frankie and Doris couldn't be here. That's one daughter-in-law I'd be better off without."

"It's her birthday," I said diplomatically. "She wanted to spend time with her family."

"We're her Family now," Yolanda snapped. I instinctively glanced at Joel, who was being led away from the crowd by Andrea.

"You never know in a marriage," Yolanda said to

Dick, who nodded.

I melted into the crowd and tried to lose myself in the festivities. I danced, sang a little karaoke, got dinner from the buffet line and chatted with my family and friends. It felt good to have them all there: Nancy, Billy's daughters Kristen and Brittany; my girlfriends Kim, Gloria, Marcia; all the people who were important to me.

But I couldn't help imagining how this party would pale in comparison to what the Family would do. I had planned a gorgeous, elegant party that anyone would to be proud of, but I didn't have the budget for the ostentatious, over-the-top blowout I felt certain Yolanda would host. I couldn't help feeling I wasn't good enough for this Family, or maybe the truth was, I wasn't bad enough for them. Either way, something just wasn't right. And I couldn't get Yolanda's words about Frankie and Doris out of my head: 'We're her Family now. We're her Family now.'

Ten cars lined the Family driveway, all sparkling clean luxury cars. I pulled my blue Accord into the line and headed for the front door. Just as I stepped onto the porch, the door flew open, and Yolanda opened her arms wide. "Sunny! So good to see you."

What a difference a week makes, I thought. "Nice to see you, Yolanda."

"Come in. Everyone's waiting."

I walked in, half glad that Yolanda was acting civil again, and half worried that she was so unpredictable.

Andrea appeared from the kitchen with a smile. "Hi, Sunny."

I wore an off-white wrap blouse over a slinky fitted skirt and high-heeled pumps. I eyed Andrea's drab pants and sweater. Didn't anyone in the Family ever dress up?

"Andrea, you look like you could be getting married today," I said politely. "You're beautiful."

"Thanks." Andrea blushed.

"Hi Mom," said Joel, walking up from behind and dressed just as casually as Andrea.

"Hi sweetie," I said, kissing him. I was amazed at how handsome he looked but didn't mention it. Why does everyone seem more comfortable in this house than in mine? Even my own son seems to be happier here. That's why I couldn't compliment Joel's looks. I couldn't validate the fact that he seemed more at home here than at home.

"Who needs a drink?" Dick said, sounding more cordial than usual.

"Maybe a Cosmo?" I thought it might relax me.

Yolanda led me outside, where several uniformed female servers carried sushi and champagne on silver trays. "Let's sit by the pool. We need to talk."

I suddenly felt like a child headed for a scolding.

Yolanda wasted no time after sitting me down at the patio table. "Sunny, we need a reception hall."

"I know some great halls." I lit up. "I used to have a party planning business before Michael …"

"… We're thinking the Rockfield Country Club," Yolanda cut in. "We need to fit four hundred and fifty people, and it's the only place I can think we can do that without going to some banquet room."

"Well," I said, rather unsure of what I should say. "I've never been there …"

"It's very private," Yolanda offered.

"I'm sure it's very nice." I was trying hard to cooperate.

"Nice? It's the classiest country club in New Jersey."

"With four hundred and fifty people, though, won't

it be expensive?"

"That reminds me," Yolanda scooted closer. "Doris's parents gave us ten thousand toward her and Frankie's wedding."

What does that mean, I wondered. Is she asking me for money?

"I'm sure you want Joel and Andrea to have only the best. Right, Sunny?"

"Well ..." I mentally calculated whether I had enough money in my savings to write a check, while at the same time wondering why the middle-class mother of the groom would have to contribute ten thousand dollars to a wedding paid for by the wealthy parents of the bride. With all that Mafia money, how they could be so blatant and rude to ask for it? "I suppose I could help."

"Ten thousand. That's not help. It's a token gesture," Yolanda laughed.

I didn't join in Yolanda's laughter. To me, ten thousand dollars is a lot of money. Certainly more than I could afford to give. But maybe it was also a chance to mend fences. With a ten thousand dollar peace offering, perhaps I could have a little involvement in the wedding plans. "Could I give you one thousand a month for ten months?"

Yolanda rolled her eyes, then nodded. "Sure, why not?"

"Thanks," I said, although I wasn't sure why.

"Now," Yolanda said, "Joel doesn't want to get married in the church. So we'll have the wedding at the country club. My uncle will perform a non-denominational service."

Her uncle, I thought. Father Louis Gigante—the Catholic priest, the brother of Mafia godfather Vincent

Gigante. I shivered, but then remembered that Yolanda said a non-denominational service. Maybe this will be OK. They're honoring Joel's wishes. That's class. They easily could have forced a Catholic church wedding, and no one could've stopped them. But they're taking Joel's feelings into account, and that was the important thing. I'd always had the sense that Joel was ashamed of his Jewish heritage. If he went as far as to say that he didn't want to get married in a church, it's a sign that he's finally embracing his Judaism.

I smiled. This is good. This is going to work out after all. I glanced over at Andrea leading Joel away from the jukebox and onto the dance floor for a slow dance to "Up Where We Belong."

Chapter 36
If You Lie Down with Dogs

Oak trees lined the street like golden red-brown mountains, dropping a myriad of autumn colors to the browning grass below. Even the air looked different in the fall, I thought ,as I drove toward the Family estate in the distance. It's cleaner, fresher. It made me feel like anything was possible.

I smiled at the thought, remembering how Yolanda offered to have the wedding in the reception hall instead of the church, simply because that's what Joel wanted. After the years of emotional struggle and despair following Michael's death, the financial terror of not being able to find a job, the fear of raising the boys alone, the only real challenge I faced now was feeling suddenly left out of Joel's life, and the Family's life. I had a boyfriend, I had a great job, I had my own side business that was starting to catch on, the boys were on their own and doing great. And now, Yolanda was beginning to open up again, too. If skipping the church wasn't enough evidence, inviting me to help choose the wedding dress definitely was.

I felt like I was a part of the Family again. Even if it did cost me ten thousand dollars. It was worth it. If that's what it took to keep the peace, to be able to participate in the plans for the wedding, it's was small price to pay. Things were changing, I thought to myself with a smile.

I got out of the car and was hit by a blast of cold fall air.

Yolanda swung open the front door, approaching with a hug that was all too familiar and pleasantly comforting to me. "Thanks for inviting me here for this, Yo."

"Hey, it's a wedding," Yolanda said, walking me past the dining room, where two seamstresses were tending to what had to be over twenty wedding dresses hung throughout the room. In the living room, Dick sat on a couch in sweat bottoms and a white tank top, the kind of shirt the kids called "wife-beaters." He eyed Andrea standing in front of a six-foot fireplace, modeling a long, flowing, white lace gown and veil.

"It's beautiful," I beamed, sitting next to Dick on the couch.

"I hate it," Andrea answered before making a quick exit from the room. Hate it? It was stunning enough to be on the cover of *Modern Bride*, but hey, who was I to say?

"There are plenty more to choose from," Yolanda said.

"Where's Joel?" I asked.

"It's bad luck. The groom can't see the bride in the dress until the wedding." Yolanda handed me a Diet Coke, and a few minutes later, Andrea came out in a new dress.

I eyed the strapless fit, the beading, satin and lace and let out a sigh. "It's even more beautiful than the last one."

"Too stuffy." Andrea turned and stomped out of the room. Okay, now I had caught on to Andrea's game. The rules were, whatever Sunny likes, I'll hate. Did any of these dresses come with matching diapers and a pacifier?

"We got your check," Dick said to me. "It was short."

"Short?" I took a nervous gulp of Diet Coke.

"It was only a grand." Dick burped. "Should've been ten grand."

I can't believe these people, I thought, quickly turning to Yolanda, who patted me on the leg. Are they purposely trying to embarrass me?

"Sunny's making payments," Yolanda told Dick. "One thousand a month for ten months."

"Why?" Dick asked. *Why do you think, you low-class sack of excrement?*

"It's just what she's doing."

I wanted to leave. I wanted to hit him even more, but I resisted. *I'll ignore this man's crass behavior, for Joel's sake.*

"Da, da, da-da!" Andrea strolled out singing the Wedding March, wearing a white chiffon, low-cut dress and a smile from ear to ear.

"A little revealing, don't you think?" Yolanda asked.

"I'm not your little girl anymore." Andrea smiled.

"But, Daddy's little girl, always. Right, Princess?" Dick said to her with what was probably the most genuine smile I had ever seen from him.

I noticed Dick staring at Andrea's cleavage. The dress was not one of the more elegant ones. But I knew just how to handle this. "I think it's very nice," I said. "And you can definitely pull it off. I think it's the one."

Andrea's opinion instantly changed. She eyed the short train on her dress and turned up her nose. "It makes me look cheap."

As Andrea disappeared again, Yolanda pulled out an overstuffed day planner. "Sunny," Yolanda said, "you're going to be so happy. We found a beautiful church for the service."

"Church?" I suddenly felt alarmed. "I thought we weren't doing the church."

"Andrea wanted to walk down a long aisle," Yolanda said matter-of-factly. "I'm sure Joel will understand."

"I don't know," I said. "He felt pretty strongly about

it."

"I'll handle it," Dick said. "All you have to do is look at my little girl and you start humming 'isn't she lovely' in your head. She was born to walk down a long aisle and make everyone there fell blessed just to be in her presence. It's a good thing she never wanted to be an actress. She would have put that Angelina Jolie bitch to shame." He said this last with a smirk.

I burned inside, falling silent. It wasn't just the slap in the face about the church. I knew now they never intended to have the wedding at a reception hall. It was just a way to make it look like they were listening to Joel. But Dick saying he'll take care of it? Like he held some kind of sway with Joel that I didn't? Like he was some type of father figure who knows just what to say to convince Joel to have a wedding in a church? Or maybe he was just going to hold a gun to Joel's head.

"Everyone will be happy," Yolanda said, avoiding eye contact with me.

Once again, I had to let it go. It was a major issue, but this one was for Joel to take up with them personally. I remained silent and watched Dick's football game on TV. After a few plays of the game, Andrea walked in again.

"You like it?" Andrea spun around.

"It's beautiful," Yolanda said, getting up to view it closer.

"Is the train too long?" Andrea asked.

"Doesn't matter," Yolanda said. "We can put on a train from a different dress. We can change the veil, the sleeves, the straps ... anything. That's what the seamstresses are for. It has to be perfect for my baby."

Even with anger and resentment creeping through

my body, I couldn't help being overwhelmed by how beautiful Andrea looked in this dress. After all, this was to be my daughter-in-law.

"You're radiant," I said, holding back a tear.

"It sucks," Andrea said, beating her well-worn path out of the room.

As the tear coursed down my cheek, the phone rang. Dick answered. After a short conversation, he handed the phone to Yolanda. "It's that Jew bitch from Gino's team."

"That what?" I asked, incredulously.

"I was talking to my wife," Dick said.

"I don't care who you were talking to, you can't talk that way in front of me."

Dick seemed a bit taken aback, then shrugged his shoulders. "What's the problem? I didn't call you a Jew bitch." "I'm sure you do behind my back".

Yolanda took the phone into the other room. I sat upright on the couch. This one I wasn't going to let go. "It's offensive to hear you talk like that, Dick. It's an affront to everything I believe in, not to mention rude and disgusting behavior," I said. "I won't stand for it."

"You don't like it, leave." Dick laughed, downing his beer and heading to the kitchen.

I sat alone on the couch, feeling like I'd been punched in the stomach and kicked in the head. There were so many things wrong, I thought. A family that once took me in as their own now treated me like shit. They're rude and disrespectful, and Joel's marrying into this? How long can I keep the peace? How long can I swallow my pride and not rock the boat? Is this what the Mafia is like? I've seen *The Godfather*. They treat their Family well. This has nothing to do with them being in the Mob, even if they say they're not. These people are just appalling. I don't care how much money they have. These are not the kind of people I want my son involved with, Mafia or not.

A hand patted my thigh. I jumped, then realized Yolanda was sitting beside me again.

"Pay no attention to Dick," Yolanda said. "He doesn't mean it."

"Yolanda, I won't stand for that kind of talk. If this is the way things are going to be between us …"

"Of course not," Yolanda interrupted. "We're Family. We've got our kids to think about."

"I just don't feel settled about this, Yo. Things have been so strange. I thought the wedding would help, but now I'm not so sure. I don't know what to tell Joel."

Yolanda put her arm around me. "There's nothing to tell Joel, except that we're all going to be one, big happy Family."

"That's all I want," I said. "For Joel's sake."

"Just like old times." Yolanda smiled, gave me a quick hug, then stood. "I'll go check on Andrea."

As I left the room, Dick walked back in with a new beer. He saw me and stopped. "You still fuckin' here?" I shook my head, trying to block him out, trying to remember what Yolanda said and trying even harder to trust her. Mumbling that Jew Bitch.

"I said, are you still fuckin' here?" "When the fuck are you leaving?" Dick didn't sound like Joel's father-in-law. He sounded like a gorilla without an iota of intelligence.

I jumped up. "I'm fucking leaving, all right?" As I passed the dining room, Yolanda looked up from Andrea's dress and eyed me, but didn't say a word. I walked out the front door and was hit by another frigidly cold blast of wind.

In wool slacks and a brown fall coat, I watered flowers on my backyard deck while Joel sat on a deck chair, playing with Koho. "It's nothing, Mom," Joel said, petting Koho, who barked back at him.

"Nothing is nothing, Joel. This is something."

"What?"

"I'm not crazy, Joel, there's something wrong with those people."

"You must have said something to them."

I put down my water can and walked over to Joel, hoping my close proximity would somehow shake sense into him. "You need to stand up to them, Joel. You can't let them walk all over you."

"I'm not the one complaining, Mom."

"So you're going to let them talk to me that way? He said 'Jew bitch.' That's OK with you?"

"You said he wasn't talking to you."

"Oh, my God, that's not the point! It was a disgusting, anti-Semitic remark!"

"If I was there, I would have said something."

"Would you have? Well, then, it's not too late, Joel. You can still say something."

"It's kind of after-the-fact at this point." Joel got up and followed Koho to the grass, conveniently away from me.

I saw him backing down, and knew I had to do something to spark the fire in him, or Andrea and this Family were going to eat him alive. "They changed the wedding to a church."

Joel kept petting Koho, who was wagging his tail

excitedly.

"Did you know that, Joel? After you told them you weren't comfortable with a church wedding, after they told you it was OK to have the wedding at the reception hall, they've now made plans for a big church wedding. Did they tell you this?"

"Andrea wants to walk down a long aisle."

"You're Jewish, Joel!"

"I'm not having a Jewish wedding anyway. What's the difference if it's in a reception hall or a church? It means the same thing to me."

"They don't give a damn about what you want! They treat me like shit! They make Jew-hating remarks! Does any of that mean anything to you?"

"Why are you trying to cause trouble, Mom? Can't you just let things be?"

"You think I'm causing this? You think this is all my fault?"

"Well, you're the only one who seems to have a problem with any of it."

In disbelief, I stared at Joel for a tense minute, but he wouldn't turn to meet my eyes. Tears clouding my eyes, I spun towards the house and accidentally kicked the water can into a row of potted begonias, knocking them over. As the porch door slammed, Koho ran up to the fallen begonias and lapped up water from the spilled can.

Chapter 37
Business Affair

I stood in my bedroom in red high heels and a sexy lace-up corset. The fabric was a rich brocade, red roses against deeper red roses, trimmed with black ribbon lace-up treatments in the front and side. I wore a matching G-string, which I had placed for convenient removal instead of black underwear, black garters and lace-topped sheer black stockings. Posing in the mirror, I slowly ran my hands up the body and pushed my breasts together. They almost, but not quite, spilled over the top of low-cut bustier. The dramatic, vivid red color showcased the creamy alabaster of my skin beautifully. I leaned into the mirror, gently applying red lipstick and black mascara.

I took another look at my nearly naked body in the mirror. From my closet, I pulled out a nondescript beige trench coat. I put it on, pulled it tight around my waist and headed for my car.

Feeling exuberant, sexy and in control, I marched through the lobby of Ted's office in my high heels and trench coat, looking like a businesswoman with a mission. I stepped into the elevator, noticing the receptionist whispering to a co-worker as the elevator door shut.

Stepping out on Ted's floor, I headed toward his office. More whispers from secretaries, women in cubicles. I thought I heard someone say 'whore". Were those women looking at me? Was I imagining things? I couldn't be sure, but my confidence started sinking. They can't see what I'm wearing, I assured myself. They can't possibly be talking about me.

I continued my march toward Ted's office, dodging more whispers and dirty looks. I pulled my overcoat even tighter still.

I stopped outside Ted's office door. That's how they know, I realized. I've been here for presentation after presentation, and they've never bought one thing from me. They know Ted's using the presentations as an excuse for us to get together.

I don't care, I said to myself. I'm not going to let a jealous secretary pool ruin my surprise. I stopped outside of Ted's office and through the glass saw that he was meeting with his partner, Martin. They both noticed me at the same time. Martin looked annoyed. Ted looked surprised, and not happily. He opened the door to his office. Before either he or I could speak, his secretary called out.

"Ted, your wife is on line one. She just wants to know if you can pick up some dinner on your way home."

On his way home? He didn't live with her. Why would he be picking up dinner? My face showed confusion, panic. Ted's secretary looked at me triumphantly.

Ted looked alarmed but his voice remained steady. He looked at me while he answered her. "Mary," he said, "tell her I'll call her back." Without missing a beat, he continued. "Sunny, do we have an appointment?" he asked.

"No," I stammered. "I-I-I just got some new samples in. I thought you should be the first to see them."

"It's not a good time, Sunny," Ted said.

"Another time, then." I fled the office, suddenly aware of how cold I was in my skimpy lingerie.

I hadn't been on the road for more than two minutes before my cell phone rang. I hit the hands-free button hard.

"Your wife wants you to pick up dinner?" I almost shouted.

"Sunny, let me explain."

I wanted him to tell me that he was just bringing her some food. That they had to talk about one of their kids, or the bills. That he was doing her a favor, just this once. I wanted him to tell me anything except what he was about to say.

"I knew if I told you I was married, you'd never go out with me."

"You're damn right I wouldn't! You told me you were separated! How dare you!"

"I had to see you! I had to get to know you! My marriage is over! I haven't been in love with Kathryn in a long time. And now, since we've been together...Sunny, I love you."

I had waited to hear him say that for so long. But not like this. Was he just saying it so I would keep on seeing him? Could I ever believe anything he said?

"Ted, I can't be involved with you. I don't date married men. You have a family."

"I love my kids, but that doesn't change how I feel about you."

"But you lied to me! How can I ever trust you again?"

"Just give me a chance. I am going to ask Kathryn for a divorce. I swear it. I want to be with you."

And I wanted to believe that. So badly I could taste it.

"Listen, Sunny, let's spend the weekend together."

"I don't know. .."

"We'll go out of town. I'll tell Kathryn it's for business. I know a great place in Maine."

"I just don't know, Ted. I don't know about anything

anymore."

"Wait, Sunny."

I hung up the phone.

I walked into my bedroom and dropped my purse on the bureau. Slowly, sadly, I peeled off my lingerie. Before I left my house, I thought my outfit had looked enticing and dangerous, but now it just looked like a cheap Halloween costume. Being with Ted had made me feel womanly and confident in a way I hadn't felt in years. More important, I had grown dependent on him as a friend. He knew everything about what was going on in my life. He called me every day, wanting to know how things were going with Joel. Asking about the family, giving me advice and support and mostly just listening. But as much as I needed him, and wanted him, I couldn't get past the thought that he was someone else's, and that he preferred it that way… or, at least, did not care enough about me to choose. That part hurt. Better to find out sooner than later, until I was in too deep to get out…because I would have to get out of a relationship with a married man. I couldn't live with myself, not to mention with him, once I found out who Ted really was: a liar and a cheat.

Why couldn't I find myself a full-time man? There had to be a better way. I had so much to give. Emotionally. Mentally. Physically. Sexually. I could be good for someone.

I knew I wanted a lot. Emotionally. Mentally. Physically. Sexually. I wasn't ashamed of that. I had needs. Ted had met them all. What if I found someone who couldn't meet my needs, but could be there all the time? Would I want that instead? Would I give up the passion of Ted for the stability of a full-time relationship? Can't I have both?

"I wish Michael were here," I whispered. Michael was the full-time and full man.

Chapter 38
Goodbye, Joel

I placed pieces of straw around my festively decorated kitchen table. The six place settings of china and crystal were perfectly placed to enhance the miniature pumpkins, squash, and dried corn cobs scattered upon the table. A cornucopia of fall flowers with leaves and twigs intertwined burst from the center of the table. Orange and yellow cloth napkins sat upright at each place setting, pleated in the shape of fanned turkey feathers.

I heard the "you've got mail!" announcement from the computer in my office. I was pretty sure who it was from, and with a glance at the simmering pots on top of the stove, I made a quick dash to my office to look at the email.

It was from Ted. I opened it, and Bugs Bunny stared up at me. The sound came on, and played a loud "Boing!" The animated card showed Bugs looking at a voluptuous female rabbit. At the sight of her Bugs fell backwards, his eyes bulging out of his head. I had to laugh. Ted loved to surprise me with emails. This one read, "I miss you today. More deeply and more madly in love, Ted." He signed all of his emails that way.

I missed him, too. He was with his family, of course, but I brushed that thought quickly out of my mind and dashed back to the kitchen.

I arranged the small, shallow bowls holding butter pats and moved to the stove to stir pots of creamed corn and homemade cranberry sauce. I tasted the mashed new potatoes and added a touch more of butter and salt. With the ding of the oven, I carefully removed a golden brown, twenty-pound turkey and set it on the counter to cool. It smelled delicious. Oh! The cornbread! I unwrapped my homemade cornbread and sliced it into little golden squares.

I used open hands to brush off any stray crumbs on my funky patchwork vest and blue jeans. I adjusted my chandelier earrings in the reflection on the oven door. "Who needs a man anyway, huh, Koho?"

As Koho barked from my bed, the phone rang. I rushed to the living room, slipping on my black high heels along the way. I picked up the phone, "Happy Thanksgiving!"

Joel's voice answered, "It's me, Mom."

"Joel, sweetie, why don't we talk when you get here? I've got to start the gravy."

"I can't come, Mom."

I stopped cold. My mouth opened to say something, but nothing came out.

"Mom?"

"What do you mean you can't come? Everything's done already. Chris and Claire are on their way. We're going to start soon."

Chris was Joel's childhood best friend. He was driving in from the other side of New Jersey with his pregnant wife, Claire. Certainly Joel would never stand them up.

"I'm going to Andrea's, Mom."

"Joel, you told me you were bringing Andrea here."

"I know, I'm sorry. But Andrea wants to spend her last Thanksgiving with her family."

"We're her family."

"You know what I mean."

"What last Thanksgiving? Is she dying?"

"That's not funny, Mom."

My voice quivered. "I'm not joking, Joel. You promised you'd be here. I've been working for days on this. Everything's ready."

"She wants to be with her mother. It's her last Thanksgiving before we're married."

"Joel, Andrea's family celebrates a lot of holidays that we don't. Christmas Eve, Christmas and Easter. They can have you on all of those days. Can't you take one holiday and spend it with me?"

"Of course, Mom. Just not this one."

"Joel, I've always done Thanksgiving. It's my favorite holiday. Please. I'm asking you. .."

"Mom, don't get carried away. It's not a big deal."

I was devastated, but tried to keep my voice even. "Do you think you can come for dessert? I know it's a long way, but I baked two kinds of pie, and …"

"I don't think so, Mom."

Being diplomatic no longer mattered. "Do you know what you're getting into here, Joel?"

"Don't start with that, Mom." After a long silence, Joel finally said, "We'll all be together at Christmas, Mom. At the Family's house. Like last year."

I held the phone in my lap and whispered, "Goodbye, Joel." As I slowly hung up the phone, Devin walked in, dressed in jeans, a black shirt and black leather jacket. I couldn't help noticing how handsome he looked. Like a big, rugged biker, or a quarterback dressed for an after-game interview..

He saw the look on my face. "What's the matter, Mom?" Devin asked.

"Doesn't matter now," I said. I stood to kiss him, but

fell into his arms crying instead.

Chapter 39
Woman Overboard

The sun rose over the Chesapeake Bay, reflecting off the blue November water like a dull mirror. I sat in a white Turkish bathrobe, sipped coffee and stared out the balcony window of the Marriott hotel, soaking up the rare euphoric feeling radiating through me. Ted, in a matching bathrobe with a Marriott logo on the pocket, hugged me from behind. Together we savored the magnificent view of the bay, dotted with luxury yachts. Ted kissed my neck. "We're going to be so sore we'll have to take a week off."

"If the next two nights are like last night," I said, settling back into his arms, "we'll have to take the whole month off."

"Happy?" Ted kissed my neck.

"Never happier." I smiled. "Just to be away from the whole mess of ... "

"Ssshhh." Ted hugged me tighter. "Don't think about it."

"But you're the only one I can talk to about it. The only one who doesn't think I'm crazy."

It was true. Through all of the ugliness with Yolanda, Dick and Andrea, Ted remained my confidante and support system. He called every day to see how I was, and how my relationship was going with Joel. Now that everything seemed to be crashing down around me, I needed him more than ever. He took me away on luxurious weekend trips, hoping that exquisite hotel rooms with spectacular views would distracted me from my pain. But for me, the most treasured thing was he was a friend who genuinely cared.

"People think weddings are joyous occasions, and they are. But there's a lot of stress involved too. Once the wedding day rolls around, everything will fall into place."

"I hope so. I hate to see Joel get stuck in a marriage he's not happy in." I sensed Ted pull back a bit. I reached to touch his arm, but he glanced at his watch.

"I have to make a call. I'll be right back."

He stepped into the other room. He was dialing the wife, and his facial expression told me he realized what time it was and he was truly concerned about his wife. Turning back to look out the window, I realized for the first time that Ted loved his wife. Maybe he isn't happy with her, but he loves her. He loves me too, or at least professes to. Can he love both of us? Is all the feeling on my side only? Could he really just be here for the sex? Is there no future here?

Feeling a bit faint, I leaned back in the chair. Am I kidding myself? I'm available for him whenever he needs me, and he's available for me whenever he needs me. How could I not see it?

"I don't care," I whispered. "I love him."

"Ready to buy a yacht?" Ted stepped out onto the balcony.

I sat up suddenly. "We're not buying a yacht."

"No," Ted said. "But don't tell the yacht dealers that."

Ted and I moved from one yacht in the boat show to the next. Each one bigger than the last, and each with an exotic spread of champagne and caviar.

"Are you buying today?" Every salesman asked Ted the same question.

"Yep, by oh-five-hundred hours," Ted told every salesman. That brought out the better champagne and the best caviar. After the eighth boat, we were stumbling back to our room, laughing, kissing and falling into bed.

"Don't even think about sleeping," I whispered to Ted as I unbuckled his pants.

"Who's thinking?" Ted moaned.

I sat in a chair by the window, half staring at the bay, half staring at Ted who looked like a log on the bed. For what seemed like hours, I had sat wondering about Joel marrying Andrea, marrying into a Mafia Family. I wondered when Devin would find the girl he wanted to marry. About how my family was changing. Grandkids soon. That alone was worth making peace with the Family, no matter how much I had to swallow to do it.

I thought about Ted. I couldn't let him go. Did he love me the way I loved him? I didn't know, but loved just loving him. I wanted him in my life, and I would have to fight for it. My argument with myself led me to wonder why was it me who always had to compromise to keep the people I love in my life? When do I get my way?

The view of the harbor from our room was spectacular. I watched the water in the bay turn from grey to golden orange to black, while the lights of the harbor emerged from dark specks of nothing into bright, sparkling diamonds.

I peeked between two candles and a vase of breadsticks at Ted, who was absentmindedly chewing his steak and staring blindly into space. I wondered where his mind was. It definitely wasn't with me.

As I took a nervous sip of wine, a gray-haired, bearded man in a paisley vest and red bow tie strolled up to the table strumming a mandolin. Before we could speak, he broke into a poignant, melancholy song in Italian. It's a love song, I thought, but a sad one. I smiled at Ted, whose eyes looked sad. "Do you know Italian?" I asked.

Ted shook his head. "I don't have to."

As the old man strummed the last note of his song, Ted handed him five dollars. "What was the song about?" Ted asked him.

The singer bowed his head and translated the words: "My love, my wife. Most wonderful woman on earth. But I didn't know it then. I cheated on her. She found out and left me. Then my girlfriend left me. Two blessings of love in my life, and I ruined both of them. Nothing's been the same since." The man slowly walked away.

"Ted," I whispered. "Let's get the check."

We walked out to the fountain in front of the restaurant. I looked at Ted, who leaned in for a long, soft, kiss that reminded me of everything I loved about him. The passion, the spontaneity, the intimacy, the freedom to be bold, the exhilaration of damning the rules and living life to the fullest. Ted handed me a penny to throw in. I closed my eyes, smiled and threw the penny high in the air. It landed on the rim of the cracked plaster fountain and bounced onto the driveway.

Chapter 40
The Breaking Point

Billy sat in my living room, dressed in a gray suit and blue shirt open at the collar that he might have worn for a night of gambling. He poured a Jim Beam on the rocks, because I didn't have Wild Turkey. "Ready for that drink yet?"

I was sitting on the floor wrapping Christmas presents and held up my hands. "Still too early for me."

"It's five o'clock somewhere." Billy sipped his bourbon and sat on the couch. Outside the window behind him, a noon snow fell fast and heavy.

"You should slow down," I said, not just talking about drinking.

"Why start now?"

"Because you're young enough to change your life."

"Fifty-six isn't young enough for anything."

"You look seventy."

"Well, aren't you in the holiday spirit."

"I'm worried about you, Billy.

I was. Earlier that year, Billy had been diagnosed with cancer. In true Billy style, he hadn't changed his lifestyle one iota. He simply added in the radiation treatments. Billy had always lived his life beating the odds. We all knew he'd win against cancer, too. Still, I wanted to care for him, to bring him soup and fresh vegetables, drive him to his treatments, give him vitamins and make sure he exercised.

"You look pale…pasty. You get winded walking from the car to the house. You smoke too much, you drink too much, you stay out too late."

"When's the last time you got laid?"

I went back to wrapping. So much for Florence Nightingale.

"I'm sorry, Skunkie, but you knew what you were getting into from the beginning."

"I don't regret it. I just wish I had gotten more time to spend with him."

"Come to Vegas with me. I'll find you a man in three hours."

"Stay here with me. I'll get you healthy in three months."

"I'd never survive here. It's too suburban. Too much happiness."

I laughed. "Just stay until the wedding."

"That's nine months from now."

"I could use the support."

"You'll have my support. It'll just be from Vegas."

"Well, promise me you'll slow down."

"I may be a drunk and a gambler, but I've never lied to you, and I'm not about to start now."

I tied a bow on the last present and added it to a large pile of presents.

"When did you start getting into Christmas?" Billy asked.

"Last year. It's fun. The Family has a big party."

"I thought you were pissed at them."

"I just don't understand them. They're hot and cold. They like me, they don't like me. They're nice to me, they're not nice to me."

"Sounds like a craps table."

"I'm just trying to keep the peace, for Joel. And they invited me to Christmas, so ... "

"You spend a boatload of money you don't have on

presents for them."

"I just have to make a few extra sales this month, that's all."

"Well, how many people are there? You've got enough presents here for the cast of *Cats*."

"Not funny, Billy." I started pointing out presents one by one, partly to fill in Billy, and partly to double-check that I hadn't missed anyone. "There's Yolanda and Dick, of course Andrea and her brother Gino, Angelo, her other brother and his wife, Nikki."

"You get presents for her brothers? And their wives?"

"It's a big Family party. I can't leave anyone out." I went back to the list. "There's Frankie and Doris, Joel ... "

"You got a present for Joel? He's Jewish."

"How would it look if I didn't get my own son a Christmas present?"

"The same as it's looked for the last 27 years."

The phone rang. I jumped to get it, knocking a vase with fresh-cut flowers to the floor. I scooped up the cordless phone and headed for the kitchen. "Hello?"

"Sunny." Yolanda's voice blasted through the phone.

"Yo, I was just talking about you."

"All good I hope."

"Of course." I grabbed a dishtowel from the over door handle and walked back into the living room.

"Sunny, listen, we're going to keep Christmas small this year. Just Family."

I started to wipe up the water on the carpet. "No problem, Yo. I'm not bringing anyone."

"But," Yolanda continued, "we're going to get together for dinner on the twenty-eighth. You should come then."

I stopped wiping. Was I just uninvited to Christmas? Is she serious? I'm not going to let her off that easy. "Well, Yo, two dinners in three days is a bit much, but I'll be there for both." I almost enjoyed the silence on the other end, and sat in a chair, waiting.

"Sunny, you don't need to come Christmas day. You're right. It's too much."

"I don't mind," I said, getting annoyed.

"Truthfully, we're going to keep it just immediate Family."

"Do you not want me there, Yo? Just say it." I noticed Billy watching me and turned away. More silence on the phone. I waited.

"Just come on the twenty-eighth. We'll have dinner."

"I've got presents for everyone, Yo. What am I supposed to do with these?"

"Bring them on the twenty-eighth." Yolanda hung up.

I slammed down the phone. "Bitch."

"Trouble in paradise?" Billy asked.

Tears welled in my eyes. "She says I can't come to Christmas."

Billy took a drink. Noticing the pain in my face, he knew better than to joke. "You're better off without them, Skunkie. Trust me, I know about these people. You don't want to play around with the Family. We're talking about the daughter of Vincent 'The Chin' Gigante. You do what you're told."

"Do you think I need to be afraid of them, Billy?"

"I really don't know. I don't think they'd do anything to hurt you, but this is a really powerful Family. They're in all the usual organized rackets—loan sharking, waterfront unions, extortion—but a few new twists."

"Like what?"

"These guys are into some more sophisticated stuff. Computer fraud, stock and securities fraud—even health-care fraud. Hell, they're in cahoots with the Russian and Cuban Mafias."

"And Yolanda insists they have nothing to do with the Mafia."

Billy laughed. "Skunkie, this is the Genovese crime Family we're talking about. They practically built the Javits Center themselves. Everyone knows that in the 1990's, the convention center was one of the Genovese Family's biggest cash cows. They have control of the Fulton Fish market. They even steal money that's supposed to go to charities. Hey, you heard of the San Gennaro feast in Little Italy?"

"Sure. Michael took me there once."

"Well, every year, at the feast, they drag this life-sized statue of the saint through the streets. People pin thousands of dollars to that statue. And guess who ends up with the money?"

"That's disgusting! How could I let Joel get involved with these people? Why didn't he see them for what they are?"

"Sounds like he doesn't want to."

"I didn't raise him to be like this. I didn't sacrifice everything so my child would get tangled in a life like this. On top of everything else, they're twisting things up, making him think there's something wrong with me and deliberately excluding me from family plans to push Joel away from me! This low-life mobster's daughter just un-invited me to Christmas, for God's sake!"

"Well, maybe Joel won't go if you don't," Billy said.

I eyed Billy and nodded in agreement, then dialed the phone.

"Joel?" My voice was still shaky.

"Mom, what's wrong?" Joel answered.

"Yo called. I can't come to Christmas."

"What do you mean?"

"She said I can't come."

"She flat out said you can't come?"

"You need to do something here, Joel. This is about family. This is setting the stage for your entire future."

"Mom, you have to be making it up. She'd never say something like that."

"Why would I make something like that up?" I yelled.

"Take it easy, Mom."

"I've been taking it easy, Joel." I was reaching my breaking point. "I took it easy after *Cats*. I took it easy at the engagement party. I took it easy at Thanksgiving. What the hell am I supposed to do with all these goddamned presents?"

"Hold on," Joel said. "Someone's on the other line."

I heard a click and waited. And waited.

"He forgot about me," I said.

"He'll be back."

I paced the floor with the phone. Finally, with another click, Joel was back. "Mom. That was Yolanda."

"So you straightened it out?"

"There's nothing to straighten out. It's a simple thing. They're not inviting Doris's parents, they're not inviting Nikki's parents. None of the in-laws' parents will be there, so they thought it wouldn't be fair to them if you were there. That's all it is. Nothing more."

"I think it's wrong to invite me and then take it away,

especially after I bought all these gifts."

"Don't make this into something it's not, Mom."

"It's something, Joel. Everyone sees it but you."

"None of the other in-laws will be there, Mom."

"The other in-laws have family to spend Christmas with. I don't."

"We don't even celebrate Christmas."

"That's not the point, Joel. They know I don't have anyone to be with on Christmas. Why would they want me to be alone, if they're having a big party? It's common decency to invite me! Why do you go along with everything they want? Don't you see how they're manipulating you?"

"What do you mean?"

"I mean, they're deliberately trying to alienate us. Don't you see? Yolanda told me that after she married Dick, she made him cut off all ties with his mother. She convinced him that his own mother was an alcoholic who was no good for him. And now, Yolanda and Andrea are trying to do the same thing to me. I don't trust them, Joel. Not anymore. There's something wrong there, and if you don't do something about it fast, you may be headed for a big mistake."

"What are you saying, I shouldn't marry Andrea?"

"No, I'm saying you need to show more of a backbone. Tell them I'm your mother and I need to be respected by the family. Can't you at least do that for me?"

"Mom ... "

I recognized the resignation in Joel's voice. "I'll see you the twenty-eighth, Joel. Merry Christmas." I hung up and shook my head at Billy. "And a happy fucking New Year."

The Family estate looked like a fairy tale. A castle outlined in tiny white lights sleeping in a soft bed of snow. Red garland streamed across every window, wrapping the home like a giant gift. I was slipping and sliding my way up the icy driveway for the second time, with a second load of Christmas gifts.

Yolanda met me at the door. "Sunny, I didn't know you had more gifts. I would have gotten you some help."

Did you think I was going back to my car for exercise? "I got it, Yo. The place looks beautiful."

"I'm embarrassed. I didn't have time to do our normal decorations this year, with the wedding plans and all."

What wedding plans? I haven't heard about any plans. How long does it take to plan a wedding? What kind of wedding are they planning that it's consuming all their time nine months before the event? "If you need any help with the wedding, I'd be happy to chip in."

"There's nothing to do, really." Yolanda faked a smile. "It's only a wedding."

I felt the chill. I walked into the unwrapped post-Christmas mess and declined the offer of a drink from Joel. Yolanda didn't say another word to me. No one did. Even when I handed my gifts out to each Family member, the most I got was a plastic smile and a mumbled "Thanks."

I felt more and more uncomfortable the longer I was there. Not even Joel spoke to me. I was an outcast. A plague.

Why did they invite me, I wondered, if they're only going to treat me like this? Am I here just because they don't want to make Joel mad? Do they enjoy torturing me like this? Not one of them gave me a present. I didn't expect anything from anyone, except maybe Yolanda. After all, she even gave Devin a shirt for Christmas. But nothing for me. Their message is coming through loud and clear. I'm to be humiliated and embarrassed.

I fell deeper and deeper into my personal rant, getting angrier and angrier by the moment.

My thoughts were racing. It's not like I needed a present, I thought, but it hurts to be left out completely. To be ignored? Intentionally slighted? This is about more than presents. This is life. Joel's life and my life, and I don't like the way it's going.

Dick walked into the room, shirt untucked over a pair of sweatpants, a beer in his hand. He glared at me.

"Hey, you still fuckin' here?"

It was like a recurring nightmare that got worse each time. I got up and found my coat on the couch.

"Are you leaving?" Yolanda asked. The first words she'd said to me in an hour. I had to escape, but the roads were treacherous.

"I'm worried about the snow," I said, conflicted. The last thing I wanted to do was ask these people for help. "It looks like it's going to start again, and I'm not good at driving at night anyway. I'd better head out."

I put on my coat, wondering if someone would ask me to stay and offer to drive me home later. No one uttered a word.

"Well," Yolanda finally said, "you know best."

I shook off the cold in my car and drove away. I had brought a dozen presents, but I was taking away only loneliness. The whole experience still tugged at me as I walked into my empty house. It was dark, except for the red answering machine light flashing by the phone.

I checked the messages, all three from Joel. "Where'd

you go, Mom?'" was the first. I deleted it. As the second message started to play, the phone rang again. I reluctantly picked it up. "Hello?"

"Mom, why'd you leave? That was really disrespectful."

"Disrespectful? Are you out of your mind, Joel?"

"You didn't even stay for dinner. That's an insult to the Family, and you know it."

"They wanted me to leave. Your future father-in-law asked me if I was still 'fucking here.' Those people humiliated me. No one said a word to me. And after I got presents for every single one of those people, they don't give me one thing."

"Yolanda got you a present, Mom."

"What? Where?"

"I don't know, but I'm sure she did."

"Well, why wouldn't she have given it to me when I gave her mine? You know what, this all sounds so trivial. It's not about presents, Joel. Nothing is what it seems with that Family. They have it in for me, and I have no idea why. I'm just trying to get along. Keep things on the level for your wedding, but I won't be treated like that. I won't stand for it, even if you will." I slammed the phone down and ignored the rings that quickly followed. There was nothing more to say.

I couldn't sleep. I watched movies on TV with the sound off. At 2 A.M. the downstairs door creaked open. I picked up the phone and quietly ran to the doorway, peering my head around to look downstairs. I heard footsteps as the door clicked shut. My heart pumped like a hammer pounding a nail. Do I hide? Do I scream? Do I run? As the footsteps started up the stairs, I yelled, "I have a gun!"

"No, you don't," Joel answered.

"Goddammit, Joel! You scared the shit out of me." I walked into my office and switched on the light. Joel followed.

"Sorry, Mom. I saw the light on." He paused. "I asked Yolanda about the present."

"Please don't tell me she had one for me."

Joel looked away. "She didn't."

I was relieved to see that this seemed to bother Joel too, although it hurt that Yolanda truly didn't think to get me anything. "What'd you say to her?"

Joel sat on the leather chair by the desk. "She said you're overreacting. She was just busy. She forgot."

"And what do you think?"

"About what?"

"About me remembering to give all of them gifts, and them not getting me a thing."

"Yolanda says you're just making a big deal over the holidays because you lost Dad and Grandma and Poppy."

Shocked, I dropped into the desk chair. I stared at the computer screen, then looked back to Joel. "She said that?"

"She said you should get over it. It's no big deal."

"No big deal? Is she some kind of moron? You don't 'get over' losing your husband, Joel. You don't get over losing your mother. You don't get over losing your father. I sure hope you haven't."

"It's been awhile, Mom."

"Three of the most important people in my life, and I lost them one after the next. I should be over that? Every time I started to, I lost someone else. The wound was ripped open again and again."

Joel looked down at his lap. I could see he knew I was

right, but he didn't want to get into it. And he didn't want to admit Yolanda was wrong.

The more I thought about it, the angrier I got. "How dare she say that about me? They have no idea what I've been through. They've never lost anyone. They've never had to struggle for money. They raised their kids on blood money from Vincent 'the Chin' Gigante, a vicious mobster. And they dare tell me how to live my life?"

"Mom ... "

"They have no regard for human life. They're pariahs....piranhas. I'm your mother, Joel. You're going to let them talk about me that way? I did the best I could for you, and I deserve your respect. I deserve their respect. They don't have to like me. Hell, they can hate me if they want, I don't give a shit anymore, but I won't stand for being disrespected that way. If they think I will, they've mistaken my kindness for weakness. That's not the way it's going to be. It's not the way I was raised, and it sure as hell isn't the way I raised you."

"You're making way too much of this."

"You listen to me, Joel, I'm tired of you rolling over for them every time they want their way. Can't you see this is about control? They're trying to control your life! They're trying to drive a wedge between us. You need to stand up to them, and you need to do it now. You need to tell them they can't treat me like this, and if they do, then you want no part of it."

"What if I like it? I mean, what if I like being there?"

Suddenly, I understood my son. Joel saw wealth, power and notoriety in the Family. The same greed and selfishness that motivated people like Vincent Gigante were motivating Joel. Those vices always clouded people from calculating the consequences of their actions.

"Do you really like it there?" I asked.

"I'm happy there. It's a happy Family. Like ..."

"Like when your dad was alive?" Joel's face was tortured. I could see that he wanted to say yes. He was happy with the Family. It was the complete, happy unit that was torn away from him when his father was murdered. At the same time, I saw that he knew the way the Family was treating me was wrong. And, I knew, Joel wasn't strong enough to stand up to them. If he were, he would have done it by now. I realized he was weak, I was ashamed this was my son. All he had to do was say this is my mother, I love her, you don't have to love her but, you have to respect her.

Chapter 41
Extended Family

A mild breeze ruffled through the trees in my backyard, sending the smell of April through my open windows. The promise of spring gave me a sense of yearning that was palpable. Ted was with his family. Joel was probably with his new Family. I poured myself a glass of Merlot and channel grazed, looking for something on television. Nothing caught my interest.

I dialed the phone. A message played on the other end. "Hi, it's Chris and Claire. We're not in. Leave a message at the beep."

"Hi Claire, it's Sunny. I just wanted to see if you were around. Give me a call when you get in. Bye."

Claire was one of my dearest friends, although she was young enough to be my daughter. Actually, it felt like she was my daughter. I had known Claire ever since she started dating Chris. I had known Chris...well, I had known Chris for 20 years. Could it be that long? I met Chris when he and Joel played youth hockey together. They were both 8-years old. Sometimes, the games were two and three hours away, so I began carpooling with Chris's dad, Bernie. Over the years, the boys grew inseparable, bonded by their love for hockey and their quick-witted personalities. There was a healthy athletic rivalry between them, but also a brotherly love. Chris used to spend almost every weekend at our house, especially after his mother died, and eventually, he became like a third son to me.

Devin grew close to Chris as well. Over the years I watched the three of them turn from boys to men. The milestones of their young lives—first dates, graduation, proms—happened far too quickly. And always they played hockey. It was the common denominator that kept them close even when they were all off at SUNY colleges. They saw each other quite often during those years, playing against one another on different teams for different upstate New York schools.

During the summer, the three of them would rent a house together in Cape Cod to skate, since New England had the highest level teams for competitive hockey players.

When Joel was 18-years old, he and Devin, Chris and two other boys rented a house together—five hockey jocks in one place. They all got jobs working for various fast food places, so they wouldn't have to waste any time performing trivial domestic duties like shopping, cooking or doing dishes. I drove to visit them one weekend. As I pulled onto the street where they were staying, I didn't even need to check the address of where they were staying. Displayed prominently on one of the front lawns were half a dozen sets of hockey equipment placed out to dry. The boys had impaled the ground with hockey sticks and hung their helmets on the sticks. I'm sure the neighbors hated the lawn scattered with scarecrows dressed as hockey players.

Nothing mattered to them but hockey. Certainly not keeping the house clean. The kitchen was littered with what must have been 200 pizza boxes. Devin was working for Gino's pizza, and the boys had decided that pizza would suffice for dinner every night – as well as for breakfast and lunch. Pizza scraps were everywhere, along with an astonishing assortment of insects feasting on the remains. Their kitchen rivaled the Insect Zoo at the Smithsonian. I took one look and refused to spend even one night in that house. Luckily, there was an available room at a nearby hotel. I watched them skate the next day, and, after feeding them their only non-pizza meal of the summer, I drove the five-hour trip home.

During their college years I drove upstate to watch them play whenever I could. On one of those trips, I met a beautiful young woman named Claire, who was in the stands, cheering for Chris. Claire was a brunette with pretty, big green eyes and lashes so thick she never needed mascara. The girl could turn heads wearing a simple tank top and shorts. She was a great match for Chris with his shock of blond hair and movie-star good looks.

After college, Claire took a teaching job in Las Vegas. Eventually, though, she moved to New Jersey so she and Chris could be together. That's when I started to get to know this admirable young woman. She visited my house with Chris to hang out with Joel and Devin. She was really special. I could see why Chris was in love with her, and she was as beautiful on the inside as she was on the outside. Claire was down-to-earth yet classy, intelligent but not pompous, honest without being mean. I was honored when she asked me to help her pick out her wedding gown. Her own mother lived in Arizona, so I helped Claire pick out the bridesmaids' dresses as well.

Chris and Claire's wedding was a memorable time for me. The hotel had overbooked their reservations, so I offered to let the ushers and their girlfriends stay at my house. My house was a hubbub of activity that weekend. The morning after their wedding, the newlyweds came back to my house and cooked breakfast for everyone. My kitchen overflowed with fluffy pancakes, spicy sausage, tender biscuits and pitcher of extra-strong mimosas. It was exactly as I hoped my house would be when my own sons were married.

I had always loved Chris like he was my own son, but Claire was a special new addition to my life. I always wanted a daughter. Claire was that to me, and more. She was a friend. She and Chris made spending Thanksgiving at my house a tradition. They were devastated when Joel decided to spend Thanksgiving with Andrea's Family. Very few people knew what was happening to my life—that my family was shredding apart before my eyes. Claire was a wonderful friend to me during this time. She had never particularly cared for Joel—he had given Chris a hard time for getting married—and now she had even more of a reason to dislike him.

It was midnight before I remembered that Claire and Chris were away at a hockey tournament for the weekend. I took a Valium, and went to sleep.

Chapter 42
The April Shower

I walked through the Farmer's Market eyeing all the spring vegetables. The mild late April day was a glorious showcase for the rainbow of brightly colored produce. It was only sixty degrees, but I didn't wear a jacket. No one did. Like everyone else in New Jersey that year, I was so chilled to the bone from a long winter that a sixty-degree day felt like a heat wave. I picked up zucchini, oranges, corn and flowers, loading my basket with the first hints of the summer to come.

"Sunny?" It was Claire. She hugged me tightly.

"Claire, hi! Is Chris here?"

"He's around here somewhere," Claire said. "I was looking for vegetables, he's looking for a cheese steak."

"Can't find a good cheese steak outside of Philly," I said automatically.

"I'm sorry I didn't get a chance to call you back. We were so exhausted after the tournament, and with work-

"Sweetie, it's okay. I understand." Like Joel, Chris had ended up coaching youth hockey. It wasn't so long ago that I was driving all over the country to tournaments, so I knew how draining it could be.

"It must be fate that you're here," Claire said. "I was going to ask if you had any suggestions for a shower gift."

A familiar pit grew in my stomach. "Whose shower?"

Claire smiled. "Duh! Joel and Andrea's shower."

I set down my basket to prevent me from dropping it onto the concrete. I had been hoping that the lack of communication was just a lull in the planning. After all, I hadn't had a fight with Joel since Christmas. Of course, I had only talked to him a half dozen times since then and, even at that, it was small talk. But I took that as a good sign. We weren't arguing. We weren't fighting about the family. I had hoped that, if I just kept my mouth shut and let Joel make his own choices, a lot of things might smooth over. I hoped I would, at least, be given the courtesy of being included in the wedding events, if not the planning.

"I wasn't invited," I said, telling myself as much as Claire.

"Get out!" Claire laughed. But the look on my face told Claire I wasn't joking. "Oh, my God! It must be a mistake, I'm sure."

"I don't think so," I said, retrieving my basket.

Chris walked up and hugged me. "Hey, Sunny!"

"She didn't get invited to the shower," Clair blurted out.

"What shower?"

"Joel and Andrea's!" Claire swatted Chris's shoulder.

Chris pulled back and looked into my eyes. It was all he needed to size up everything. "Damn that Joel," he said. "Let's talk to him right now."

One phone call and fifteen minutes later, we were all standing together at the hockey rink—Chris Claire, Joel and me. Meeting at Joel's was out of the question, because he was already living with the Family.

Joel spoke first. "Is something wrong?" He was looking directly at me, but I didn't know how to begin.

"You're telling me," Chris jumped in, "you don't invite your own mother to your wedding shower?"

Joel's face went blank. He looked down at the floor, shaking his head.

"The engagement party, Thanksgiving, Christmas …

what are you doing here, Joel?"

I watched Chris with pride. It was a joy to hear him defend me, as much as it was painful that he had to do it against my real son, my blood.

"It's not that simple," Joel said.

"Simple? You want to know what's simple? Treating your mother with respect. Grow a pair! Be a man, Joel."

"You don't know the whole story, Chris," Joel said weakly.

"I know more than I want to know. I'd have given anything to have my mother with me when I got married. I miss her every single day of my life, and I swear to God, if she were here now, I'd be waiting on her hand and foot. But you ... you have your mother wanting to be a part of your life, and you're disrespecting her. And why? What has she done to you but give you her entire life?"

"She's the one causing all the trouble." Joel looked straight at me. "The Family doesn't think you're a good mother. And I'm starting to think they're right. A good mother wouldn't be acting like this. Causing all this trouble."

Anger suddenly swept away all the other emotions I had been feeling. "What trouble am I causing? How can you possibly say that about me?"

"You don't like the Family," Joel yelled. "You think they're Mafia."

"They are Mafia!"

"Not anymore."

"Once Mafia, always Mafia," I said. "They've brainwashed you, Joel, can't you see it? Yolanda and Dick are interfering with the relationship between a mother and son. It's a sacred bond. No one should ever come between that … between us!"

Joel looked away. "I owe my loyalty to Andrea now, not to you."

"Fuck that!" Chris yelled, his voice echoing through the nearly empty hockey rink. "Grow a set of balls".

"Did Andrea hug you when you scraped your knees?" I said softly. "Rock you to sleep when you were a baby? Did she drive you all over the country for hockey games?"

"No, and she didn't make a fool out of me by cheering in the stands either."

"What?" I couldn't believe I heard that right. "What are you talking about?"

"You used to cheer so loud at the games. You were always the loudest parent. It was embarrassing."

I slumped to a bench seat. "If cheering the loudest makes me a bad parent, then take me away in chains. And if that shit is the best excuse you can up with for treating me like this, then you're further gone than I thought."

Joel, almost tearful, couldn't look me in the eye. "Yolanda says you did all the traveling for yourself, not for me. And the cheering too. Always drawing attention to yourself. Why couldn't the attention have ever been on me?"

Chris and Claire remained quiet, though it looked like Chris wanted to let loose. I rose and took Joel by the chin, gently drawing his gaze up to mine. "Now, I know you're brainwashed, Joel. Because this isn't you at all. If you can honestly sit there and tell me all of this, the engagement party, Christmas, the shower was because I cheered for you at games." I was having trouble getting words out of my mouth. "Can you look me in the eye and tell me that? If you can, I'll leave now."

Joel met my gaze and, mustering up a line that he looked as if he didn't believe himself, said, "I'm sick of you."

I let go. Joel lives in a toxic environment now and it's too late to cure his cancer that has spread through his body.

As I walked out of the hockey rink, I paused, turned toward my son and said, "Your dad was the one always leading the cheers. I was only trying to take his place."

Chapter 43
Panic Attack

I had lobsters boiling in water on the stove, corn buttered on plates, biscuits steaming in a basket, and a table decorated like a giant picnic. At the table, Devin poured beers for Chris and Claire, who drank and toasted, "to family."

I joined the toast, but my face revealed my true feelings.

"He'll come around, Mom," Devin said.

"He hasn't called in two months."

"He's busy with the wedding," Chris said, not believing it himself.

"Sunny," Claire said as she got up to help carry food to the table, "it'll be rough going for a bit, but things will work out. It's Joel. Come on. He'll come to his senses."

"Weddings are great healers," Devin said. "Everyone comes together for weddings and funerals."

I laughed and gave Devin a kiss. "My son the philosopher. Still, I think I'll wait to buy a dress."

"You don't have dresses in your closet?" Devin asked.

"Devin," Claire joked, "You need a girlfriend. You have no clue about women."

"I know they buy dresses when they don't need them."

As Chris and Devin exchanged a high five, the phone rang. I picked it up, smiling and a little giddy with the beer. "Hello," I said.

"YOU CAN'T COME TO THE FUCKIN' WEDDING!" Dick's voice boomed through the phone. The only other sound was Dick slamming down the receiver.

Wide-eyed, I looked at the other three, whose faces made it clear they'd heard it, too. I sank into a chair, crying. Claire rushed to me, throwing her arm around my shoulders, pulling me close.

Devin threw his beer can against the wall. "Goddammit, Joel." Devin stepped past me, grabbed the phone and dialed furiously. While he waited for an answer, he punched the wall, knocking a picture off its hook. The glass shattered on the floor.

"Joel, what the fuck?"

Devin listened to the response, but didn't like what he heard. "Bullshit Joel, this is bullshit. Are you serious? Do you know what you're saying?"

Chris walked over and stood by Devin, motioning for the phone. Devin blocked him from taking it. "I'll tell you what, asshole, if Mom's not going to the wedding, then neither am I." Devin started to slam down the phone, but Chris grabbed it.

"Joel, it's Chris. Looks like you better find another best man." Chris slammed down the phone for all of them, then followed Devin, who was cussing, yelling and punching his way into the backyard.

I let out a moan and started kicking at the nearby wall, then stomped my feet on to the floor. Oblivious of the pain shooting up my calves, I pounded my anger into the tiles beneath my feet. I clenched my hands and pounded on my knees. My nails dug into my palms, as I felt a primal scream emerge from my soul. Shaking, gasping, gulping for air that wasn't there, I bent over double, rocking back and forth on my kitchen chair.

Before the night was over, I was in a hospital emergency room with anxiety pain and heart palpitations.

The doctor said I was having a panic attack.

Billy's voice on the speaker phone was a comfort to me, even if he was making fun of me again.

"Bitter, bitter, bitter, Skunkie."

"You'd be bitter, too, if you were banned from your own son's wedding." I twirled a lock of blond hair in my fingers, trying to control my voice and contain my emotions.

"Nobody would ban me from a wedding, Skunkie. I'm too much fun."

"They sent my check back. The thousand bucks."

"Good. They should have been embarrassed to have asked for it in the first place."

"Maybe I can use it to leave town the weekend of the wedding."

"September fifteenth? That's the day before Independence Day in Mexico. We can make a weekend of it." Billy sounded excited.

"You're not going to the wedding?" I knew how he would answer, but I needed to hear it again.

"If you don't go, I don't go. Nancy's not going, Cara's not going, and I'm not going. We're all with you, Sunny."

"What about Becca?"

"Have you ever known Becca to turn down free country club food?"

I laughed and moved closer to the speaker phone. "Well, let's hope it gets straightened out so we can all go."

"Sure. I wouldn't want to miss being surrounded by wall-to-wall wiseguys. Maybe John Gotti will be there." Billy slurped a drink on the rocks. "The wedding's in two months. What makes you think it'll get straightened out?"

"Devin's over there right now, trying to talk some sense into them."

It was several days later when Devin came over for dinner and told me the story of his attempted reconciliation with the Family. He was still upset by what had transpired and it came through in his voice:

I stood just inside the front door of the house, ready to walk out, but Andrea blocked my way, with Dick and Yolanda backing her up.

'Devin', I heard Andrea say in her New Jersey twang. Then Andrea actually pleaded with me and she said that it was' my only brother's wedding and then whined, 'How can you do this to him? Joel won't be happy unless you go.'

'What about his only mother not going?'

Yo added her very special form of wisdom to the argument. 'It's the biggest day of his life.'

'It's non-negotiable. Mom doesn't go, I don't go. End of story" I told them. There wasn't anything more to say, so I started to leave, but Dick blocked the doorway and screamed, 'That Jew bitch has no right coming to the wedding after all she's said about us."

I looked him in the eye and said, 'That 'Jew bitch' is my mother.' I guess I was losing it because I leaned in to take a swing at Dick. Andrea grabbed my arm. She said, 'Devin, it's my big day. I just want it to be perfect.'

I was shocked but managed to shake off her arm. I mean, what was she thinking? Did my brother's family not coming to the wedding some how make it perfect?

'Mom's not going, I'm not going,' I repeated. I was holding my ground.

Dick just yelled, 'That's bullshit. She's not paying for

the fuckin' wedding, why should she be there?'

I guess that was my breaking point. 'She is his mother, asshole,' I said, immediately regretting the name calling—not because Dick wasn't an asshole—but because you and dad raised me better than that.

I said, 'Let's take this outside,' so Dick yelled at me 'Take your ass outside!'

"I couldn't remember when I had been as angry as I was at that moment. At the same time, I realized I was the only sane person in the room.

Looking around I saw the faces, but none of them looking at me—not even my blood, my brother. He was looking anywhere, everywhere, but at me. Andrea looked beautiful until I looked into her eyes and saw only hatred and fear.

Yolanda was so used to having it her own way that she stared at me wide eyed. I think she felt confident that no matter what happened next, she could fix it with a word, a gesture, an action, a reaction.

I turned and looked at Dick. He was fat, ignorant, an inflated ego in a Sergio Tacky warm up suit, and he knew the Family had his back

So, I said again, 'If Mom's not going, I'm not going.' Firm, but gentle, clear, but non-threatening. As I took a breath, I now could see my future sister-in-law—a stunning girl with the eyes of a devil, a medusa.

Yolanda, in her role as the mother hen, looked back and forth and then stepped forward, taking charge. She grabbed my forearm, her fake fingernails dug into me, to emphasize what she was saying. 'Devin, Family is the most important consideration here—Andrea, Joel, you … we're Family, we stick together, we take care of …'

'Our own,' I told her. 'My mother deserves respect and she will attend her eldest son's wedding. She will be welcomed at Joel's wedding or …'

'Or, what? Shithead?'

Dick stepped toward me, so I had to think fast and smart. I learned in school that discretion is the better part of valor, so I said, in as level a voice as I could muster, 'Our mother is welcomed at her son's wedding, or none of Joel's family will be there. Your choice.'

Devin looked at me, his eyes wide, "Mom, did I do the right thing? I mean these guys don't get mad, they get even."

I stood and walked toward my youngest son and gathered him into my arms summoning a mixture of pride tempered by maternal fear. He had just put himself into harm's way, for me, for our family. Regardless of what happened, he did the right thing.

A few days later, I was drinking my morning coffee when the phone rang. I picked it up and heard Dick yell, "You can come to the fuckin' wedding." As the phone slammed down in my ear, I looked at the calendar. July 15, 2001. Two months, to the day, until the wedding. What a fucked up family this is. I guess not having a best man or a mother present, upset Joel.

Chapter 44
A Marriage Made in Hell

I drove through the valley on a single-lane road winding through green pastures. I could see the road far ahead and, in the rear view mirror, far behind. It reminded me of the journey I'd traveled to get to this day. Joel and Andrea's wedding day.

Two months since Dick said I could 'come to the fuckin' wedding,' and I hadn't spoken to him, Yolanda, Andrea or even Joel since. Not a word. They didn't know if I was coming to the wedding or not, and I liked it that way. Keep them off guard for a while. I'd long-since given up the illusion that biting my tongue, swallowing my pride, and giving in was going to accomplish anything with these people. Those days were over. I hadn't even returned Joel's calls.

The only call I wanted to place to Joel came four days earlier—September 11, 2001, but Joel was living with the Family, and I didn't have anything to say if Dick or Yolanda answered. The city's phone circuits were overloaded, anyway. Nine-eleven would put a damper on the wedding. A lot of people couldn't get flights, so the crowd was going to be thinner. My three sisters were not able to fly from Florida.

Devin said Andrea wouldn't postpone it. She didn't want to let down all the workers who needed the money. The country club that was counting on the income, the band, the valets, the florist with the family to feed. Too many people were counting on this wedding, Andrea had told her parents. Yeah, I'm sure that was it, I smiled to myself.

"We're lost." My friend Gloria, in an elaborate blue dress cascading all over the passenger's seat, threw her arms up. "We're going to be late, and it's your fault."

"I lost the directions," I said, "but it's a church in the middle of nowhere. How hard can it be?"

Gloria's son Michael was no help in the back seat. "We'll never make it," he warned, gazing out a side window.

I knew he was right, but didn't want to admit it. It would kill me to miss the wedding. My oldest son getting married. How could I have been so careless? Besides, I'd hated to miss seeing the looks on Dick and Yolanda's faces. They had to be freaking out—not knowing if I would ruin the wedding by showing up or by not showing up. Either way, I thought, they were screwed. Finally, I thought, I'll be in the driver's seat here.

"I should've driven," Michael said.

I looked at the clock and tried to speed up without Gloria noticing.

"We're not going to make it," Gloria said.

The car climbed a small hill out of the valley and, as they rolled over the crest, a giant church steeple popped up in the distance. "There it is," I said with a smile.

"How do you know it's the right church?"

I studied the building. It was more like a cathedral. It was giant, ornate, gaudy and overshadowed the entire landscape around it. Far from blending in or complementing the small town, it towered up in the center of it, casting such a shadow that it blocked out and overpowered everything around it.

"That's it," I said.

Devin opened the door and helped me out of the car. He stood back to admire my strapless, Victorian style, antique gold gown. With full-length black gloves and a shawl that matched the netting and lace appliqués of the dress, I felt like Grace Kelly. "Wow, Mom, you look ... I mean you look ... "

"What?" I kissed Devin.

"You look amazing. Beautiful." Devin kissed me back.

I winked my thanks.

"You know they're going to hate you for this," Devin laughed.

"They hate me for everything," I said. "It wouldn't matter what I wore."

As I started up the steps, I saw Joel waiting at the church door. He looked so handsome in his tux, I couldn't help but feel a wave of joy. Joel walked down to meet me and gave me a soft kiss on the cheek. "I'm glad you're here," Joel whispered.

I hugged him. "So am I, sweetie. So am I."

"I gotta get inside, Mom."

"Go, Joel, it's your big day."

As Joel jogged back inside, I called out, "I love you," but Joel was inside the church already and missed it.

The photographer, a tanned, young man with long hair and an electric blue suit, took my arm and led me to a nearby lawn. "Wow! Nobody told me the mother of the groom was stunning."

His compliment had me glowing. "Did they tell you I was the out-law?"

Around the side of the church, in a quiet enclave, the photographer started taking pictures of me. Billy's girlfriend, Denise, stood nearby in a sexy black dress, smoking a joint with Billy's daughters, Brittany and Kristen. Denise held it out to me, and I accepted it and sucked in a lungful of smoke. As I blew out a thinner cloud of smoke, I handed it back to Denise. "I'll need more than that if I'm going to get through this day."

"I've got a lot more," Denise assured me, handing the joint back to me. I took another hit and shared it with the photographer.

Maybe it was the joint, maybe it was the pressure, maybe it was one of the other three joints, or the extra-dry martinis that seemed to fall into my hand every time I turned around, but the rest of the day went by in a blur. It was the first time I had been to a wedding that featured FBI men lurking outside, spying on the proceedings and taking notes. Billy pointed them out.

Andrea said "I do" a little too loudly, and Joel said it a bit too quietly, but other than that, the church ceremony went well.

The bridesmaid and flower-girl dresses looked tacky, and I mused over the contradiction. With all its money, the Family could afford to show refined and elegant taste, yet most of them just seemed crass and low-rent. But what do you expect, when Grandpa walks around the streets of New York in his pajamas?

Grandpa Vincent "The Chin" Gigante couldn't attend the wedding. He was locked up at Springfield Prison in Missouri, serving a 12-year sentence after being convicted on 41 different counts of racketeering and conspiracy.

At the receiving line after the wedding, Joel gave me a big kiss, while Andrea pretended to be in a deep conversation with a friend behind her and, amazingly, completely missed me in the line.

Dancing at the reception, I saw the photographer

constantly clicking away, his lens focused on my every move. I knew the Family wouldn't like it – seeing so many photos of the confident, attractive mother of the groom, looking so different from the overstuffed mother of the bride. But what could I say? Stop taking my picture? Besides, I loved every minute of it.

During the mother-son dance – the only time I got to dance or even talk with Joel, Dick sent out a woman to cut in one minute into the dance. They couldn't even let me have that little moment of pleasure.

Billy quickly moved to the rescue, keeping me out on the dance floor.

"I've never seen you look more radiant, Skunkie." Billy held my right hand and moved smoothly to the rhythm of "Come Fly with Me."

"They won't let me do anything, Billy." I tapped my forehead in frustration on my brother's shoulder. "They're watching my every move, telling me what to do, where to go. Sometimes I just want to …"

"Easy, Skunkie. Look at all these wiseguys around you. It's a damn Mob convention. The last thing you want to do is make a scene here. Deep breaths. Let it go for now."

This was not a fun day, I thought, as I walked alone into my dark, empty house. Heartbreaking, emotionally draining, bittersweet. The hardest part was that I knew the wedding could've been such a joyous union. Instead, it was to be tainted by the family's petty games. Going through the motions, pretending things were normal for a while, only made it worse. It was like walking a little girl around the outskirts of a carnival, letting her see the rides, hear the games, smell the cotton candy, but not letting her in.

"What happens from here?" I whispered to myself.

Chapter 45
And a Happy New Year to You!

New Year's Eve was going to be a quiet one. I had not made any plans on purpose. Aside from Ted, there was no one I really wanted to spend it with, anyway. New Year's Eve was one of those holidays where people just tried too hard to have fun. I was still recovering from the stress of Joel's wedding, along with the sadness at not being invited to the Family's Christmas party, and basically from being totally cut off from my son. I decided to rent some movies and eat take-out. The next day, the first day of a new year, I had a festive New Year's brunch for Claire, Chris, and their two daughters, Trinity and Abigail.

The day after New Year's Day was a Sunday, and I spent it puttering around my house, organizing my closets, catching up on phone calls and emails. I was more than a little disappointed that there were no "Love you more madly and more deeply" emails from Ted. The one cliché about dating a married man is that you don't get to see him on the holidays. I understood that, but I was excited to hear his voice when he called after the long New Year's weekend.

"I need to see you, Sunny."

"Did you miss me?" I purred into the phone.

"Can you meet me at the Bridgeway Diner?" It was a cozy little place about halfway between Cream Ridge and Pennsylvania, where Ted's office was. We had had many lunches there – usually after spending time at a nearby motel.

"Sure, sweetie, but wouldn't you like to have dessert before lunch?" I offered, suggestively.

"How about one o'clock?"

Ted was all business today. Maybe somebody was in his office.

"I have an appointment in the morning, but I think I can get away this afternoon. Are you sure you want to meet in the diner?"

"I'll see you then."

He hung up. I was puzzled. He wasn't usually that abrupt with me. Oh well, holidays were a stressful time for everyone. I knew they had been for me. Maybe spending all that time with his family had drained him. I chuckled to myself. If he needed a little resuscitation, I was just the person to do it.

I pulled into the Bridgeway Diner parking lot. Ted's car was already there. I was wearing a jewel green silk suit with a crisp silk organdy flower on the lapel. My suit was understated; attractive, without being overtly sexy. It said "I'm a professional business woman." The sexy lingerie I wore underneath, however, said. "I want to have mad, passionate sex with you – now!" Ted may have been all business on the telephone, but I was sure we would end up in our favorite motel after lunch.

"Sunny!" Ted waved me over to a booth in the back, near the restrooms.

God, he was so handsome. I hadn't seen him for several weeks, and had almost forgotten his sexy, rugged good looks. My heart raced a little as I slid next to him on the leather booth. I gave him a chaste kiss on the cheek, but squeezed his arm intimately as I settled next to him.

"Happy New Year, sweetie!"

"Happy New Year, Sunny." Ted looked around nervously. "Uh, maybe you'd better sit across from me."

I looked around, but didn't recognize anyone from his office. What would they be doing all the way out here? Still, it was better to be safe than sorry.

"Sure, baby."

I went around to the other side of the table and slid into the booth, while a busboy filled our waterglasses.

"How were your holidays?" I was hoping he'd tell me that they were awful, miserable; that he'd pined for me the entire time and realized he couldn't spend another holiday without me. That realization had sent him straight to a divorce lawyer's office, where he immediately filed papers. His divorce would be final in the spring, when we'd go to Europe—Rome, possibly?—to celebrate.

"Terrible, actually."

I looked up at him, startled out of my reverie. It was the answer I'd hoped I'd hear—but somehow, his delivery wasn't what I expected He seemed not sad, but somehow tenss—almost angry.

"I know – I missed you, too."

A waiter appeared with our menus, and Ted disappeared behind his. I waited for him to tell me he missed me as well. Why was he scrutinizing the damn menu? We'd eaten here dozens of times. Why would he care so much about lunch, anyway? Wasn't it beside the point?

"Coffee, ma'am?" The waiter stood, pad in hand and pencil poised.

"Yes, please. and I'll have the grilled chicken Caesar salad, with the dressing on the side, please."

Ted appeared from behind his laminated curtain. "I'll have a burger, medium well, and coffee."

I waited a bit until the waiter left.

"Ted, are you okay? You just don't seem like yourself today."

Ted looked out the window for a moment, as the waiter returned with our coffee. When the waiter left, he turned back to me. "Katherine knows."

Time slowed down and then stopped completely. A million thoughts jockeyed for position in my brain like cars in a traffic jam.

Oh my god!—How could this happen?—This is wonderful!—This is terrible!—Now we can be together.–– His poor children.—This is for the best.—Will we get married?—No more sneaking around.—He'll need a place to stay.—Maybe he'll move in?—How did she find out?

I looked at Ted. He looked so deeply disturbed it was obvious that displaying anything other than shock and horror would be inappropriate.

"How did she find out?"

"Someone sent her a letter."

"What? Why would someone do that?"

The waiter arrived with our food, and Ted busied himself with condiments. I took a sip of coffee, waiting for him to answer. He didn't.

"Ted."

"Yes?"

"What's going on? Who would send Katherine a letter?"

He swallowed his mouthful of food. He seemed to be stalling, and I didn't understand why. I started to feel impatient with him. I wanted some answers. I was entitled to some answers.

"Ted?"

"Anita sent it."

"Your secretary? Why would she do something like that?"

And then it dawned on me why she would do something like that. Why she always seemed to treat me with such disdain. Hell hath no fury ...

"Did you...were you...involved with her?"

He let a big breath out, and answered. "Yes. Yes, I was."

It was like a car accident I couldn't turn away from. I didn't want to know, and yet I had to ask.

"Was it serious?"

"She thought it was."

The blood rushed to my face, and there was a strange buzzing in my ears. 'She thought it was.' Just like I do.

Ted continued. "She's always been angry that we're seeing each other. I guess she decided to get even. I just don't know why she had to do this now."

"You mean, during the holidays?"

He didn't answer, and suddenly I had all the answers. He meant, now, as in, with this affair. He'd had them before, many, many times. I wasn't special. I was another in a long string of "other women." I wanted to get up and storm away from the table, but I stayed. Maybe, I prayed, maybe he'll tell me that this time is different. Maybe, if I just sit here, and don't say anything, don't push for answers, maybe he'll say what I need to hear...

I looked at his face, searching for the reassurance I needed. His eyes were puffy and bloodshot. He looked bone tired. He chewed his food mechanically, but he wasn't even tasting it. I saw in his face that he loved his wife, and more importantly, that he would never leave her. That he never had any intention of leaving her. How could I even have hoped for that? He has kids, for God's sake. I never thought I'd be this person. How could I ever have settled for this? When did I become someone that would be some married man's little plaything on the side?

I took a long look at him and thought, "He's miserable. He's not angry with me. He doesn't think I wrote this letter. He's just completely devastated because the woman he loves, the mother of his children, is hurt. He can barely look at me. He can't even chew his food."

On some level, I must have known he would never leave her. But I thought I loved him. I was so alone. I don't know how I would ever have endured the whole wedding fiasco without Ted's attention. He had been the one bastion of comfort I could always escape to whenever Joel and the Family tried to crush me. But I had survived. It was time to move on.

I stood. The diner suddenly looked small and shabby. The Formica tables were chipped, some of the leather banquettes worn and frayed. I had never noticed before what a tacky little place this was. And I had no reason to be there, with him.

"Sunny." Ted looked up at me. I waited for him to tell me not to leave, that he loved me and couldn't live without me.

He said nothing.

As I gathered up my coat and bag, the busboy rushed over, gesturing towards the plate of food I hadn't even touched.

"You're done, ma'm?"

"Yes," I told him. "I'm completely done."

Chapter 46
It's a Boy

Eyes puffy red, I sat on my living room couch, dabbing tears with a dishcloth. I was exhausted. "You're the only one I have left, Billy."

Billy's voice crackled through the speaker phone. "If I'm your last hope, you're in a lot of trouble, Skunkie."

I laughed through my tears. "Devin's got his life to live …"

"Joel has Andrea's life to live," Billy said.

I laughed again, then let out a little sob.

"You're not alone, Skunkie. The boys haven't forgotten you. They're just busy. They'll come around someday."

I shook my head, finding it difficult to speak. "I mean," I hugged myself for comfort, "I miss having someone to love and care for. I miss Michael, too."

The long silence told me what I already knew, that not even Billy could fill that void in my life. My big brother, my best friend since childhood, the only family member to pick me up when I fell, to make me laugh when I was down and to hold me close when I was in pain—Billy couldn't solve this one. The long pause told me what I'd known for years. I was alone. Yes, Billy loved me, he'd be there for me. But when it came right down to it, without Michael, I was alone at heart, and always would be.

"Hey," Billy finally said. "You're going to be a grandma. Think how busy you'll be!"

I smiled, then wiped another tear. "I haven't seen Joel in six months. What makes you think I'll see the baby?"

"Things change with babies," Billy said. "Believe me, things change."

"That'd be nice," I said, a hint of hope in my voice. "But I didn't even find out Andrea was pregnant until I heard about the baby shower I wasn't invited to."

"You're the grandma, Skunkie. You'll see the kid. Besides, you think Yolanda's going to baby-sit?"

I laughed again. "Yeah, she will. Don't you know how Italian women are slaves to their children?"

"You're going to be fine, Sunny. You're going to be just fine."

Devin sped down the interstate while I sat in the passenger seat, talking on my cell phone.

"We're going to be there in ten minutes, Joel. But if they're in the room, I'm not coming in." I paused, listening. "I'm being unreasonable? Don't even get me started. No one even called me when the baby was born!"

Devin turned off the highway.

"I'm calling you now, aren't I?" Joel said.

"The baby's two days old, Joel," I said. "You don't get a lot of credit for calling me two days after he's born."

Devin motioned with one hand, palm down, for me to be nicer. I rolled my eyes and nodded. "But thanks, Joel. For calling me. All right, sweetie, we'll be there in five."

The hospital elevator stopped on the third floor and I left with Devin right behind, lugging two overstuffed baby bags.

"I can't believe you spent four hundred dollars on baby clothes." Devin said. "They're never going to let the kid wear them."

I realized he was probably right, but it didn't matter. I was a grandmother, too, and I'd buy my grandson whatever I wanted. As we approached the room, Yolanda stepped through the doorway and blocked it. I burned inside. Joel promised he'd have them out of there.

Yolanda gave a fake smile and started to hug me, moving toward a kiss on the cheek. I recognized it as a typical Mafia ploy, kissing your enemy when what you really wanted was to shove a knife into her back. I was having none of that phoniness. I pulled away and ducked around her and into the room.

Andrea, holding the baby on the bed, saw me and immediately turned away. I realized Andrea hadn't spoken to me since before the wedding. Who is this girl, I wondered, and what had I ever done to her? One again that evil she-devil surfaced. Billy had said things change with babies. Apparently, not enough.

While Devin and Joel hugged, I stepped toward the baby, but Andrea cradled him tighter, like a football, and turned her back. Once more, I found myself not wanting to rock the boat. Instead, I hugged Joel and whispered, "he's beautiful, Joel."

"We named him Michael. After Dad."

The pain in my heart was confusing. Was it for Michael? It couldn't be about being excluded from the family. I thought I was past the point of caring about that.

Joel gently took the baby from Andrea and handed it to Devin, but Devin looked awkward and obviously felt uncomfortable holding a newborn, as most single men would. What's he doing, I thought, giving the baby to Devin? Then Joel stepped between Devin and me and took the baby back. I realized he was sneaking the baby over to me. Overwhelmed with joy at the sight of the tiny mouth, nose, eyes and the delicate, flailing hands, I forgot how absurd it was that Joel had to go through this charade just to let me see my first grandchild.

I instinctively held out my arms and took little Michael from Joel. I held him close, cooing, calming him, rocking him. The baby relaxed into my arms and softly fell asleep. His new-baby smell overwhelmed me. It made my heart ache. There's something so deeply primal about the scent of a baby; it brought up all these longings from deep inside me.

Yolanda appeared and took the baby from me, literally jerking him awake. "He needs his rest." Yolanda plopped him into the plastic hospital bassinette.

"We should leave them alone," Yolanda said, taking me by the arm and leading me out of the room. I looked back to Joel, expecting him to extend his moment of bravery, but Joel mouthed "goodbye" as he poured a glass of water for Andrea.

When Yolanda shut the door, I felt light, expanded, overjoyed at being a grandmother. The euphoria was what I'd remember most, and the way it felt to hold baby Michael. That was enough to mask the sick feeling that I knew I would never see him again.

Chapter 47
Still Crazy After All These Years

Billy freshened his drink, poured me a glass of wine and helped himself to a piece of shrimp. I had lured him to my house with the promise of a home-cooked meal. Of course, the fact that he was on his way to Atlantic City didn't hurt any. More important, I had all sorts of news about "the Chin." Who better to share it with than someone who had rubbed elbows with his share of Mob guys?

Billy, of course, indulged me. He was always willing to listen to me when no one else would. Billy looked handsome as ever in a tan blazer over a crisp white shirt. But he looked tired and a little too thin. Chemotherapy was supposedly keeping his cancer at bay, but it was knocking the crap out of him. Not that he would ever admit it.

I had a roast in the oven and some delectable cheeses, crackers, shrimp and pâté on the kitchen table. The Merlot Billy poured me was fine and dry. I was happy to see him. I never felt I had enough time with my favorite brother.

"So, the Family has to eat a little crow, huh?" he asked. "You don't exactly look broken up about it."

"After everything these people put me through, I'm glad to see them getting a little back."

Billy spread some pâté on a cracker and took a bite. "I guess Joel will finally have to admit that the family is Mafia." He swallowed and looked surprised. "Hey, this is great, Skunkie."

"What, you think the only place you can get gourmet food is in a casino? Come on, you know better. I've got a roasted garlic and peppercorn rub on the prime rib, rosemary roasted new potatoes and …"

Billy waved his hand to cut me off. "Yeah, yeah, let's skip talking about the menu and talk about the old guy. That's why you dragged me here, isn't it?"

"I didn't drag you here! And by the way, I'm sure Joel will not be admitting that the Family is Mafia. He's far too brainwashed for that. Billy, I think Joel is suffering from Stockholm syndrome. It's a real paradoxical psychological phenomenon—hostages express empathy and have positive feelings towards their captors. They actually defend their captors. That sounds like Joel to me. I recall Patty Hearst suffered from that."

"But didn't Andrea's grandfather finally admit that he's been pretending to be crazy all these years? It was all over the news. Even I saw it."

"Yes, he did. He pleaded guilty to obstructing justice with his crazy act, and got three more years added to his sentence. And Andrew, Yolanda's brother, got sentenced to two years in jail. He also has to forfeit $2 million to the government. Even after his two-year jail term, he's never allowed to set foot on the waterfronts in New York, New Jersey and South Florida."

"So, Joel will finally have to admit he's been wrong." Billy took a sip and crunched down on an ice cube.

"No. Joel will just say they forced "The Chin" into admitting his guilt. The FBI was going to drag the whole Family into it—not just Andrew. They were going to prosecute Yolanda, "The Chin's" wife, all his other kids—everybody—for obstruction of justice, for helping him with his crazy act. So, to prevent that, he gave himself up… or at least that is the story I hear."

Billy chuckled. "Too bad. I bet you would have liked to see Yolanda spend a little time in jail."

"No, not really. Although it might have humbled her."

"Wow, the Feds really played hardball with this guy. They really wanted to nail him. Well, that Family has been controlling the docks for fifty years. I guess the Feds are cracking down."

I checked my roast. It smelled divine. I pulled out a salad bowl with spinach, arugula and endive and began tossing it with a champagne vinaigrette.

"Jesus, Skunkie, you've got enough food for an army here. You're gonna get me fat."

"You could use it. Are you taking all the vitamins the doctors told you to take?"

"Please, lay off. You sound like Brittany." Billy's daughter had been spending a lot of time taking care of her father; shopping, cooking, cleaning for him. I was proud of the woman she turned out to be.

I checked the dressing. It needed a little something. I sprinkled a little freshly ground pepper in it and took a sip of wine.

"So, back to the Family. Did I ever tell you that when "The Chin" and Andrew were both charged with extortion, they called in Yolanda for questioning? She had to give up ownership of the real estate holding company."

"How did you hear that?" Billy sampled one of the cheeses with a Carr's cracker.

"Joel told Chris, and Claire told me."

"Quite a little chain of info you got rolling here."

"Well, I wouldn't have to hear things from my son's friends, if my son was talking to me, but he's not." I attempted a cavalier tone of voice, but failed. I took a sip of wine and pretended to check the roast again.

"You just looked in there, Skunkie. It hasn't cooked any more in the last five minutes."

I closed the oven door harder than I planned to.

"I'm just so disgusted with my son. Do you know, I heard through the 'info chain' that he can't even take a vacation at his own timeshare? Andrea's parents just show up, whenever Joel and Andrea go on vacation, without telling him in advance. Apparently, they tell him what he can and can't do. What kind of life is that?"

"It's the one he chose for himself, Skunkie. There ain't a damn thing you can do about it. Besides, you never know. Maybe, eventually, Joel will come around. Look, I didn't have a great relationship with my daughters for the longest time, and, now, things are really good between us."

"Joel's never going to come around, Billy. He doesn't have the strength of character to stand up to them. Maybe that's one of the reasons Andrea zeroed in on him."

Billy changed the subject, hoping, I'm sure, to avoid the depressing conversation that would ensue if we continued to talk about Joel.

"So, the newspapers had some stories about the old guy's crazy act. This is a good one. Once, FBI agents with subpoenas found him standing naked in the shower of his bathroom, holding an umbrella over his head to keep himself dry!"

"Let me tell you something. Not only was this guy not crazy, I think he was brilliant. Come on, Billy. He's been acting like a lunatic, checking himself in and out of mental hospitals for thirty years—all to avoid prosecution. That's straight from the *New York Times*."

"Since when do you read the *Times*?" Billy interrupted.

I continued, ignoring him. "According to the *Times*,

he fooled some of the most respected minds in forensic psychiatry. You have to admit, that's damn good."

"Forensic psychiatry? Maybe you'd better stop reading the *Times*, Skunkie. You're starting to scare me."

"Shut up!" I jabbed Billy playfully. "Apparently they had hours of taped phone conversations with him from jail, talking to his wife, his girlfriend, his kids. All with him sounding completely sane. And you know what's really ironic, Billy? The most damming evidence against him was a taped conversation after 9-11. The first thing he did was call his kids and make sure they were safe. They have him on tape saying he would pray for the children who were on the flights that were hijacked and crashed."

Billy freshened his drink. "What's ironic about that?"

"Don't you remember? Joel and Andrea got married right after September 11. They got married on September 15. Rather than postpone the wedding, because nobody could get flights, she had the wedding anyway. It didn't matter to her. Everyone important to her was nearby, but all the members of our family from Florida who couldn't make it in. I just think it's fitting that, in the end, that's what really did him in."

Billy sniffed the aroma of prime rib exaggeratedly.

"Enough about these Mafia idiots. What's a guy gotta do to get fed around here?"

Chapter 48
Good Riddance to Joel's Rubbish

I had finally had it. Joel had completely turned his back on me, and it was time to move on. Time to get rid of all the old hockey posters, yearbooks, CDs, trophies, clothes—everything that Joel had left behind in the house. Time to dump the memories. Through Devin, I'd sent word that Joel could come claim them, or they would be trashed.

"Why, Mom?" Joel said as he looked at the boxes on the floor. "This stuff's been here over ten years and it never bothered you. Why throw it out now?

"You cut me out of your life, Joel."

"I did not, Mom."

"You didn't even tell me about the Christening, Joel. You invited everyone but me."

"I didn't think you'd come."

"Not even an invitation!" My face turned red with the anger that had been stewing below the surface for two years. "I didn't even get a phone call from Dick saying I'm not invited to the fucking Christening!"

Joel bowed his head to avoid my stare, but I squared off in his face. "I'm done, Joel. Finished. You've pushed me over the top. I don't know why, but you treat me like I don't exist. Or worse, like I don't matter."

"Mom, it's not that bad."

"This is the first time you've been to my house in two years, Joel. And you're only here because you don't want me throwing out your stuff!"

"It's not like that."

"Oh, yes it is. That family has you wrapped around

their little fingers. You're not a man, you're a puppet or worse, you're a muppet with their hands up your ass.. You don't have the strength or the decency to stand up for me or even yourself."

"Mom, I ... "

"All you had to do was say to them, 'Look, she's my mother. She might not be perfect, but she did the best she could.' All you had to say was, 'I know you don't like her, but she's my mother and I love her. She's a part of my life, and if you want me to be a part of your life, you need to welcome her as well.' Would that have been so hard?"

Joel's eyes were wet.

"I'm not asking for the world, Joel. I'm not asking for them to love me, be my friend ... not anymore. I just want respect. If not from them, at least from you. You know, all this time I kept hoping you'd fix things and finally stand up to them. Three years, this has gone on, and you've done nothing but cave in to them. Well, you think they're going to be there for you when things go bad? God forbid your marriage doesn't work out, are they going to support you then? Are they going to come to your rescue then?"

Joel looked out the window, trying to hide the torment on his face.

"This Family controls everything . It's their background, their life. They wanted to control me, but they couldn't. I wouldn't let them. You did. They control you now, and unless you do something to change that, they always will."

"What do you want me to do, Mom?"

I stepped closer, gently putting my hands on Joel's shoulders. "Stand up to them, Joel. If not for me, then for yourself."

I looked into Joel's eyes, but instead of seeing my married, 30-year-old son, I saw the broken-hearted ten-year-old who didn't make the championship goal. The crushed teen whose girlfriend just broke up with him. The young adult on the day he realized he would never make it to the NHL. For a moment, I knew I had gotten through to him.

Joel took a deep breath, looked away for the slightest second, then looked me in the eye. "This is all your fault, Mom. Not anyone else's. You're the problem here, not the Family. Not Andrea. You haven't done enough to make her feel welcome in our family. You haven't given her the attention she deserves. The whole Family sees it. It's you, Mom, not her, not me."

I stepped back like I'd taken a blow to the gut. I couldn't speak, couldn't breathe. Joel stared me straight in the eye with a steely strength that wasn't his, then turned to walk out.

I stopped him with a voice that sounded cold and dead.

"It makes me so sad to say this, Joel, but you are less than you pretend to be," I said. "You're the one who'll have to live with your shame and embarrassment. In your heart of hearts, you know what you're doing is wrong. But I don't expect anything of you anymore. It just hurts to see that the boy I raised has turned into a coward."

He left without a word, without taking any of the boxes of his possessions. One by one, I dragged the boxes downstairs and outside my front door. I didn't want them in my house.

Chapter 49
Bitter No More

I slumped in the steel chair next to the hospital bed. It was three in the morning, and the rhythmic sound of the ventilator kept me awake, unlike every other night for the last week, when it lulled me to sleep. I sipped cold coffee from a Styrofoam cup and followed the length of the feeding tube up to an IV bag, then tracked the line of oxygen back down to Billy's unshaven face. I didn't recognize him. His cheeks were sunken, his gambler's fat lost months before to chemotherapy. He was an empty sack of skin loosely draped over a withering skeleton.

Billy would be furious at the medical folks for keeping him alive like this. **I** was enraged that they were keeping him alive like this. I remembered how Billy used to say, "If I can't gamble, I have no use for living." He would have hated this, I knew. But the doctors were fighting—insisting he be kept alive against his will, against our family's will.

One of the doctors was thoughtful enough to furnish us with honest, frank advice based not on medical science but personal experience. He told us that the cancer had metastasized to all of Billy's vital organs which were shutting down. Worse still, he would probably always be like this, hooked up to cold steel that breathed for him and rubber tubes that fed him. Billy's other doctor was not as compassionate. He seemed to think that Billy should be kept on life support endlessly. Either way, we were screwed. Since Billy did not have a living will, the hospital insisted that all immediate family members must be in total agreement before they would take Billy off life support.

Deanne was there, of course, as was Brittany, who

lived near Billy in Queens. I was in from New Jersey the minute I'd heard he was hospitalized. Kristen had flown in from the Bahamas. But it wasn't enough. Even after Deanne, Brittany, Kristen and I had given permission to have Billy taken off life support, the hospital informed us that there were other family members on their way in, and they had to be in accordance as well. All of these formalities seemed ridiculous to me. Of course Cara and Nancy, on their way in from Florida, would agree. Then my cherished brother could finally be pain-free and at peace.

Billy's doctors insisted that he was not in pain. How can anyone possibly make that determination for someone in a coma? We wanted to believe them, because the alternative was too horrible to contemplate, but we had found out differently. When Devin first arrived at the hospital to find his beloved uncle in a coma, he got angry. "You'd better get out of this fucking coma," he'd railed at Billy, "because everyone is here and everyone wants to talk to you." I was standing next to Devin when Billy opened his eyes. My heart leapt. He opened his eyes for Devin. Gently, we all explained what was happening to him. I sat down next to him, and looked into his eyes. He looked back at me, completely lucid.

"Billy, are you in pain?" I asked him. "Blink for me if you're in pain."

He blinked. That was all I needed to know. Immediately, I felt searing pain move through my body, deep into my bones. His pain became my pain.

Brittany, brave girl that she was, told him what the doctors said, that he would never be any better. Told him that he would never be able to play cards again.

"Daddy, do you want us to keep you alive? Because

we will, as long as you want us to."

Billy's eyes filled with tears. So did Brittany's. I knew she meant it. She had been taking care of Billy for months, bringing him food, cleaning his house. She was the one who had found him collapsed in the shower, covered in his own feces.

"Billy," I said. I dabbed at his eyes with a tissue. "Do you want us to keep you alive? Blink once for yes, and twice for no."

Slowly, deliberately, Billy blinked twice.

So now the hospital was making us go through the charade of having all family members in agreement. This must be a financial thing, I thought. The hospital must make a lot of money keeping Billy on all this machinery. Even in matters of life and death, the bottom line is always the bottom line. It's all about the money.

Brittany and Kristen sat quietly in the room, barely awake.

It broke my heart that Billy's daughters had to see their father like this. He might not have always been there for them, but he loved them, and they both knew it. Funny, how estranged a family can be, yet still come together when it matters most. Warm tears formed in my eyes. God, I thought, the tears I've cried in this lifetime would fill an ocean. And now Billy, my last friend, my last ally.

"You've already left, haven't you?" I whispered to Billy. "Not even a chance to say goodbye, a last hug, one more role of the dice."

My voice gained force.

"I never thought you'd go first. I know, I know. The fast lifestyle, the drinking, smoking. But you always defied the odds. Surprised everyone. But I guess you've used up your nine lives. I didn't expect this. Not this soon. I don't mean to be selfish, but I still need you, Billy. You're my best friend. "

Billy's fingers might have moved, or my tears might have made it look that way. I watched Brittany rise and walk to the bed, sliding her hand under her father's head and pulling him closer as she leaned in to kiss him. She whispered in his ear, "Tomorrow the doctors will increase the morphine. A day later, you'll be free."

I was moved by Brittany's strength and courage. I was inspired by both Brittany and Billy. As if, not by words but by feeling, Billy had given her one last gift. One last hint of encouragement. As if Billy had given me his very last ounce of willpower, with the promise that I keep it alive in myself.

My mind began to wander. I thought of Michael, and for the first time since he died, it didn't make me sad. Instead, I felt an odd sense of calm. Is that what fourteen years of grieving has led to, I wondered. To peace?

I thought of Devin, a grown man, good job, a girlfriend or two, still so good to me. I must have done something right, mustn't I?

I thought of work. Of all the menial jobs I went through, then the better jobs. And now, I had my own business. I was successful. I didn't have to depend on anyone. Not Michael, not an employer, I could make it on my own. And, as much as I always wanted to be taken care of, I felt stronger, more at home taking care of myself. I had done well, I assured myself. And I knew I could keep doing better.

"The thing is," I whispered to Billy, "I've lost so many people I've loved. Michael, Mom, Dad. It was hard, but at least it was final. They were gone, and there was no way they were coming back. Now you're leaving, and it's breaking my heart, because I'll know you'll be gone for good, too. But, with Joel, it's an open wound. He's gone, but it's not final. That's what's ripping me apart. I've learned to deal with loss from death, but losing my son when he's still alive?"

I sat crying quietly for a while, then felt a strength rise within me. Billy's strength. My strength now. I looked up to Billy, then over to Brittany and Kristen. The daughters who loved him unconditionally, no matter how little he was around. The father who loved his daughters unconditionally, even if he couldn't show it in the way most parents could.

"Aunt Sunny, why don't you go back and get some sleep?" Brittany was standing over me, her hand on my shoulder. I looked up at her. I would go back to Kristen's condo where I was staying, but there would be no sleep for anyone tonight.

The next morning, Brittany picked up Nancy and Cara at the airport. When they came into the condo, we held each tightly for a long moment. Nancy stepped back and looked up at me.

"Sunny, you look terrible," she said.

"Thanks, Nancy. Hospital rooms do wonders for my looks."

"I just don't understand how the hospital can do this, knowing Billy could be in terrible pain," Cara said.

"They don't care, Cara. That's the whole point. They just don't care."

Brittany, her face swollen with tears, said, "We need to get to the hospital and do this."

Kristen hugged her, just as Nancy, Cara and I had

hugged. Sisters giving each other support in their darkest hour. "It's okay, Brittany. You know Dad would have wanted this."

The doorbell rang. "That's probably Joel," said Kristen. "I told him we were all meeting here to go to the hospital."

Joel and Andrea walked in. It was the first time I'd seen Joel since I'd thrown out all this belongings. He hugged Kristen, then Brittany, then me. "Mom...I'm sorry..."

"I know you are, Joel. I know."

He was talking about Billy, or about everything else. In my grief-stricken state, I didn't care. I just couldn't process my relationship with Joel at the moment. My brother was dying.

Cruel and insensitive to the end, Andrea wouldn't talk to me. There was no room in her heart to offer any condolences to me, or to anyone else for that matter. No one really spoke much that morning. We were all so grief-stricken at the thought of going to Queens Bay Hospital to say goodbye to Billy. Could this really be happening? It was so surreal, almost cinematic. I felt like a character in a sad, sad movie heading toward its foregone, tragic conclusion.

There were so many of us, and not enough cars, so we had to figure out who would drive with whom. Cara and Nancy got in the car with Joel and Andrea, who were going to follow us to the hospital. I was to go with Devin, Brittany and Kristen. Before we even pulled out of the condo parking lot, Nancy dashed out of Joel's car and into the car with us.

"That bitch!" she cried.

"Who?" I asked, stupidly. Who else?

"That Andrea is carrying on that no one is talking to

her, and how unfair it is to her. I'm not driving with her. She's an idiot!" She's making this all about her.

I said nothing, but inside I fumed. This spoiled, self-centered princess was so narcissistic that all she cared about was how people were treating her, and at a time when we were all about to do the hardest thing we'd ever had to do. It never even occurred to her that perhaps no one was talking that to her that bleak April morning, because there wasn't much to say.

By the time we got to the hospital, Cara, easy-going Cara, was completely beside herself.

"My God," said Cara, "all this girl can think about is herself. I'm not getting back in the car with her! I'll slap her, I swear to God!"

"Don't worry," said Devin. "I'll make two trips, if I have to."

When we got to the hospital room, we were met by the hospital administrator. I could tell by her cold, dead eyes and lackluster voice that she had stopped caring about people a long time ago. She was explaining all the formalities that surrounded discontinuing life support.

"Decisions regarding withholding or withdrawing life-sustaining treatment are based on substituted judgment."

"What does that mean?" I asked.

"Mrs. – I'm sorry, you are?"

"I'm Sunny Rubin. Billy's sister."

"It means, what the patient would have decided."

"Well, we all know what Billy would have decided. And it wouldn't be to live like this."

"I understand. But without an advance directive that designates a proxy, the patient's family becomes the surrogate decision maker. Family includes persons with whom the patient is closely associated."

I was tired of all this medical mumbo-jumbo. I wanted my brother out of pain—now.

"What are you getting at?"

"Apparently, the patient had a 15-year relationship with a woman who isn't here to give her consent."

Deanne looked stricken. I wanted to crawl under a rock and stay there. Without Deanne knowing, we had been sneaking in Denise every day to see Billy, after Deanne left. It was an elaborate charade we conducted to protect the feelings of the woman who had given birth to Billy's children. Denise was Billy's true partner, but he had never legally divorced Deanne, and she was still his wife. Deanne had never stopped loving Billy. Not for a minute. Estranged though they may be, she was at the hospital every day.

And Denise was there every night.

But what did all of this have to do with making legal decisions on Billy's behalf?

"I'm still his wife," Deanne said. "We were never divorced, all of his sisters are here and his children, and this is what we want."

"I understand, Mrs. Matus. But unfortunately, without Denise's permission as well, we simply cannot withdraw your husband from life support.

"How dare you!" I screamed at her. "We're his family! How dare you do this to us! To him!"

"I'm sorry, ma'am, but this is hospital policy. And I'll thank you to keep your voice down."

"Fuck you! My brother is in pain! We're not going to stand for this another minute!"

"I'm afraid you don't have a choice."

Wild eyed, breathing heavily, I ran into a nearby waiting room. "He's in pain!" I screamed. "My brother is in terrible, terrible pain. The cancer is eating away at him and these bastards won't take him off life support!"

The few people in the waiting room looked up, alarmed. I must have seemed insane to them. I didn't care.

"This fucking hospital! Don't get treated here! They don't care about the patients. They won't unplug my brother from life support, and he can't take it anymore! Help us!"

Two guards came to remove me from the room. When they put their hands on my arms, I slapped at them, and they jumped back.

"I'm not leaving this fucking hospital until you fucking people take my brother off life support! Get off of me!"

Suddenly, Devin was lifting me up in the air. I kicked at him, tried to get him to put me down.

"Get off me! What are you doing? Don't you give a shit about your Uncle?"

"Mom, they called the police!"

"I don't give a fuck! Let them arrest me!"

Devin carried me through the hospital lobby, out into the street, and to his car. He put me down on the ground, hard.

"We don't need this, okay, Mom? There's enough going on right now without you getting arrested. Okay? Now cut it out!"

I broke down with sobs that came from 15 years of death and struggle. Devin opened the passenger door of his car, and I climbed in, defeated. I had no more fight left in me.

Later that day, Kristen finally located Denise, who rushed to the hospital and gave her consent to have Billy removed from life support. They increased his morphine drip, so he would could slip into a morphine-induced coma. This way there would be no suffocation, no discomfort of any kind once they withdrew life support.

The hospital said I wasn't to be allowed back in, but I sneaked back as soon as I heard that they had unplugged him. I went to his room. He lay on the hospital bed, surrounded by all the people who loved him. I took his cold, boney hand in mine and squeezed it tightly. Leaning in to kiss him, I whispered, "I'm not bitter anymore, Billy. I'm not bitter."

It took 12 hours for Billy to finally pass away. We were all there when he did. You think it might have been awkward to have his legal wife and his long-time girlfriend in the same room, but it wasn't. Some people die without anyone at their bedside who loves them. On April 24, 2004, at 9:36 P.M., Billy Matus went to that great casino in the sky. He had not one, but two women, at his side, when he passed.

I bowed my head, smiling that he was able to do it his way, one last time.

Chapter 50
No Good Deed

It may be clichéd to say that death brings people together, but in the case of Devin and Deena, it was completely true.

It was a terrible time when Billy lay dying in his hospital room in Queens, but some good actually came of it. Billy had two nieces who visited him in the hospital—Deena and June. They were the daughters of Deanne's sister. At the time I was too grief-stricken to notice, but Devin was hitting it off with Deena. They began dating, and a year after Billy died, decided to get married.

I was thrilled. My relationship with Devin was as good as my relationship with Joel was bad. And now I would have a new daughter-in-law; a chance to redeem myself as a mother-in-law and an opportunity to grow close with a woman whom I could treat as the daughter I never had. And, on some level, Deena was a connection with Billy. After all, hadn't she met Devin while both were visiting their favorite uncle in the hospital?

Deena seemed like a nice enough girl. I hadn't had much of a chance to get to know her, but I assumed that would all change after they got married. Devin loved her, and that was good enough for me.

I wanted to throw them a beautiful engagement party in my backyard. Hopefully, it would erase the memory and the bitter taste in my mouth left from the engagement party I had thrown Joel and Andrea. We planned it for July. When I telephoned Deena to ask for her input regarding colors, she was quite specific.

"I'd like the colors to be the colors of apples," she

said. "Not just red, but all the other colors that apples come in.

I liked her decisiveness, and her taste in colors.

"Those sound beautiful," I answered truthfully. The party was going to take place in July, starting in the afternoon and scheduled to go on into the evening. I envisioned my backyard glowing during dusk on a warm summer night, enveloped in vermilion red, pale gold, and Granny Smith green.

I spent months planning the décor, the entertainment, and the menu. I rented a tent and tables. I ordered tablecloths in juicy apple colors. Inside the tent, I strung lights and garlands of red and yellow roses. For each table, I made individual centerpieces from purchased flowerpots filled with fragrant roses and several varieties of apples, all matching the color scheme. I ordered bags and bags of glittering red confetti, all shaped like tiny lips, and scattered them on each table. I purchased dozens of candles to add to the ambiance for later, after the sun had dipped below the horizon.

I outdid myself on the menu. Crab salad in cucumber cups, tender filet mignon on toasted bread with horseradish cream, shrimp kabobs in spicy citrus sauce, a champagne fountain and open bar. For later, the guests would enjoy a full dessert table and gourmet coffee bar.

Because there would be many small children at the party, I hired a clown for entertainment. I also purchased enormous inflatable animals—monkeys, lions, tigers and zebras—and "hid" them in the bushes. Nancy had flown in from Florida with her two daughters, Michelle and Melissa, and the girls took all the small children on a safari "hunt."

The day of the party, I had to pat myself on the back.

Children and adults alike were having a spectacular time. I was flushed with wine and happiness, and radiant in a white silk halter dress. Crisp linens, flickering candles, glorious hors d'oeuvres—that night, my backyard was the most magical, romantic place on earth.

By early evening, many of the guests were pretty tipsy. An open bar on a balmy summer night does that to people. Joel and Andrea had made an appearance; of course, Andrea was still not talking to or acknowledging me in any way. I chose not to focus on that. The evening was supposed to be about love and happiness, not grudges and negativity.

Deena had a pretty good buzz going herself, and Andrea, sober as a judge, zoned in on her like a predator. I couldn't help but notice that Andrea had corralled her in a corner, and was giving her an earful.

Many of the guests, including Nancy, overheard them. Andrea was not drinking, but she might as well have been for the crap she was spewing. It seemed she took this opportunity to try to poison Deena's mind against me. She was explaining to Deena what a horrible person I was, and how she had managed to completely estrange Joel and me. At least that part was true.

"If you know what's good for you, you'll do the same thing with Devin," she warned Deena.

Even Deena's own friends were taken aback by what happened that night. Here was this lavish, entertaining and great fun engagement party, and my daughter-in-law was bad mouthing me, her hostess in my own home. Although many people saw fit to report back to me what was happening, no one intervened.

Certainly there was nothing from Joel, who was far

too frightened of his wife to stop her. Joel was afraid of tiny, stick-thin Andrea—the skinny mouse that roared.

Devin was too busy drinking and yucking it up with all of his buddies to notice what was going on. I'm sure now if he had, he would have put a stop to it.

There were still more problems to come. Melissa, who was 13 at the time, decided to go home and post pictures of the party on her "My Space" page. Under my picture she wrote, "A Crazy Aunt." Okay, I thought it was funny. I am crazy, but in a good way. However, she wrote under Deena's picture, "Wasted before the clock struck 12." It was a very inflammatory statement, which of course made Deena and her family livid. The worst damage was done with the captions she wrote under Andrea's picture, "A Mafia Princess." True, but dangerous.

Gino had been in touch with Melissa since Joel and Andrea's wedding. Nancy and her daughters had stayed at Yolanda and Dick's house for a couple of days. Just long enough for Gino to fall in love with the beautiful Melissa. And they'd been chatting through My Space ever since. Of course, when Gino saw pictures of his sister with that caption, he went ballistic. He showed it to his family, and started threatening Melissa. He warned her to "watch her back," and demanded that she never post pictures of the Family again.

Everyone was angry with Melissa; and with Nancy for letting her daughter post these things, but this was different. This was real danger. We finally made Melissa understand that these are not people you want to piss off, and she removed the pictures.

I've run out of sons to make engagement parties for. But if I'm ever tempted to make a party like that for anyone else, do me a favor. Smack me in the head with a two-by-four, and remind me that no good deed goes unpunished.

Andrea did a great job of poisoning Deena's mind against me. She was young and impressionable, just the type of person a predator like Andrea would zone in on. At first, I worried that I had lost another son. Do you know, if you type "evil mother in-law" into Google, you get back over 36 million hits? Andrea had convinced my new daughter-in-law that I was one of those.

Devin, however, never faltered in his love, or defense of me. He was always diplomatic, but found a way to get his point across. He would choose times when it seemed that Deena was having a hard time allowing herself to get past the things Andrea had been telling her, to tell stories of how I had driven in the snow and ice for 5-to-6 hours to be at every one of his and Joel's hockey games, and then back again, to go to work. He would joke about how good I had gotten at warding off unwanted advances by fat, smelly hockey coaches and scouts. He never complained about how I had cheered the loudest, as Joel had. Instead, he bragged about it, saying how his mom had always been his number one fan. Devin would often complain, in front of Deena, about how my other son, his brother, allowed his wife's family to treat me. He would say firmly,

"I would never allow anyone to treat my mother that way. Joel allowed that family—a Family of criminals, no less—to treat our mother like she was the one who was trash.

Devin told Deena: "This is a woman who worked to raise two boys on her own, who was always there for us no matter what. She sacrificed everything to make sure we had the best. Chris isn't even her own flesh and blood, and even he knows she deserves the respect that Joel refuses to give her."

I was so proud of Devin, the good son. He was the one who would always be there for me. I knew that had he been the one to meet Andrea and fall in love with her, he would have had the backbone his brother lacked, to stand up to her and that whole Family.

Devin continued to advocate for me, and I also talked to Deena myself. I told her that the gossip Andrea had spewed to her about me was hurtful, and in most respects, flat out false.

Andrea had pled a pretty strong case against me, and the waters were rough there for a while. What I had going for me was a son who never backed down—A son who loved me so dearly, that he wanted his wife to love me as well. Devin was a good-hearted man who, no matter what, would never turn his back on our relationship.

At a time when I was unsure if I would ever break through the walls that Andrea had helped construct between Deena and I, Devin said to me, "You are my mother, and I love you, and that will never change. Regardless of what happens, you will always be a part of my life."

I knew he meant it, too.

Ultimately, Deena and I ended up with another champion for our cause. His name is Jack Michael Rubin, and he is my grandson.

As a mother, I was well aware of the magic that takes place when the nurse or doctor first places that new baby in your arms. Your heart, mind and even your very soul are consumed by the way they look, the way they feel, even the way they smell. Your first thought is usually how amazing it is to love something so strongly, that you've barely laid eyes on.

As a grandmother, I knew I would love my grandchildren, but again, was not prepared for the enormity of that feeling. When Jack was born, my relationship with Deena was still a bit on the tense and uncomfortable side. I was afraid at first, when I visited them at the hospital. Flashbacks of what had happened when Joel's first child had been born kept creeping back into my mind, but I needn't had worried. My son Devin, truly the strongest and most compassionate man I know, told his wife whom I know he also loves very deeply,

"This is my mother, and she is Jack's grandmother and I will never allow what Andrea did be done to her again. My mother loves baby Jack. She is a warm loving person and will always be there to help us."

Things were not instantly all wine and roses from that point on, but Devin wasn't going to be satisfied until it was. His tireless support was eventually enough to cause Deena to give me a fair chance. She was able to see how strong my love was for my son, and for Jack, her baby. She was finally able to see how much family means to me. Motherhood changes the way we look at the world, and I think it also helped Deena look at our relationship from a different perspective. There was no denying that Jack and I needed each other.

We have all come a long way. Deena and I are friends now. We even email and talk on the phone. Deena has become aware of the importance to teach love and acceptance rather than hate and prejudice. It's amazing what a child does when they enter your life.

I am now invited to celebrate Christmas and Easter along with her family. Making me feel like a part of Devin,

Deena and Jack's life. This year Christmas and Chanukah were the same week. During this holiday season I made the traditional Chanukah dinner, brisket, potatoes Latkes, with applesauce, stuffed cabbage and let us not forget my special matzo ball chicken soup! After dinner we light the Menorah, which is Jack's favorite time. Enthusiastically he holds the burning Shamash, the middle candle that is used to kindle the other lights. His eyes open wide and he begins lighting the other candles, I can't help but wonder if in another life our sweet Jack was a pyromaniac. As the Menorah is flickering and we watch the yellow and amber flames light up the room, I also wonder if perhaps we should have disabled the smoke detectors, and take solace in the fact that the fire extinguisher is close at hand.

Afterwards, as we experience relief that Jack has made it through another Festival of Lights without burning down the house, we open presents. We watch little Jack's eyes light up when he opens the packages of Chanukah gelt (chocolate money), dreidels (spinning top) and lots and lots of toys. Almost as joyous as watching Jack is knowing that Deena hasn't forgotten me. She gave me a beautiful collectible Elephant, and wished me a Happy Chanukah. I am grateful to my daughter-in-law, as she has chosen to be caring, loving and respectful, as family should be.

My favorite moment came minutes later, when I looked up and saw Jack jumping up and down excitedly saying,

"Grammy, Grammy come with me, I want to show you Christmas, it's downstairs!"

Totally overwhelmed by the sparkling Christmas tree all dressed in lights and garland we all shared the joy and love of the Holiday season together. Devin, Deena and Jack have truly made me feel like we are not only celebrating the holidays, but most importantly are celebrating the fact that we are family. I no longer feel like I'm standing outside Saks Fifth Avenue in the cold, looking in the window at things I can never have, but instead I am right there in the middle of that beautiful holiday display.

Chapter 51
Death of the Chin

I spent Christmas Eve with my good friends Mark and Tina and their daughter Jennifer. It was a small, intimate gathering of close friends. We had a lovely dinner, and afterwards, opened gifts in front of a roaring fire, with Christmas carols playing in the background. Afterwards, I came home, and treated myself to a long, luxurious bubble bath. I snuggled into a cozy robe, poured myself a glass of wine, and eyed the pile of Barbie and Bratz dolls, Disney Princess pajamas, Dora the Explorer DVDs. I had pretty much cleaned out the girl's department at Toys 'R Us when I shopped for Chris and Claire's three adorable daughters. I was going to spend Christmas day at their house, and had still not wrapped their gifts. I wasn't going to be arriving at their home until 3 the next afternoon, so I decided the wrapping could wait. At the moment, I was sipping a dry Merlot and channel surfing, with Koho snoring contentedly next to me.

Suddenly, the news anchor on the eleven o'clock news programs declared:

"Yesterday, the funeral of mob figure Vincent "The Chin" Gigante was held in Greenwich Village. Vincent 'The Chin' Gigante, the man described by The New York Times Magazine as "the last great Mafioso of the century," died December 19th from complications of heart disease at the same federal prison hospital in Springfield, Missouri, where John Gotti died three years earlier.

After a service at Saint Anthony of Padua Church on Sullivan Street, Mr. Gigante was cremated at the historic Green-Wood Cemetery in Brooklyn, NY. He is survived by eight children, 5 from his wife and 3 from his mistress, and his prominent cousins from Boston.

Gigante's lawyer, Flora Edwards, has said that the family intends to sue the federal government over Mr. Gigante's health care treatment while in prison.

Gigante was best known for walking through his Greenwich Village neighborhood in a bathrobe and pajamas, a tactic, which he later confessed, was an act to depict him as mentally ill and escape criminal prosecution. Gigante was 77 years old."

As much as Joel was no longer a part of my life, I was still curious about this turn of events. Was Yolanda broken up about the death of her father, or doing a happy dance over a substantial inheritance? What about Andrea? How would she explain to Joel the presence, at the funeral, of various Mafioso, police and FBI agents?

Turns out, no one had to explain anything to Joel. The next day at Chris and Claire's house, Chris offhandedly mentioned Joel while his three daughters were playing with their new toys.

"I spoke to Joel yesterday."

"Oh, did you?" I didn't mention the Chin, or anything about the Family for that matter. I never did when I was with Chris and Claire. Joel's treatment of me was a great bone of contention between Joel and his childhood friend. I tried not to aggravate the situation and avoided discussing Joel with Chris and Claire whenever possible.

"Andrea's grandfather died."

"Oh, I'm sorry to hear that." I kept my tone light and my focus on the girls playing. If he wanted to give me any information, it wouldn't be because I was prodding.

"Yeah, Joel said it was kind of a drag. Andrea just stuck him with the kids and went off to the funeral. It was just assumed that he would baby-sit so everyone else could go to the funeral."

"Well, he isn't a blood relative. He never even met her grandfather. So I can understand." I played it cool and calm, almost defending Andrea's actions. I found it amusing to be the bigger person. Andrea would never defend anything I did. It wasn't necessary to stoop to her level.

"That's not the point!" Chris seemed almost impatient. "It's just that he wasn't even given a choice. He was just told that he was going to stay home and baby-sit."

"Honey, why should that even surprise you?" Claire had a sardonic look on her face. "They tell him when to jump, and he asks how high. End of story."

"Yeah, let's talk about something more pleasant. It's Christmas! Hey, girls, who wants to have a sleepover at Sunny's house during Christmas vacation?"

"We do! We do!"

The three abandoned their toys and came running over, climbing on me. Trinity, their six-year-old, got to me first and climbed next to me on the couch, staking her territory. It seemed like only yesterday that she was born, and here she was, already looking like such a young lady. Abigail, their four-year-old, climbed up onto my lap. Cali, their precious two-year-old with enormous, sea green eyes, wasn't far behind. She scrambled up onto the couch and threw her arms around me. The three of them, in velvet Christmas dresses, tights and black patent leather shoes looked like they belonged on a Christmas card.

I took the girls for sleepovers regularly, since Claire and Chris had no family nearby and no one to ever give them a break. The girls adored me and it was mutual. It was my pleasure to have them over; even though it took my house several days to recover from having three active toddlers run through it.

"Okay," I said. Let's ask Mommy and Daddy what would be the best night for you to sleep at Sunny's house."

They covered my face in kisses, and for the moment, I was the happiest woman on earth.

The drive home took an hour, and I had plenty of time to ruminate over the death of The Chin. There was no Billy to call and discuss it with; nobody I knew would be remotely interested. When I got home, after taking off my makeup and settling into comfy pajamas, I sat at my computer.

"Vincent Gigante funeral" I typed into a search engine. Several web pages turned up. I clicked around, reading bits and pieces of information. One website, The Chicago Syndicate, offered quite a bit of information on Gigante's funeral:

"Pallbearers carry a coffin with the body of former Mafia boss Vincent (Chin) Gigante out of St. Anthony of Padua Church in the Village after a simple service attended by few mobsters. There were no garish floral arrangements yesterday and only a few shiny limos with refrigerator-size guys. Hardly a capo showed up. Mostly, the funeral of the legendary Mafia boss Vincent (Chin) Gigante was a quiet reminder of an Old World Greenwich Village that is disappearing day by day.

Gigante, after all, was an underworld dinosaur, an old-time gangster who dodged prison for decades by shuffling unshaven about the Village in a bathrobe, muttering that

Jesus was his lawyer. His final tribute reflected the fallen state of the Mafia, with hardly any mobsters seen paying their final respects at the St. Anthony of Padua Church on Sullivan St.

It was a modest affair, nothing like the 2002 funeral for mob boss John Gotti, when 19 open-air cars packed with flowers paraded about Queens.

The attendees mainly were family and friends, including Gigante's brother, Mario, a reputed captain in the Genovese family, Gigante's wife, Olympia, and several of his children.

The service was held a few blocks down Sullivan St. from the tiny apartment where Gigante lived for years with his mother. It was presided over by another of his brothers, the Rev. Louis Gigante.

Rev. Gigante, who stood by his sibling even after Vincent had admitted the crazy act was just that, did his best to preserve the image of his brother as a man misunderstood. "The world had a different view of him through the media," he declared. "But we, his family, his friends, the people of Greenwich Village, me, his brothers, his mother and father, we all knew him as a gentle man, a man of God."

To a church three-quarters full, the priest presented the powerful gangster as a lonely throwback wedded to his rapidly changing neighborhood. "Vincent never traveled," the priest said. "He was always on Sullivan St., walking and helping others, neglecting himself." No mention was made of Gigante's status as Godfather of the most powerful crime family in America. No one recalled that Gigante once parted the hair of mobster Frank Costello with a bullet, shouting, "This one's for you, Frank!"

Instead there was the story of a 77-year-old man dying alone in a prison somewhere in the Midwest, neglected. As the priest saw it, the government that pursued his brother for decades finally did him in. "In the eight years Vincent was in prison, I visited him 19 times. There wasn't a day he didn't suffer," said Rev. Gigante. "He did his time like a man. He was going to come home. He was dying to come home. But he couldn't. They allowed him to die."

Then the white-gloved pallbearers did their job, carrying the coffin piled high with red and white poinsettias down the aisle and into the pre-Christmas chill.

In the end, Vincent (Chin) Gigante emerged from his childhood church, carried out into a Village the old mob boss would have barely recognized."

I scoffed inwardly at the remarks made by his brother, the Reverend. There wasn't a day the Chin didn't suffer while in prison? Well, hello, what do you think prison is for, you idiot? And what about all the people who suffered at the hands of this Mafia kingpin? Just because he eventually became a frail, sickly old man it didn't mean he wasn't, at one time, a ruthless thug. And what about this drivel about Gigante wanting to come home, but he couldn't? Again, must we remind the Family that prison, is by definition, a place you don't leave just because you "want" to come home? And this nonsense about the prison "letting" him die – people get sick in prison, and they die. You can point fingers all you want, but old people with heart disease who aren't incarcerated die all the time. The only difference, in my opinion, was that the Family knew a lawsuit when they smelled one.

Interesting that this website should compare his funeral with that of John Gotti. Gotti had been enough of a legend so that even I knew the details of his funeral. I recalled the news showing clips repeatedly of throngs of onlookers lining the streets to catch a glimpse of his larger-than-life funeral procession. His hearse led a procession of what had to be over 100 vehicles; many of them black stretch limousines. Several were decorated with elaborate floral arrangements. His casket was made of gleaming bronze.

Of course, the most interesting aspect of Gotti's funeral was not newsworthy. In June of 2002, June, Deena's sister, had gotten married. Deanne, Billy's wife and June's aunt, asked me to accompany her to the wedding as her "date." I readily agreed. It was a low-key affair, and after the reception, many of the guests continued to celebrate at a local restaurant/bar in Queens.

The bar was packed. It was the week of the US Golf Open, which that year was being played locally at Bethpage State Park on Long Island, not far from Queens. It was a big year for professional golf and there was a lot of hype surrounding Tiger Woods, who won the US Open that year. Still, we managed to find tables and squeeze our way into the bar, ordering rounds of drinks and getting as rowdy as the rest of the crowd.

Nearby there was a table full of attractive men, who were a little more subdued than the rest of the crowd. Kristen and Brittany challenged me to go and talk to them. Since I'm not one to back down on a challenge, especially one involving attractive men, I introduced myself to two of the men, who turned out to be a father and his son.

They were sweet, even with their tough guy "I'm Italian so don't fuck with me" kind of attitude. Eventually, with their tongues loosened by alcohol, they said they had just been to a funeral, and that they were part of the craziest, most powerful family in New York. Gotti. They had to be talking about John Gotti.

I guess I'd had a few too many, and I in the spirit of "when in Rome," I declared that no, my son had married into a family was more powerful.

"Oh, yeah?" They answered. "What Family is that?"

"Well," I answered. "Who would be more powerful than Gotti?"

Their eyes grew wide, their jaws dropped.

"No way!" they exclaimed. "You're shittin' me!"

If they only knew how I wished I was.

As I sat pondering my memories, and the ramifications the Chin's death may have on my son's life, Ying was back in her little Sullivan Street apartment, watching the news as well.

Zhong had gone to bed early, he had worked hard that day, and then gone out for pizza with his friends. When he came home he had kissed his Grandmother's cheek and said,

"Turn on the news, Grandma. It will make you happy, I think." With that, he said goodnight and left Ying on her own. When she turned on the news, she saw why.

The same story was playing in Ying's living room that I was watching in mine. The death of Vincent "Chin" Gigante. Ying watched, unable to take her eyes from the screen. The man was finally dead, she could hardly believe it. Ying knew someday she would have much to atone for, but nonetheless, she had prayed hard for this day to come. Some days, she even prayed for his death to be a long, slow, violent one. Other days, just knowing he would no longer breathe the same air as she and her grandson was enough. Tonight, she didn't feel ecstatic, as she had thought she would. She was left somewhat numb, and slowly, as she processed the fact that the Chin was really, actually, truly, finally dead, her mind started to go back to a place she wished she never had to go again. Another death, that of her precious Jing.

Ying had taken the baby out of Jing's arms slowly, and before the reality of what and whom she was holding in her arms had hit, Jing was back in the big, black car that had brought her to the curb in front of the newsstand. Ying yelled out to her to wait, but the car sped off, windows tinted so she couldn't even know if Jing had heard her. She looked down at the bundle in her arms. Unwrapping him from the dirty towel, she saw that he was a boy, and on the surface at least, looked healthy.

"Well, hello my grandson. You look just like your mother did…so long ago."

She wrapped him quickly in a blanket that hung from the back of her chair, and said,

"I will name you Zhong. It means loyal and devoted in our country. I can tell by your eyes that you will be that for me, little one."

Zhong had closed the stand for the day, and gone shopping to get items the baby would need. She also took him to the neighborhood clinic, to make sure he was healthy on the inside too. The doctor there knew Ying, and he also knew the situation with Jing. He didn't ask any questions, and when his tests showed that the baby was positive in his system for opiates, he didn't call any one to take him away. The doctor knew that this boy was where he belonged. He schooled Ying on how to care for him and things to watch for. He gave the baby a medicine to counter-act the drugs, and sent them on their way. Ying hired the neighbor boy to run the newsstand for a while. She needed to stay home and care for this little one.

Two days later, was the worst day of her life. As Ying sat rocking and feeding the baby, there was a knock on her door that changed the course of her and Zhong's lives forever.

To this day, Ying remembers everything about that day, vividly. Opening the door, she saw the two young detectives, and knew what they were there to tell her before they even introduced themselves. She invited them in, and sat stoic in the chair, baby in her arms, inwardly bracing for the news.

"Maam," the one who had introduced himself as Taylor began, "Do you have a daughter, about seventeen or eighteen?"

"Yes," Ying replied, "I do, her name is Jing."

"Is that her baby?" the other detective asked, indicating Zhong.

"Yes, she left him here two days ago. What has happened?" Ying asked, wanting them to just hurry and get it over with.

"I'm sorry, Maam," the one called Taylor said, "but we were wondering if you may have a recent photograph of your daughter that we may look at?"

Ying rose slowly, Zhong still in her arms, just going through the motions now. She could feel it already in her heart. She knew her Jing was gone. She didn't tell this to the detectives though. Instead, she reached up to the shelf that hung above the television and took down a small, framed photograph. Going back across the room, she handed it to the detective and said,

"This is almost two years old. We haven't seen each

other much since then."

The detective took a photo out of his briefcase, careful not to let Ying see it. He looked as if he were comparing the two, and then showed it to his partner who nodded.

Looking a little nauseous, the detective said those words that every mother never, ever wants to hear,

"I'm sorry to tell you this maam, but your daughter is dead."

And with that simple sentence, Ying's whole world had changed.

"How?" she asked, still sitting calmly with the baby to her chest.

"We believe she was murdered, maam. We don't have a lot of information yet. Her body was found this morning, in an alley a few blocks away. She didn't have any ID on her, and her fingerprints came back to a Jade Wei. We, um, thought that was probably an alias."

"Her hooker name." Ying stated bluntly.

The detectives exchanged a glance, and then the older one; Ying couldn't remember his name, asked her,

"You knew she was, um, a prostitute, Mrs. Woo?" and when Ying nodded, he went on,

"Do you know what area she was working, or who she was working for?"

Ying looked at him and said,

"No, I do not know where she 'worked' or who she 'worked' for. Tell me how she died."

The detectives looked at each other again, their discomfort apparent.

"Well, the medical examiner is not finished with their report just yet. I can tell you that she was strangled, and that she had a lot of drugs in her system. We are not sure yet which killed her. We, um, also believe, um…she may have been sexually assaulted."

Ying continued to sit quietly, but the room seemed to be spinning. She had to hold onto the baby with one hand, and steady herself by putting her other hand on the arm of the chair.

"Tell me, what makes you believe she was 'sexually assaulted'?" she asked.

"There are indicators, maam. She was nude, when we found her, and the Medical Examiner says there was, um, trauma, um to her 'private areas'." The detective pulled at his collar, looking like he needed some air.

"Can I see the picture you have?" Ying asked.

"No, Mrs. Woo," the detective said, "I can't show you that. It's a crime scene photo. You really wouldn't want to remember your daughter that way, I'm sure, anyways."

Ying looked at him, ready to argue that she needed to see it, and then changed her mind. He was probably right. She hugged the baby close to her, and asked them to show themselves out. The detectives tried to ask her more questions about who Jing's friends and 'business associates' may have been, but she just waved them off and said,

"Gentlemen, unfortunately I did not know the woman my daughter had become. If she was here, she would have told you that herself."

Ying spent the next few days at home, tending to baby Zhong and mourning the loss of his young mother, and the girl that had once been her reason for getting out of bed each day. Now, she resolved, she would get out of bed for Zhong.

When Ying returned to the newsstand, she took Zhong with her, setting his cradle up in a corner of the covered area where she sat and took her breaks and had her tea. On the second day she was back, the big, crazy Italian man that walked the street in his bathrobe stopped by. Ying didn't like this man. She already knew then that he wasn't crazy. She heard the exchanges that went on between him and his men. She had heard him talking about her Jing, calling her 'a pregnant whore'. She wondered, even then, how much this man and his way of life had to do with the death of her daughter. Today, she would find out.

The "Chin" made his purchase, today a New York Times, and as he started to amble away with that crazy shuffle of his, a black car stopped near the curb. It looked very much like the one that had brought Jing to drop off Zhong. A man got out of the back seat and, glancing around in all directions, approached the Chin. Chin stopped walking, and looked at the man, but as if he didn't know or recognize him. They both stepped back toward the newsstand, and once under cover of the awning, they began to talk.

"We have a...situation." the man told Chin

"What?" Chin asked.

"A whore, the Chinese girl, she's dead. I think the pimp, the one who calls himself D-Licious may have... gone too far."

The Chin looked at the man. From where Ying watched, quietly in the shadows, she could see his face was completely without emotion. Obviously unaffected by the misery of others he stated in a monotone voice,

"I guess those are the chances you take when you decide to be a whore."

Then, like nothing had happened, the Chin shuffled

off down the street, rambling aloud to himself, and twitching for his FBI audience. The other man, momentarily unsure of what to do next, finally turned and got back in the car and it left. Ying continued to stand silently in the shadows at first, and then whispering in her native tongue, said two prayers. The first was for her daughter's immortal soul, and the second was for the long, slow, painful death of the Chin.

The next day, Ying had another unexpected visitor that cemented her hate of these people.

As she was readying herself and Zhong to leave for work in the early dawn hour, there was a soft knock at her door. She opened it and was surprised to see a young African American girl standing there. She held a plastic grocery bag in one hand, and was dressed shabbily, and way too skimpy for the temperature that morning.

"Yes?" Ying asked.

"Mrs. Woo?" the girl said.

"Yes, how can I help you?"

"I brought some things for you. Things that were Jade's. Your daughter, right?" she said, her voice was shaky, and she glanced continuously over her shoulder.

"Come in," Ying told her. The girl started to protest, but something about the look in Ying's eye changed her mind and she stepped inside.

Ying gestured at the couch, and the girl perched herself on the edge of it, ready to run if she had to.

"Here, I thought she would want you to have these." she held the bag in Ying's direction and Ying took it.

Opening the bag, Ying could feel the tears rush to her eyes. So far, she had only cried in private, with no other witness than Zhong, but she couldn't stop them now. She reached into the bag and pulled out an old photograph. It was well worn, looking as if it had been carried in someone's pocket. It was a photo of Ying, Wei and a very young Jing, just after arriving in New York. Ying kissed the photograph, and sat it on her knee. She reached in again, and pulled out the last Cheongsam Ying had ever made for Jing. It was a green silk, and it was still brand new. It was folded with care, and attached to one of the buttons was a gold chain. A charm dangled from the chain in the shape of a heart. Inscribed on the back were symbols that read "forever in my heart" in Chinese. It was not an expensive necklace, but it was one that had been given to Jing by Ying for her fifteenth birthday, before...

Ying looked up at the girl, tears flowing freely now.

"Thank you," she said, "What is your name?"

"Felicia," she replied in a small voice, "I have to go now."

The girl rose and started to leave, but Ying's voice stopped her,

"Was she your friend?" Ying asked.

The girl hesitated momentarily, and looking at Ying she said,

"Yes, she was good to me."

"Will you tell me what happened to her?" Ying asked, quickly adding, "I will tell no one, I just need to know."

Sighing, and looking like she'd rather be anywhere else, Felicity sat back down.

"Miss Woo, they will kill me too, if they knew I told."

"Just between these walls," Ying said, "You have my word.

"It was so bad...I couldn't help her...they would a hurt me too." she looked at Ying, tears filling her own eyes now. Ying nodded, and she went on, "You see, Jade had this pimp. His name was D-Licious. Big, mean, nasty Italian man. Tried talkin' like he was black, he sounded so stupid, but he was so mean, no one would tell him that. Anyways, he was real mad when Jade got pregnant. He used to hit her a lot then and tell her she was stupid and that pregnant whores didn't sell good on the street. He would a made her have an abortion, I think, but she had got too far along. Anyways, he gave her more and more drugs. I think he thought that would kill the baby. That didn't work either. Jade had her baby. Me and another girl was there. We helped her, and cut the cord and cleaned and wrapped him up. D-was not around that day, so me and Jade talked another guy, I guess his name is not important, but we asked him to take us to where you work, to drop off the baby. Jade was afraid D- would kill him, or sell him or something. So Louie, this other guy agreed, that's how I knew where you lived. She pointed it out to me that day. Made me promise if she ever got dead I'd bring that stuff to you.

A couple days later, D-got back. I heard him and Jade arguing; the walls in that place are pretty thin. I heard her tell him she wanted to go home. She didn't want no more nasty men rutting all over her. She wanted to go home and be a mother to her baby. He laughed at her. He told her she was 'nuthin' but a 'cheap Asian whore' and that's all she will ever be. They fought for a long time. I had me a couple of John's in between, so I didn't hear it all, but for a while, us other girls couldn't even work, 'cause Jade was screamin' so much it scared the Johns away. Then it got real quiet. I saw a lot of guys; most of D's crew comes out of the room. One of them was carryin' something over his shoulder, wrapped in a blanket. I didn't know it then, but it was her." Felicia paused there, and looked at Ying to see if she still wanted her to go on. Ying nodded, but the tears continued to trace their path down her cheeks.

"Like I said, I wasn't in the room, but that other guy who helped us bring the baby here, Louie? He kinda likes me. He came to me later that night and wanted to…well, you know. I pretended like I wanted to be wit him too, and I started asking him about Jade. At first, he didn't want to tell me, but then we started doing things and he got kinda talkative. He said that D- told Jade he would kill her if she tried to leave. She said she was goin' and he wasn't going to stop her. So, after a while, he tied her down to the bed. He tied her off, you know, so her vein would pop, and he gave her some brown sugar. Then, he fu..Sorry, he had sex with her in all of her places. Louis said that's when he called in the rest of the crew. They all had sex with her. They used empty beer bottles and other stuff in the room, that's why we kept hearing her scream. D- kept giving her more sugar, hoping she would shut up. Louis said D-had to choke her 'cause she wouldn't shut up. He said she was gonna get us all busted. Anyways, after they was done with her, D-told a couple of the guys to "take out the trash". I'm real sorry, Miss Woo. Jade was a nice girl. She didn't mean no harm to nobody. She didn't deserve that. I really gotta go, though. I'm gonna get me killed." Felicity stood once more and headed for the door. This time, Ying let her go.

She sat there as the sun came up that day, not even thinking about opening up the newsstand, not hearing Zhong's cries from his cradle, not processing any sight or sound around her. The hate started as a minor irritant in her head, like a fly that you could slap away, but then it would come right back to annoy you. She eventually got up, and she took care of Zhong, and she went to work, and she tried to be a good person, but that hate continued to grow inside her. She would see the Chin's daughter on television, defending him, acting proud of him, and she would remember that her own daughter would never come home. She would watch his brother the priest drape a protective arm around him, and she would hate him that much more. She did not, and would never have any proof that he had anything to do with the death of her beautiful Jing, but in her heart, she knew. So Ying just watched, and waited. She knew that some day, even he would have to die.

So, on the day that Ying heard of the death of "the Chin", she smiled. She closed her eyes and envisioned his spirit being taken by Ch'eng Huang, who conducts a kind of preliminary hearing. Ying knew that after 49 days, sinners descend to hell, located at the base of the mythical Mount Meru. There, she envisioned all of the levels of hell that Gigante would have to pass through, before having to drink the elixir of oblivion in preparation for his next reincarnation. Her favorite part is imagining him being dropped off of the bridge of pain into a river that would sweep him off into his next life.

She opened her eyes, and spying a fly caught in a spider's web hanging in the corner of the room, she laughed and said to herself in Mandarin,

"I hope that is where your re-incarnation leads you." Ying's heart was finally at peace.

After the death of Vincent Gigante in 2005 the leadership of the Genovese Crime Family appeared to be in Limbo. However, as was true when Gigante lived, the members are tight-lipped about the organization and leadership of their family. The position of Boss is listed as vacant or unknown on all of the most current watchdog lists, but the estimated membership is about 270 "made" members. By all accounts, the family still appears to be the most organized crime family, and still remains powerful. The "Code of Omerta" also seems to have kept this family afloat. Since the 1980's, mobsters all over the country have testified against their crime families, whereas the Genovese Crime Family has only had five members turn state evidence in it's history.

Chapter 52
The Sunny Side of the Street

Joel now has three children. I know because I heard about him from all my family members.

Andrea is careful to send every single one of my relatives a birth notice. Just not me. But those are my grandchildren, so at the beginning I sent gifts for every birthday, every holiday. She always sends them back. I try and be clever, and send them from places other than my home. At Halloween, I sent pumpkin cookies from the Cookie Factory. On Valentine's Day I had chocolates shipped from Harry and David. I imagine that she would open these packages in front of her little toddlers, who will clamor for the sweets. How would she be able to pack up such delectable goodies and send them back? But she does…every time.

I hear other news about Andrea through the "info chain." She's lost all of her hair, and has to wear a wig. The last time I saw her, at Devin and Deena's wedding, her hair was thinning in spots. Now she's bald. I know enough about anorexia to know that alopecia, the fancy name for baldness, is a major sign that someone is starving herself. How ironic. Andrea is the classic case of the poor little rich girl. This spoiled, entitled Mafia princess, who can have anything, denies herself the most basic of necessities—food. I don't particularly care if she wastes away, but I worry about the example she is setting for my grandchildren, particularly the little girl. Of course, Andrea blames her hair loss on stress—me. She'd rather blame her cue-ball head on me than on the fact that she exists on water, oxygen, and large servings of familial dysfunction. It doesn't surprise me.

What is it about this woman who doesn't seem to understand the importance of family; who doesn't understand the respect that is owed the mother of her husbands?

As a young bride I was not particularly fond of Michael's mother. But I honored her because it was expected of me. "Honor your father and your mother, so that your days may be long in the land that the Lord your God is giving you."

This is not just a religious, but a moral imperative. The obligation to honor one's parents is an obligation that one owes to God. I would never think to disrespect my husband's mother, let alone manipulate my husband into cutting off contact with her. She was family. For better or for worse. The bond between mother and child is sacred. Nothing, no one, should ever be allowed to interfere with that bond.

And yet, there is a tremendous loyalty that Andrea, and now Joel, show toward her side of the family. I wonder if some of what I've seen on *The Sopranos* is true. I try not to be deluded by what is, after all, cable TV's ability to "push the envelope" on sex, drugs, profanity, and violence.

One episode of the popular HBO show reverberates in my mind: Tony Soprano is making his nephew, Christopher Moltisanto, a captain. He tells Christopher to cut his arm; Tony cuts his arm and they press their blood together. This blood oath is an oath of loyalty. He made Christopher repeat, "Fuck ya mudda, fuck ya fadda; ya loyalty is to us. Ya only family is us now."

Is that what the Family has done to Joel? There must be some explanation for how easily he was able to disown me and be completely absorbed into Andrea's Family. A friend of mine, an expert in domestic violence, has likened what has happened to Joel to what abusive husbands do to their battered wives.

Popular emphasis has tended to be on women as the victims of domestic violence, although there is now some awareness of men as victims. And the abuse is not always physical. Psychological and emotional abuse is just as damaging. Preventing the victim from seeing friends and relatives, actively sabotaging the victim's social relationships and isolating the victim from social contacts—this is an effective technique for a dominating spouse to gain full control of their partner.

Did I somehow let this happen to my son? I believe I tried to prevent it. Maybe I didn't try hard enough...

I think of Michael's mother, unable to face the loss of two sons. She couldn't even bear to see Devin and Joel, her two grandsons, because it was so painful to acknowledge them. She never sent birthday cards.

I refuse to abandon my grandchildren. I'll find a way to stay in the lives of my grandchildren, whether I ever get any acknowledgement from Joel or not.

Three grandchildren, and a fourth on the way. They will get this letter, and know who I am, who Michael was, who Billy and Minna and Maxie were.

"My dearest grandchildren,

When you open this, you will first wonder who I am. No doubt you have been told that I died long, long ago. Perhaps, in a way, I did. Perhaps I died and came back to life many times over the years.

Please know that I wanted to be a part of your life. It was never my intention to not know you. I never wanted to miss out on special memories with you. I never wanted to miss the chance to indulge and spoil you. Many years ago, you were taken out of my life. Now, through the grace of God, you have found this letter. I can only pray you will somehow find your way back to me.

This letter is the story of my life; it is also the story of the grandfather you never knew. I want you to know about your great-grandparents and your grand-uncle, Billy. You come from a long line of strong, kind, proud, loyal, devoted, courageous, loving people. Your grandfather Michael, in particular, was a remarkable human being. He was a wonderful father to your father. He lives on, in all of you.

I hope you will never suffer the kinds of misfortunes that I have endured, but I cannot protect you from whatever destiny has in store for you. In many ways, your life was mapped out for you the moment you were born. We all have a contract with God when we enter this world, and it's up to us to live up to our side of the bargain: in exchange for life on earth, we will live it to the fullest, with honesty, dignity and grace.

God's plan is only an outline, and you can fill it in however you wish. You have the ability to create, from God's plan, your destiny. You can walk tall and live your life with grace no matter what happens to you. You can choose to be happy no matter what life deals you. You are the common denominator in every day you live, in every choice you make. You are a Rubin. You are a survivor...and you are always welcome in my life."

Joel's children are innocent pawns in a game devised to hurt me. They're as innocent as lambs. I'm missing that magical time of their life when they live in a world that they see as all perfect and pure. By the time his children are old enough to understand the concept of "innocence," they will have lost theirs.

If there's one thing I've learned in life, it's that things don't turn out the way we want them to. We can complain and be bitter, or we can decide to accept them.

We have to move on—find our joy in the small pockets of life where the light still shines. That's the choice I've made, even if I was forced into it. Even if it took years to realize it. I'm a survivor. I'm not someone who lets life bury me. I'm someone who accepts where I am, but also knows when to move on. I've lifted myself out of the abyss and found my way through the shadows and back to the light in my life.

I remember as a child, how Billy used to tell Fat Marty to leave me alone. "Don't give her grief," he'd say. "Let her walk on the sunny side of the street."

I was an optimist then, even if it was because Billy forced me to be one. And who couldn't be optimistic around Billy? In Billy's light, life was a game to squeeze every ounce of fun and joy out of. He did that, by God. No cancer would ever take that away from him.

As for me, I might have done it the hard way... but I made it. My son Joel

on the other hand, surrendered to cowardice. In other words, he took the easy

road. The thought of that, no matter how true it is, sickens me. The feelings of

shame that I have towards him lie coiled in my gut like an evil snake, ready to

rear it's ugly head at a moment's notice. I have to

remember Devin, to quell the nausea that those thoughts provoke. In him I see all of the morals and values

that I tried so hard as a parent to instill, and I realize that the character flaws have to be Joel's and his alone. I cannot take responsibility for the poor choices he has made, and continues to make. His outright betrayal had finally sent me a clear message and I had to admit that this was the end of the road. I think of him now and am sadly reminded of the Cowardly Lion from The Wizard of Oz with his tail between his legs, trembling and whining. It breaks my heart to know that although a mother lives to save her children, Joel had become too contaminated. He is the only one who can save himself now... If only he had the antidote.

I, on the other hand chose the more difficult path of endeavoring to not be afraid to do the right thing, make the right choices. I've discovered that there is no "true happiness" but only the security that comes from knowing our own strengths and weaknesses and continuing to strive to be one's own person. That's how I have spent my life, and will continue to spend my days to come. Being my own person, and liking the person I see in the mirror each day, will be my proof of victory.

And by the way, I'm still walking on the sunny side of the street.

Reading Group Questions & Topics for Discussions

1. Which Character was your favorite in the beginning?
2. Which Character was your favorite at the end.
3. If your favorite character changed, why?
4. Can you relate to the predicaments to your favorite character? To what extent do they remind you of yourself or to someone you know?
5. How would you have dealt with the situation?
6. Did you feel that the family was using their power and control to influence Joel?
7. What other characters to you think fell under the influence of the family?
8. Did you enjoy the Mafia history and if you did, what parts did you enjoy most and why?
9. What parts of the book made you feel emotional and why?
10. Did Sunny inspire you in any way, please explain the situations.
11. Were there any funny moments that you enjoyed reading?
12. What part of Sunny's life was the most tragic? Explain how you felt when reading about them?
13. Did you feel Sunny was courageous when dealing with family or was she foolish?
14. How would you deal with the situation?
15. Do you think it's common that many Mother In Law's experience their son giving into their wife's family demands? Do you think it's always the Mother in Law's fault?
16. How did you feel about the ending and did you feel there was no other outcome for her.

28938382R00223

Made in the USA
Charleston, SC
26 April 2014